The Henry McBride Series in Modernism
and Modernity

Institutions
of Modernism

Literary Elites and

Public Culture

Lawrence Rainey

Yale University Press

New Haven and London

Published with assistance from the Frederick W. Hilles Publications Fund of Yale University and from the fund for the Henry McBride Series in Modernism and Modernity established by Maximilian Miltzlaff.

Printed in the United States of America.

Library of Congress Cataloging-in-Publication Data

Rainey, Lawrence S.
 Institutions of modernism : literary elites and public culture /
Lawrence Rainey.
   p. cm. (The Henry McBride series in modernism and modernity)
 Includes bibliographical references and index.
 ISBN 0-300-07050-0 (alk. paper)
 1. American poetry—20th century—History and criticism. 2. Modernism (Literature) 3. Eliot, T. S. (Thomas Stearns), 1888–1965—Appreciation.
4. Marinetti, Filippo Tommaso, 1876–1944—Appreciation. 5. H. D. (Hilda Doolittle), 1886–1961—Appreciation. 6. Literature and society—History—20th century. 7. Authors and readers—History—20th century. 8. Authors and patrons—History—20th century. 9. Joyce, James, 1882–1941—Appreciation. 10. Pound, Ezra, 1885–1972—Appreciation
I. Title. II. Series.
PS310.M57R35 1998
811'.5209112—dc21   98-8300

A catalogue record for this book is available from the British Library.

The paper in this book meets the guidelines for permanence and durability of the Committee on Production Guidelines for Book Longevity of the Council on Library Resources.

10 9 8 7 6 5 4 3 2 1

This book is for Sonia

The Henry McBride Series in Modernism and Modernity

The artistic movement known as modernism, which includes the historical avant-garde, produced the most radical and comprehensive change in Western culture since Romanticism.

Henry McBride (1867–1962) wrote weekly reviews of contemporary art for the New York *Sun* (1913–1950) and monthly essays for the *Dial* (1920–1929) and was one of the most perceptive and engaging of modern critics. He discussed difficult artistic issues in a relaxed yet informed style, one that is still a model of clarity, grace, and critical responsiveness. The Henry McBride Series in Modernism and Modernity, which focuses on modernism and the arts in all their many contexts, is respectfully dedicated to his memory.

Contents

Acknowledgments

I am grateful for fellowships that helped support the research and writing of this book from the American Bibliographical Society, the American Philosophical Society, and Yale University.

I am also grateful to the many institutions where research for this project was conducted, and particularly to their directors and staff: Don Skemer, curator of the Rare Book and Manuscript Collection at Princeton University Library; Robert Bertholf, curator of the Poetry and Rare Books Collection at the State University of New York, Buffalo; Thomas Staley, director of the Harry Ransom Research Center for the Humanities at the University of Texas, Austin; and Piero Meldini, director of the Biblioteca Civica Gambalunga, Rimini, and his assistant, Paola Delbianco. I am especially grateful to my longtime colleagues at the Beinecke Rare Book and Manuscript Library of Yale University: Ralph Franklin, its director; Patricia Willis, curator of American literature; Vincent Giroud, curator of modern books and manuscripts; Diane Ducharme, archivist; Stephen Jones, library service assistant; and Al Mueller, public services assistant.

Portions of various chapters in this book have appeared in the *Times*

Literary Supplement, the *James Joyce Quarterly,* the *Yale Review,* and *Modernism/Modernity,* as well as in *Representing Modernist Texts,* edited by George Bornstein (University of Michigan Press). To the editors and publishers of these publications I am grateful for their kind permission to use them here, albeit with significant alterations.

I owe a special debt of gratitude to friends and colleagues who read and commented on various portions of this work in manuscript: Ronald Bush, Jerome McGann, Annabel Patterson, and John Sutherland. And I am deeply grateful to Michael Keller, whose generous counsels were invaluable.

Introduction

Charles Dickens, rising to his feet, stood at the banquet table and surveyed the vast hall in which the leading citizens of Birmingham had gathered in early 1853 to pay him homage. It was his duty to thank them now, and he proceeded to offer his tribute:

> To the great compact phalanx of the people, by whose industry, perseverance, and intelligence, and their result in money-wealth such places as Birmingham, and many others like it, have arisen—to that great centre of support, that comprehensive experience, and that beating heart,—Literature has turned happily from individual patrons, sometimes munificent, often sordid, always few, and has found there at once its highest purpose, its natural range of action and its best reward.

"The people," Dickens concluded triumphantly, "have set Literature free." And in return for that gift of liberty, he opined, "Literature cannot be too faithful to the people."[1]

Within thirty years of Dickens's death in 1870, authors were far less confident about the beneficent effects of literature's dependency on "the people" or the prospects for a public literary culture. In that

period, as many critics have noted, British popular fiction underwent a profound transformation, one in which the novel gradually acquired a class structure analogous to that of the social world surrounding it. By the decade 1900–
1910, the later years of Henry James and the period when Joseph Conrad most
acutely felt the tension between the claims of his art and the imperatives of the
marketplace, the polarization between "high" and "low" literature had firmly
crystallized, and the modernist project issued its claim to aesthetic dignity by
repudiating that Victorian literature, above all fiction, that had sold itself to a
mass reading public. Leopold Bloom, the protagonist of *Ulysses* who concludes
his first appearance in the novel by cleansing himself of feces with pages torn
from the popular weekly *Tit-Bits,* epitomizes the modernist contempt for
popular culture.

For some scholars, that contempt is modernism's salient characteristic. "Mass
culture has always been the hidden subtext of the modernist project," one
influential critic has urged, a project in which popular culture is construed as a
threat of encroaching formlessness, gendered as female, and held at bay by
reaffirming and refortifying the boundaries between art and inauthentic mass
culture.[2] Viewed as modernism's defining trait, hostility to mass culture also
furnishes the grounds for drawing a firm distinction between modernism and
the avant-garde. Whereas modernism reaffirms the boundaries of traditional
art, the avant-garde "attempts to subvert art's autonomy, its artificial separation
from life, and its institutionalization as 'high art,'" an impulse that accounts for
its "urge to validate other, formerly neglected or ostracized forms of cultural
expression," chief among them popular culture.[3] Modernism, in this account,
becomes little more than a reactionary, even paranoid fear of popular culture.
In stark contrast, postmodernism seeks "to negotiate forms of high art with
certain forms and genres of mass culture and the culture of everyday life" and
therefore stands as the legitimate heir of the historical avant-garde.[4] The result
is clear: modernism is naive and irremediably reactionary, while the historical
avant-garde and postmodernism are self-aware and emancipatory.

Such formulations have brought welcome attention to the ongoing dialogue
between modernism and popular culture and its bearing on the status of art and
aesthetic autonomy. But their tendency to postulate a rigorous opposition
between "high" and "low" culture may be inadequate to account for the growing complexity of cultural exchange and circulation in modern society, a development epitomized in three events that occurred between 1902 and 1906. In
1902 Alfred Harmsworth (later Lord Northcliffe) piloted the *Daily Mail*—a
recently founded newspaper (1896) and one already notorious for blurring the

distinction between information and entertainment—to sales in excess of one million a day, the largest circulation in the world. His success hinted at the arrival of a new age of mass media, presaging the future triumph of film, radio, and, much later, television. In 1904 Oswald Stoll constructed the Coliseum in London, an institution that was "the largest music hall ever built," as contemporaries noted, and also something new and quite different: as Stoll called it, a "palace of variety." It was a site from which the stars of traditional music hall such as Marie Lloyd were conspicuously excluded, precisely because the audience the new "palace" addressed was no longer the working and lower middle classes that had formerly filled the halls, but rather an emerging group of suburban consumers who rejected equally the "low vulgarity" of the popular halls and the contemplative ethos of traditional, autonomous, or "high" art. In 1906, finally, the first appearance is reported of the word *middlebrow,* a term that acknowledges not just increasing stratification but also increasing interchanges among different cultural sectors.[5] These events, all occurring within a span of four years, point to an institutional field of cultural production being rapidly and radically transformed into one more variegated and complex than the rigid dichotomy between "high" and "low" allows. Modernism's ambiguous achievement, I shall urge, was to probe the interstices dividing that variegated field and to forge within it a strange and unprecedented space for cultural production, one that did indeed entail a certain retreat from the domain of public culture, but one that also continued to overlap and intersect with the public realm in a variety of contradictory ways. Modernism is commonly considered "a strategy whereby the work of art resists commodification, holds out by the skin of its teeth" against the loss of aesthetic autonomy. But it may be that just the opposite would be a more accurate account: that modernism, among other things, is a strategy whereby the work of art invites and solicits its commodification, but does so in such a way that it becomes a commodity of a special sort, one that is temporarily exempted from the exigencies of immediate consumption prevalent within the larger cultural economy, and instead is integrated into a different economic circuit of patronage, collecting, speculation, and investment—activities that precisely in this period begin to encroach upon and merge into one another in unexpected ways.[6] Modernism marks neither a straightforward resistance nor an outright capitulation to commodification but a momentary equivocation that incorporates elements of both in a brief, necessarily unstable synthesis.

That equivocation, in turn, demands new strategies of authorial self-construction that can accommodate a rapidly changing configuration of cultural institutions. The theme of authorial self-construction has been crucial to a great deal of recent scholarship, from Stephen Greenblatt's well-known exploration of self-fashioning in the courtly culture of the Renaissance to Jane Tompkins's study of literary elites in the emerging nation-state of nineteenth-century America.[7] In this book exploration of the theme is extended into the early twentieth century, when new strategies for reputation building—involving theatricality, spectacle, publicity, and novel modes of cultural marketing and media manipulation—responded to increasingly international cultural interchanges, the growing prominence of the early mass media, the rising pressure of advertising, the unprecedented fusion of information and entertainment, and the challenges presented by a dense, highly differentiated array of institutional arenas in which to speak to an increasingly fragmented public. Strategies of authorial construction changed as authors sought to address different publics, ranging from patron-*salonniers* to mass audiences, or from patron-investors, dealers, and speculators to a broader (if numerically restricted) corpus of critics and educated readers.

Those strategies, diverse and contradictory as they were, must be situated within the institutional field in which they unfolded. More typically, instead, scholars and critics have tried to define modernism through a unilateral focus on formal devices or ideological constellations. It is urged, for example, that "collage and its cognates (montage, assemblage, construction)" constitute "the central artistic invention" of modernism and the avant-garde, that these practices "call into question the representability of the sign" and, in ways that are left unspecified, "reflect" some "larger desire to break down existing economic and political structures."[8] Or it is asserted that the avant-garde's defining trait is its dismantling of aesthetic autonomy, the view that art is a conceptual category predicated on its divorce from material and social reality: the avant-garde "can be defined as an attack on the status of art in bourgeois society," an assault against "art as an institution that is unassociated with the life praxis of men."[9] Such claims typically draw on arguments derived solely from the reading of literary texts or artworks, a procedure that evinces excessive faith in our capacity to specify the essence and social significance of isolated formal devices and to correlate them with complex ideological and social formations, slighting the intervenient institutions that connect works to readerships, or readerships to particular social structures. To focus on those institutions, instead, is to view modernism as more than a series of texts or the ideas that found expression in them. It becomes a social reality, a configuration of agents and practices that converge in the production, marketing, and publicization of an idiom, a shareable language in the family of twentieth-century tongues. To trace the institutional profile of modernism in the social spaces and staging venues where it operated can teach us a great deal about the relations between modernism and popular culture, the fate of aesthetic autonomy, authorial self-construction in advancing modernity, and the troublesome place of literary elites in public culture.

Public culture is used here as a colloquial counterpart to Jürgen Habermas's notion of the public sphere, that social and discursive space in which, during the later seventeenth and eighteenth centuries, norms of rational argument began to take precedence over status, tradition, or the identity of participants in civic discussion.[10] For Habermas the public sphere is a historically specific set of sites and institutions (salons, coffee houses, journals of opinion, webs of social relationships) as well as a practice of rational and critical discourse on affairs (at first cultural and aesthetic, then civic and political in nature), a practice that institutionalizes a procedural ideal of unfettered critical exchange and a social one of inclusive participation. The transformation of that sphere, its gradual distortion and partial disintegration, occurred under the impress of its continual expansion to include more and more participants and the development of large-scale social organizations that mediated individual participation: channels of communication became more regulated, and the public sphere, now "dominated by the mass media," was transformed into an "arena infiltrated by power," one in which the ideal of rational discourse and its critical function have been eviscerated.[11] Habermas's work has generated debate far too extensive to be summarized here, but its general tenor remains challenging and suggestive, and it stands in the background of this study.[12] Modernism, poised at the cusp of that transformation of the public sphere, responded with a tactical retreat into a divided world of patronage, collecting, speculation, and investment, a retreat that entailed the construction of an institutional counter-space securing a momentary respite from a public realm increasingly degraded, even as it entailed a fatal compromise with precisely that degradation.

"Like all history," one critic has observed, "the history of literature is economic and institutional as well as personal."[13] But the question of institutions has been little discussed in Anglo-American literary theory. In general, as Theodore Ziolkowski observes, the term is appropriated as a metaphor to help in understanding the functioning of generic coherence (Austin Warren), the interpretive community (Stanley Fish), or professional and academic criticism (Harry Levin, Frank Kermode, Leslie Fiedler, and Gerald Graff), and in such usage it typically refers to a set of protocols internal to literature or the profession, not something that exists outside them.[14] German theorists, influenced by the work of Peter Bürger, have used the term differently to describe a concept or framing category, "the epochal function determinations of art in its social contingency," an approach that remains so stubbornly theoretical that it can say little about the specific social structures that mediate between works and publics.[15] For sociologists, institutions are the structures that interpose themselves between the individual and society; they are both social subdivisions of human beings and the regulative principles that organize various zones of activity and behavior.[16] That sense predominates in this study, though the Anglo-American and German senses of the term (the literary profession, the concept of aesthetic autonomy) also come under consideration.[17]

Anglo-American literary modernism was unusual in the degree to which its principal protagonists interacted with one another through shared institutional structures during a brief but important period from 1912 to 1922, roughly from the formation of Imagism to the publication of *Ulysses* and *The Waste Land*. These dates, with excursion into the 1930s and the aftermath of World War II, constitute the parameters of this study. Such historical boundaries are, of course, arbitrary, slighting the extent to which Anglo-American modernism drew on cultural traditions that extend much further back in time, minimizing developments that occurred in the decades that followed. Still, they acknowledge the special density of the social and institutional space that bound together the authors whose works have been deemed central to discussion of the modernist moment. Further, they allow one to take advantage of the especially rich archival heritage of Anglo-American literary modernism, a heritage that has become far more accessible in recent years (with the massive publication in the past decade of letters to and from Ezra Pound, for example, or the *Dial* papers, first made public in 1988, or Sylvia Beach's *Cahier de vente* for *Ulysses,* first made public in 1993). The chronological limitations of this study, and its exclusive focus on English-language modernism, are strategic decisions aimed at facilitating a more probing exploration of a subject that has been otherwise neglected in recent literary studies.

One omission of this study needs to be acknowledged. Some readers, especially those with literary critical training, will find far too little of the detailed examination of actual works that is sometimes held to be the only important or worthwhile form of critical activity. I reject the idea that history or theory are acceptable only if they take on the role of humble handmaiden to the aesthetic artifact. Further, juxtaposing the analysis of specific works with discussion of institutional networks would encourage, however inadvertently, a vulgar materialism that I also disclaim. That is not to say, of course, that certain modernist themes might not be usefully scrutinized from the perspectives suggested by my study. If *Ulysses,* as is often said, is the archetypal narrative of modernism, it may not be an accident that its two male protagonists spend their day not in aimless wandering about the city of Dublin, as is often reported, but in a tireless search for patrons and patronage; or that Buck Mulligan, the character who partially mediates between Stephen and Leopold Bloom, is described on the novel's first page as resembling "a prelate, patron of arts in the middle ages," a description promptly followed by Buck's offer to finance Stephen's journey to Athens and his request that Stephen borrow a quid from the Englishman Haines. Another frequently discussed motif of *Ulysses,* the search for a missing father, may also owe much to obvious etymological play: *pater,* the Latin word for father, is the root word of the Latin *patronus,* the term that eventually becomes the English word patron. Perhaps it is no accident that the theme of the dead or missing father is also prominent in *The Waste Land,* that other exemplary work of Anglo-American modernism. Contemporaries, at any rate, were quite willing to draw connections of just this sort. In 1926, when Hart Crane informed his parents that he would soon receive financial support from the prominent patron Otto Kahn, his father, who had recently refused to sustain his son's literary efforts, reacted this way, according to Crane's mother: "He said to me over the phone . . . 'I understand Harold has a new Daddy'—an expression that revealed a whole lot to me."[18] It might reveal something to us, too.

Modernism's interchanges with the emerging world of consumerism, fashion, and display were far more complicated and ambiguous than often assumed. At times they came perilously close to being the kind of phenomenon that art critics deride with the scathing term "smart art." To acknowledge that, however, is not to encourage a view of the modernist moment as an extended exercise in bad faith, to imply that the classical status of modernist works is the result of a conspiracy, or to indulge a spurious moralism that condemns the modernists for their engagements with mundanities. (Indeed, in Chapter 5 I urge that the demise of those engagements was an influence for the worse in the career of H.D.) But it is to suggest how deeply flawed is the common narrative that currently structures accounts of modernism and postmodernism. One sees its effects in the work of one scholar, who, commenting on modernism's decline in prestige, remarks: "the administered culture of late capitalism" has "finally succeeded in imposing the phony spell of commodity fetishism even on that art which more than any other had challenged the values and traditions of bourgeois culture." Another urges that the twentieth century has witnessed two distinct revolutions in the field of culture—the first a "real" revolution in which artistic activity was urgently politicized and innovation swept through all the arts, the second an equally important but less noted revolution in which universities and other cultural institutions appropriated modernism's formal repertory, canonized its works and artists, and sapped its political energies.[19] Both accounts rehearse a fall narrative in which an Edenic state of subversion imperceptibly yields to appropriation, assimilation, and containment by "late capitalism" or its cultural instrument, academic criticism. Informing such accounts are two related though not identical paradigms. One is the adversarial model of culture, the belief that only cultural activity inimical or in opposition to dominant social values can be genuine or true culture. The other, paradoxically, is a variant of the concept of aesthetic autonomy that the avant-gardists are held to have destroyed, the assumption that aesthetic virtue and commerce are antithetical principles. Both notions presuppose a conception of cultural activity that has been distilled of its material complexity, one that bears no relation to the realities of cultural production within complex, modern societies. They are fairy tales of good and evil that have been given a specious aura of profundity by being garbed in academic diction; but they cannot serve as the basis for critical accounts of cultural activity in the twentieth century, in which cultural institutions and artifacts interact with a highly differentiated and complex civil society.

Chapter 1 of this study considers the formation of Imagism and Vorticism, the two movements that mark the emergence of the avant-garde in Anglo-American literature, and assays the role of mass culture and patronage in their formation. Chapters 2 and 3 turn to the publication of *Ulysses* and *The Waste Land* in 1922, examining the deluxe edition and the little review as institutions. Chapters 4 and 5 study turning points in the careers of Ezra Pound and H.D., transformations that are an outcome of the institutional affiliations outlined in previous chapters. In Pound's case, the turning point is the beginning of his admiration for Fascism, in H.D.'s, the development of a coterie poetics that affects the genres, style, and institutional arenas in which her career unfolds.

A final word about the form of these essays is in order. Each reconsiders an event that has become the subject of a familiar, generally hagiographic narrative, and each explicitly offers a counternarrative that rewrites our received accounts. Analysis, it is true, jostles alongside narrative in every essay, but for many academic literary critics the presence of any story at all has become an object of suspicion. Narrative is thought to be a linear and monologic form that offers factitious coherence at the cost of analytic complexity, storytelling a form of pandering to popular tastes depraved by mass media. Expository prose, written albeit in rebarbative jargon, is the sign of resistance to the culture industry and the seal of academic legitimacy. But is it necessary to remind literary critics that a story is not an object that has merely been happened upon? No less than expository prose, stories are complex and contradictory artifacts. The apparent ease with which they may be recounted should not be confused with a resistance to analysis. Stories *are* analysis—by other means.

Chapter 1 The Creation of the Avant-Garde: F. T. Marinetti and Ezra Pound

Debate about the significance of the historical avant-garde has reached a feverish pitch in recent years, a level of intensity suggesting that more is at stake than academic questions of historical accuracy or comprehensiveness. Like an antique mirror from which the mercury has seeped and faded, the avant-garde has become the ambiguous glass in which we seem to scrutinize a perplexing image of ourselves, an image that is haunting precisely because it is simultaneously so alike and unlike, because it bears so many of the features by which we recognize ourselves and the contemporary cultural milieu, even as it also evokes a world that is already feathered at the edges, already remote. Although it would be impossible to catalogue all the salient features that have been held to define the avant-garde or its significance for today, two questions have gradually acquired special importance in the course of recent critical discussion. One is the extent to which, to use Peter Bürger's formulation, the avant-garde "can be defined as an attack on the status of art in bourgeois society," or as Bürger further clarifies, an assault on "art as an institution that is unassociated with the life praxis of men."[1] The other is how that attack overlaps with the avant-garde's use of motifs, materials, and artifacts from mass or popular culture. That usage has been damned by Marxist critics as "a colonization of other, formerly independent" cultural practices and defended by others for "subvert[ing] . . . the hierarchical distinctions between high art and mass culture," or for proposing a "critique, not only of prevailing market conditions, but also of the futility of the Symbolist [or high-art] response to these conditions."[2]

Such views sound either glib or unduly dogmatic in their bald assertiveness. Partly that results from disembedding quotations from their context, but partly it reflects the growing polarization and increasingly schematic formulations that have characterized recent discussion about the historical avant-garde. Yet such well-defined dichotomies prove strangely inadequate when tested against the complex social realities informing the interaction among avant-garde, elite bourgeois, and popular cultures in the formative moments of modernism and the avant-garde. This interaction might be traced in many cultural exchanges of the period, but perhaps nowhere better than in the dialogue of actions that took place between Filippo Tommaso Marinetti and Ezra Pound from 1912 to 1914. Marinetti, after all, is typically viewed as one of the founding fathers of the historical avant-garde, and his creation of Futurism in 1909 is considered one of its paradigmatic moments.[3] Pound, too, is widely treated as a representative of the avant-garde, sometimes in contrast to T. S. Eliot with his more symbolist or modernist style, sometimes by virtue of Pound's role in the formation of first Imagism, then Vorticism, the two movements in the Anglo-American literary tradition that most nearly resemble the Continental avant-gardes.[4]

For the most part, however, critics have paired Marinetti with Pound only in order to dismiss the importance of the connection, and in doing so they have largely been following a script that originated with Pound himself. Writing anonymously already in 1917, Eliot set a precedent followed by subsequent critics when he characterized Pound's relationship to Futurism as one of implacable but informed opposition: "Pound has perhaps done more than anyone to keep Futurism out of England. His antagonism to this movement was the first which was due not merely to unintelligent dislike for anything that was new, and was due to his perception that Futurism was incompatible with any principles of form. In his own words, Futurism is 'accelerated impressionism.'"[5] Eliot, in these remarks, was not rehearsing a history he had witnessed himself, having first arrived in England more than two months after Marinetti's final visit in June 1914, and these comments more than likely were dictated or suggested to him by Pound.[6] Yet Eliot's assessment—or, more accurately, Pound's own—has been taken at face value and repeated again and again. "Pound was never a Futurist," writes Noel Stock, the appointed biographer of Pound, and he remained "indifferent or opposed to most of their principles."[7] Pound, states James Wilhelm, "was strongly opposed . . . to the gimmick-ridden futurists with their odes to automobiles and desire to sweep away all existing art."[8] Both scholars, it is true, concede that Futurism may have stimulated Pound's thinking, but only insofar as it coincided with a general climate of "artistic rebellion" (Wilhelm) that was "[already] 'in the air'" (Stock), or only insofar as Futurism may have led Pound to think: "something saner might succeed" (Wilhelm). Such remarks bespeak a puzzling wish to dismiss the possibility that Marinetti may have played a role in Pound's development, a wish so fervent that it has transformed itself into fact. Consider the standard edition of Pound's *Selected Letters,* first published in 1950, a volume that includes two letters in which Pound refers to Marinetti by name, both from 1915; in their published versions, however, the first is presented without the sentence that mentions Marinetti, and the second is given with Marinetti's name disfigured into "Mennetti."[9]

If it is true, as the logic of poststructuralism asserts, that every erasure will leave its trace in such a way that the very thing one is trying to exclude is disclosed as the hidden center of a contaminated order, then it will come as no surprise to suggest that Marinetti, far from merely prompting Pound to issue or encourage hostile remarks about Futurism, may have stood behind two of the most significant turning points in Pound's career. Futurism in London in 1912 to 1914 mounted a sustained interrogation of the concept of aesthetic autonomy, blurring the boundaries of a category formerly deemed self-evident, precipitating a species of legitimation crisis in the concept of art itself. Yet the crisis was not purely or solely conceptual: it derived its special power from the ways in which Marinetti's activities elided and confused the distinctions separating different spheres of cultural production—most important, those associated with art and those linked with the production of entertainment as a commodity. The effect of Futurism on Pound and the London avant-garde was to make the social space of cultural production into an urgent question, to problematize the settings in which the work—the business, if you will—of modernism and the avant-garde might get done. It was no longer the polite salon or the genteel review, it seemed for a moment, but the concert hall, the mass circulation newspaper, or perhaps the music hall that might serve as the new agora of literary and cultural debate. But only for a moment. For the efforts to address the new challenges raised by Marinetti also proved to be failures: paradoxically, the twin turning points in the career of Pound and the London avant-garde were significant, not because they led to the resolution of an intractable problem, but because they revealed themselves as dead ends—and dead ends not just for Pound's poetic or intellectual development but for the avant-garde as a viable cultural institution. It was when this was finally understood that the avant-garde turned elsewhere: to a third alternative in which the opposition between elite and popular culture, or between art and commodity, could be resolved in a brief but uneasy synthesis—resolved, one might almost say, by the creation of the avant-garde itself; resolved in such a way that we who live on the other side of that dramatic moment have inherited a conceptual and institutional impasse that will probably remain unresolved for some time to come.

Though Marinetti's activities in London before World War I have been poorly chronicled, they can be reconstructed in considerable detail.[10] What emerges is a portrait of some complexity, one that shows an ongoing dialogue between Marinetti's evolution and a rapidly changing intellectual and social milieu. Marinetti visited and lectured in London at four distinct moments. The first was in 1910, when he delivered several lectures to the Lyceum Club for Women, then located at 128 Piccadilly. Pound, however, was away from London at the time, and the scant attention the lectures received makes it unlikely that he heard about them upon his return.[11] The second and more important of Marinetti's visits to England occurred in the spring of 1912, when he appeared in conjunction with the first exhibition of Futurist paintings at the Sackville Gallery, located at 28 Sackville Street and owned by Max Rothschild.[12] Even before the show opened on 1 March, it was attracting media attention prompted by reports about the controversy it had provoked during its run in Paris. Most of the coverage came from mass circulation newspapers—the *Daily Mirror* (7 February), the *Sketch* (14 February), and the *Illustrated London News* (17 February).[13] On the day before the opening of the exhibition, Sir Philip Burne-Jones offered his view of Futurism in an interview that appeared in the *Pall Mall Gazette,* and his comments anticipated the terms of subsequent debate. He called the exhibition "something hideous and incompetent" and dubbed the Futurists "a band of maniacs."[14] But when challenged to defend his assertions a few days later by Max Rothschild, Burne-Jones retracted his specific comments about individual works and formal practices, only to reassert a more fundamental critique. He should not have commented on the exhibition at all, he said now: it wasn't "really worthwhile discussing the matter seriously" because "we are not dealing with Art in any form." The Futurist paintings, he summarized, were "outside the pale of Art altogether."[15] This was the question that Futurism would press to its ultimate consequence: where was the pale, the boundary line, of Art?

The stage for a confrontation had been set, and when the show opened the next day it set off an avalanche of newspaper reviews, commentary, and publicity. In part the exhibition attracted so much and such intense discussion because it coincided with a deepening political crisis. On the day that it opened, more than a million miners led by self-proclaimed syndicalists declared a strike that seemed to threaten vital natural resources in an unprecedented way. Newspapers called the day "Black Friday," suggesting a religious cataclysm, and printed cartoons such as one portraying a massive Satanic figure with hairy arms, cloven hooves, and the word "strike" written across his emaciated chest, who strides across a coal yard and infuses the spirit of chaos among a crowd of tiny humans fleeing in fright. The title above reads "Black Friday, 1912," and below is a second title, "The Masque of Anarchy," a reference to the unions' anarchist-syndicalist leaders.[16] Simultaneously, militant suffragists suddenly intensified their window-breaking campaign, an activity that left contemporaries profoundly shocked.[17] By a kind of metonymy facilitated by the modern newspaper's juxtaposition of disparate events, Futurism was becoming the cipher of a contemporary crisis, and it was in this tense environment that Marinetti himself arrived, ready to give his lecture of 19 March at Bechstein Hall.[18] Ironically, it would mark a turning point in the career, not of Marinetti, but of Ezra Pound.

By a curious coincidence, Ezra Pound was also giving a lecture on 19 March 1912, the second in a series of three. The talk he had planned for that day was one that encapsulated the central motifs of his career to that point. From the moment he had arrived in London in late 1908, Pound had staked his claims to literary authority on the poetry and culture of Provence. The first poem he had published in England was a sestina, a verse form from Provence, that depicted the Provençal poet Bertrans de Born, and his first books of poetry (*Personae, Exultations,* and *Canzoni*) offered readers a steady diet of sestinas, albas, planhs, ballatas, madrigales, and tenzoni. His first work of critical prose treated the same subject, the poetry of Provence. Pound had established his earliest literary identity by offering readers a species of erudite exoticism, recondite material updated with pungent obiter dicta, a learned mode of writing that could appeal only to an upper-middle-class audience with significant cultural capital (to use Pierre Bourdieu's term) and ambitious cultural aspirations. As one approving reviewer of *Canzoni* put it, Pound had become "The Modern Troubadour."[19] It was a telling oxymoron: Pound had become a living archaism. For just as the sestina and the canzone were literary genres linked with a distinctly courtly way of life, so the troubadour presupposed an aulic mode of cultural production—something poles apart from the late industrial society in which Pound actually lived.

Yet if Pound could be accurately described as a form of living archaism, perhaps it was because he was living archaically. Though he had generally received warm reviews of his early verse, Pound had also soon learned that his writings could scarcely earn a sufficient income. Indeed, he would not have been able to survive had it not been for the stroke of good fortune that befell him in March 1910, when he was introduced to Margaret Cravens, a thirty-year-old American expatriate bohemian—a member of the aristocracy of sensibility, in other words—and friend of the pianist Walter Morse Rummel, studying music in Paris.[20] Two days after they met, Cravens offered to become his patron. The evidence suggests that he received about $1,000, or £200, per annum, a sum that was neither mean nor quite princely. On the eve of World War I in England, the average wage for adult male industrial workers was about £75 per annum, whereas the average annual income of the salaried class was £340. The gap between these figures represented the divide between the working class and the rest of society, a great and accepted gulf that one historian has termed "the major social fact of the day."[21] Patronage meant that Pound's tent was pitched just on the other side of that gulf, yet never far from the abyss that yawned behind him. On 12 March 1912—one week before Marinetti's lecture, and his own—Pound reported to his prospective father-in-law that his income from his writings had risen to £38 for four months, a figure that would yield £114 per annum; in addition, he had recently secured a contract with a publishing firm that guaranteed him another £100 per annum. Together with his £200 from Cravens, he noted proudly, his income amounted to "about £400 per year, with reasonable chance of increase." To be sure, "this would not go very far in England," but at least he was approaching the promised land of the salaried class.[22]

It is in this context that we can best understand Pound's plans to lecture in March 1912, for these were plainly conceived to supplement his income. The strategy was clear enough: by presenting a series of lectures with limited admission and relatively high prices per ticket, he could maximize the returns from the small audience for poetry, capitalizing on its appeal as a marker of social distinction. The series would comprise three lectures, each at 10s. 6d., or the whole series at £1 1s. (that is, a guinea; notoriously, the guinea was a monetary unit of social nuances, used until 1971 in place of the mundane pound to state professional fees, rents for better premises, and similarly impressive purposes). With the hall or salon furnished by a well-to-do friend, there were no expenses to cover, and if the house was full, even with the audience limited to fifty people, Pound would earn between £50 and £60.[23] The site for the series was the "private gallery" of Lord and Lady Glenconner, located at 34 Queen Anne's Gate, a sedate residential street in one of the choicest locations in London, parallel to the southeastern edge of Saint James's Park. Then, as now, the street was a museum of eighteenth-century architecture: its houses, all built around 1704, were handsome three-story buildings with brick fronts and interiors that retained many of their original furnishings—oak staircases, carved wood paneling with pediments over doorways, marble fireplaces, and so on. The nearby residents were no less choice, with Lady Assheton-Smith the owner and occupant of number 30, and dowager Lady Allendale residing next door at number 32. Yet they were nothing compared with the residents of number 34.[24]

The house boasted new inhabitants, Edward and Pamela Glenconner. Edward was the eldest son of Sir Charles Tennant (1823–1906), the third in a succession of enterprising Scotch industrialists who had established their wealth by creating a new system for bleaching fabrics in 1795, just when the British linen and cotton industries were entering a period of sustained growth, then expanded the operation with a range of manufactured chemicals necessary for processing raw materials. Charles Tennant had outdone even his predecessors. Investing shrewdly in railroad stocks and other speculative ventures, he launched firm after firm: in 1866, the Tharsis Sulphur and Copper Company, which mined pyrites (necessary for making sulfur) in Spain and employed some twelve hundred workmen; in 1872, the Steel Company of Scotland, centered in Glasgow; and in 1881, the Mysore Gold Mining Company, a company that revived defunct mines in India with such success that its dividend returns remained consistently better than 100 percent from 1896 to 1905. A Liberal member of Parliament from 1879 onward and later a close friend of William Gladstone, who made him a baronet, Sir Charles eventually became chairman of fourteen companies and director of nine others.[25] His career signaled a shift away from an industrial economy based on local resources to more speculative wealth obtained through investment and organization on an international scale.

The change in economic activity was matched by alterations in residence and lifestyle. Sir Charles purchased a four-thousand-acre estate at Glen, sixty miles outside Glasgow, that became the site of a massive architectural fantasy in the Scots baronial style, fifty rooms amid a phalanx of towers and turrets surmounted by carved gargoyles. In London, however, he purchased a neoclassical edifice in Grosvenor Square, the traditional abode of Tory aristocracy, and after 1880 he began to collect paintings, acting on advice from the dealer William Agnew of Agnew's Gallery and swiftly assembling a collection of British art that was among the most notable of its time. Whereas previous Tennants had been educated in Scotland, Sir Charles consigned his son Edward (1859–1920) to prep school and Eton, educating him to be a courteous country gentleman. Edward became just that: absorbed in shooting, fishing, and forestry, he lacked his father's passion for politics or ambition to make money. The chief events of his life were sparked by the initiatives of others. In 1894 his sister, Margot, married Sir Herbert Henry Asquith, already the home secretary in Gladstone's third Liberal government and a rising star in the party; dutifully, Edward ran in 1896 and 1900 for his father's former parliamentary seat, losing both times, though in 1905, the year of the Liberal landslide, he was finally elected M.P. for Salisbury.[26]

His father's death in 1906 left Edward free to dispose of a vast inheritance, though his subsequent decisions were strongly influenced by his wife, née Pamela Wyndham (1871–1928). Pamela was the fifth and youngest child of Percy and Madeline Wyndham, parents of aristocratic backgrounds who shared an interest in the arts. From 1881 to 1885 they had devotedly constructed Clouds, a massive country house that was the principal work of Philip Webb, an architect closely associated with William Morris and the Arts and Crafts movement. Here Pamela passed her youth and adolescence, nestled amid the Pre-Raphaelite splendor of original works by Dante Gabriel Rossetti and Edward Burne-Jones, tastefully displayed against the background of carpets and curtains by Morris himself. Her literary interests were shaped by the deeply romantic tastes of her older brother, George. (Pamela would write and edit ten books.) She married Edward in 1895, having met him during one of her family's visits to the country house of Sir Charles, and by 1906 she had given birth to five children.[27]

Adjusting to her marriage with Eddy, as he was known, required some effort. Pamela felt that the Glen and her new in-laws were conspicuously lacking in poetry. Their interior decorations, she complained, looked "as if Morris were not—nor had been"; Eddy's sisters, she noted coldly, could "not see the *colour* of other minds quickly"; and conversation with Sir Charles, she reported, trailed "like a winged bird, lower and lower till it gradually settles down among

1. Edward Tennant (1850–1920), first baron Glenconner, heir to the Tennant family fortune. Courtesy of David Tennant.

2. Pamela Wyndham Tennant (1871–1928), Lady
Glenconner, whose "private gallery" hosted three
lectures by Ezra Pound in 1912. Drawing from the
Sketch, 10 December 1913.

stocks and shares, or the indifferent among the poems of Burns."[28] Pamela
soon took steps to remedy the situation. In 1900 she and Eddy acquired an
estate of two thousand acres conveniently located near her parents, and from
1904 to 1906 they were engaged in constructing Wilsford Manor. Though
designed by Detmar Blow, a student of the same Philip Webb who had designed Clouds, it lacked the impress of Webb's eclectic originality. Instead, its
deliberately archaic and Jacobean style oscillated between elegant pretension
and meretricious pretense, the latter painfully evident in the nursery wing that
culminated in a thatched roof—as if the Tennants were rustics!—over the
"Stone Parlour" that looked toward the Avon River below.[29]

On the death of Sir Charles, Edward and Pamela sold the house in Grosvenor Square and purchased 34 Queen Anne's Gate, commissioning Detmar

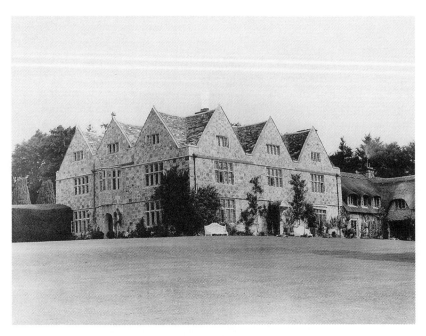

3. Wilsford Manor, near Amesbury; designed by Detmar Blow for Edward and Pamela Tennant, 1904–1906. Courtesy of Country Life Library.

4. Wilsford Manor, the nursery wing. On the lawn stands Dick Wyndham, nephew of Edward and Pamela Tennant. Courtesy of Caroline Dakers and David Tennant.

Blow to add a substantial extension to the building and reorganize its haphaz-
ard spaces. Plans were finalized in 1908 and construction completed in 1910.[30]
The front of the building remained unchanged; the back of the building, which
looked out on St. James's Park, was reorganized with sober refinement: a central
block of three windows in each story was complemented by a bowed wing of
windows on the left, a pattern that followed the building's internal structure.
Thus, the ground floor was devoted to a formal dining room (central block)
and drawing room (bowed wing), and the first floor housed a gallery to hold the
collection of paintings that had been assembled by Sir Charles, complemented
by a smaller salon. It was here on the first floor, in what was termed "the private
gallery," that Ezra Pound would give his lectures on Provençal poetry. The
room, recorded in photographs commissioned by Edward in 1910, contained
nearly all the most valuable paintings of the Tennant collection: thirty-seven
works by the masters of British art from the eighteenth century, together with
others by Antoine Watteau, Jean-Honoré Fragonard, and nineteenth-century
British artists such as George Morland and J. M. W. Turner.[31] On the north
wall that overlooks St. James's Park, placed between two windows, we see Sir
Joshua Reynolds's portrait *Robert Mayne* and Sir Henry Raeburn's well-known
The Leslie Boy; to the right of the door we can see George Romney's portrait
Mrs. Inchbald and Reynolds's *Girl Crying,* and just to the right of these hung
Reynolds's magnificent portrait *Lady Diana Crosby.* On the opposite wall stood
another series of masterpieces: Romney's portrait *Elizabeth, Countess of Derby,*
William Hogarth's *Peg Woffington,* Thomas Gainsborough's *Miss Hippisley* and
The Ladies Erne and Dillon, Allan Ramsay's *Lady Erskine,* and John Hoppner's
Mrs. Gwynn.[32]

The "private gallery" was a deeply ambiguous space that fulfilled several
conflicting functions. The room contained a specially built "sprung floor" that
furnished an ideal surface for dancing, and at times it served as the setting for
the Tennants' infrequent but lavish entertainments. It was also a "gallery" in the
ordinary sense of the word. The Tennants, moved by a mixture of impulses that
included genuine generosity, a sense of liberal guilt, and an impulse to self-
display, had decided to make their gallery open to the general public free of
charge for four hours each on Wednesdays and Saturdays, making theirs one of
the first private collections made available for public view.[33] And it was a space
in which other meanings could be invested, some of which were elaborated in
Pamela's entertaining book *The Children and the Pictures,* which recounts a
fictional story of how her children "meet" and respond to the paintings held in
the gallery. Awakened one evening by the sound of conversation below, Pamela's

5. 34 Queen Anne's Gate, London, front entrance. Photograph by E. Badford Lamere, November 1910, commissioned by Edward Tennant. Courtesy of the Royal Commission on the Historical Monuments of England, © Crown copyright.

oldest daughter discovers that the people depicted in the paintings return to life at night and conduct spirited discussions about the past and the present. Slightly put off at first, Clare soon warms to an entire cast of characters, and it is not long before she has also involved her siblings in a series of nightly dialogues and adventures with the dead. Eventually the children conclude that the world of the dead is infinitely freer and fresher than the world of the living, and it requires some effort on the part of their mother to convince them that they must learn to keep the paintings in their proper place in the realm of night and dreams.

A testimony to Pamela's devotion to her children and a fine specimen of her

6. 34 Queen Anne's Gate, London, rear facade, facing St. James's Park. Photograph by E. Badford Lamere, November 1910, commissioned by Edward Tennant. Courtesy of the Royal Commission on the Historical Monuments of England, © Crown copyright.

gift for whimsy, *The Children and the Pictures* is also a tale of cultural pathology that implies a world grown so loathsome that life is now conceived as residing only in dialogue with the dead, with shadowy figures whose comforting comments offer an untroubled escape from the living. A similar escapism is affirmed in Pamela's first book of poems, *Windlestraw,* published two years earlier, in which she praised the rural peace of Wiltshire as an ideal that promised tranquillity to her readers:

7. 34 Queen Anne's Gate, London, first floor, north wall of the "private gallery" where Ezra Pound lectured in March 1912. Photograph by E. Badford Lamere, November 1910, commissioned by Edward Tennant. Courtesy of the Royal Commission on the Historical Monuments of England, © Crown copyright.

> Here may I dwell content. And when the day
> Dawns that shall recognize thy task complete
> Thou too, from busy crowds shalt turn away
> To some sublime retreat.

The "private gallery" was exactly such a "sublime retreat." And Philip Burne-Jones, son of the great Pre-Raphaelite painter and a companion of Pamela in her youth—the same man whose indignation would shortly be roused by the Futurists—was only too happy to accept the consolatory poetry of Pamela. As he wrote to her in 1905 when he had finished his copy of the book, "I do love 'Windlestraw'—do you mind my telling you so, dear Pamela? Such sweet little verses about such delicious things—all sorts of things I'd like to have said *myself!*—(and one can't give any higher praise than that!) They seem the echoes of such a happy country life—and there are beautiful thoughts, too, beautifully

8. 34 Queen Anne's Gate, London, first floor, south wall of the "private gallery."
Photograph by E. Badford Lamere, November 1910, commissioned by Edward Tennant.
Courtesy of the Royal Commission on the Historical Monuments of England, © Crown
copyright.

expressed."[34] The ensemble of cultural values embedded in the "private gallery" of Lord and Lady Glenconner—the Tennants acquired their title in April
1911 when Asquith, by then the prime minister, rewarded Edward's faithful
financial support with a peerage, making him the first baron Glenconner—
constituted the stage for Pound's performance of March 1912. Speaking in this

room and amid these paintings, Pound was turned into yet another picture from the past, another voice from an era both dead and comforting—indeed, comforting because dead. Cast within the scenario outlined by *The Children and the Pictures,* his performance restages a drama of cultural regression, one in which the auditors are turned into children who are enthralled by the voice of remote romance that speaks in "some sublime retreat."

Access to that "retreat" was not available to all and sundry; admission to Pound's lectures was almost as difficult to obtain as a house on Queen Anne's Gate, and care was taken to distinguish them from other offerings of the contemporary economy. The program that announced them, for example, was privately distributed. Tickets were not commodities that could be purchased but favors that might be courteously requested. "TICKETS may be obtained on application to Lady Low," stated the program. Lady Ann Penelope Low, the daughter of General Robert Percy Douglas, fourth baronet, had been widowed in 1905 and now resided at 23 De Vere Gardens amid a row of houses nestled just off the southern corner of Kensington Gardens, where she kept an informal salon and sponsored "evenings at home." A close friend of Olivia Shakespear, the mother of Pound's fiancée, Lady Low frequented a circle of upper-middle-class intellectuals such as G. W. Prothero, editor of the *Quarterly Review.*[35] Here was the realm of elite bourgeois culture in which Pound's career had been fashioned before 1912: a world withdrawn from public life and insulated from the grim imperatives of a commodity economy, a sphere in which literary culture had been largely privatized, serving as a medium of exchange for an exiguous aristocracy of sensibility, a court of intellect. Access to this world was strictly controlled: the audience, as the program noted, was "limited to FIFTY."

Pound's three lectures were scheduled for the fourteenth, the nineteenth, and the twenty-first of March, and immediately after the first one he wrote his father to report his success: "Have just got my first lecture off my chest and am ready to rest. Have cleaned up $90 so far."[36] Yet there were some obvious disadvantages to these proceedings, which required that Pound maintain good relations with a network of people with influence and power—people who could oblige others to attend his lectures—and it left him little room to provoke an audience on whose goodwill he was patently dependent. Further, his access to these circles was mediated largely by Olivia Shakespear, his pro-spective mother-in-law, creating private tensions that must have been all but unbearable. That there were other avenues to an audience would become apparent in the unexpected events that attended Pound's second lecture, the one scheduled for Tuesday, 19 March 1912.

EZRA POUND, M.A.

(Author of "Exultations," "Canzoni,"
"The Spirit of Romance")

WILL GIVE

THREE LECTURES ON

MEDIÆVAL POETRY

AT

34 QUEEN ANNE'S GATE, S.W.,

AS FOLLOWS, AT 3.30.

THURSDAY, MARCH 14TH.

TUSCANY, A.D. 1290: GUIDO CAVALCANTI.

In the Chair—FREDERIC MANNING.

TUESDAY, MARCH 19TH.

PROVENCE, A.D. 1190: ARNAUT DANIEL.

In the Chair—

THURSDAY, MARCH 21ST.

ENGLAND, A.D. 790: ANGLO-SAXON VERSE.

In the Chair—W. B. YEATS.

The Three Schools will be considered in part, in their possible relation to the Art of to-day.

TICKETS may be obtained on application to LADY LOW, 23 De Vere Gardens, Kensington, W.

For the Course of Three Lectures, £1 1s.
Admittance to Single Lectures, 10s. 6d.

As Audience is limited to FIFTY an early application is desirable.

9. Program for a series of lectures by Ezra Pound, March 1912; 12.5 × 10 cm. Hamilton College Library, courtesy of Omar Pound.

The topic of Pound's first lecture, on 14 March, had been Guido Cavalcanti. His second was to treat "Provence, A.D. 1190: Arnaut Daniel." Pound was on familiar ground here, discussing the master of "trobar clus," or "closed verse," the most hermetic vein of troubadour poetry. Characterizing such poems two months later in an essay based on this very lecture, Pound would write: "They are good art as the high mass is good art," works that must be "approached as ritual" because they sought "to make their revelations to those who are already expert."[37] Pound, very plainly, was describing not just the work of Arnaut Daniel but his own poetry as well. His lecture on Daniel's poems and audience was a wholly self-referential discourse that bespoke Pound's own situation. Appropriately—and yet how ironic, when compared with Marinetti's lecture that same day—the program for Pound's lecture stated that he would discuss Daniel's "possible relation to the Art of to-day." (Like Philip Burne-Jones, Pound still conceived of art with a capital *A*.) The time was set for 3:30 P.M.

On the morning of the lecture he received a letter from his fiancée, who told him that she would be attending a lecture that evening—not his, however. She was going "to hear Marinetti lecture . . . about les Futuristes" at Bechstein Hall.[38] This was Pound's first experience of what might be termed ephemeral seduction, the powerful allure of art conceived as public practice, as a spectacle capable of attracting an audience much larger than fifty, as performance that could arouse curiosity, debate, desire. The next day must have been unforgettable for an avid reader of newspapers such as Pound. Not a one took note of "Provence, A.D. 1190: Arnaut Daniel." But Marinetti's performance was fully reported in the morning edition of the *Daily Chronicle,* with a headline reading "'Futurist' Leader in London," accompanied by the subtitle, "Makes an Attack on the English Nation." The next day a second article on Marinetti appeared in the *Morning Leader,* and yet a third was published on the second page of the *Times,* as a lead editorial![39] Odder still, Marinetti had not flattered his audience but berated it, castigating the English as "a nation of sycophants and snobs, enslaved by old worm-eaten traditions, social conventions, and romanticism." And though the *Times* reported that "some of his audience begged for mercy," the *Daily Chronicle* noted that "the long-haired gentlemen in the stalls and the ladies with Rossetti eyes and lips rewarded him with their laughter and applause." Still another observer, writing a year later, recalled an audience that "wildly applauded his outspoken derision of all their cherished national characteristics."[40]

Marinetti's lecture achieved instant notoriety. After only six weeks in England, he reported in mid-April, the Futurists had elicited 350 articles in newspapers and reviews and had earned more than 11,000 francs in sales of paintings ($2,200, or £440).[41] More important, Marinetti had achieved his success not by addressing only an educated elite but by speaking in a public forum to a wider audience. Whereas tickets to each of Pound's lectures had uniformly cost 10s. 6d., only the most expensive tickets to Marinetti's lecture had cost that much, and the lowest-priced tickets had sold for 1s.; and whereas Pound's audience had been deliberately "limited to FIFTY," Marinetti's may have reached 500. (Seating capacity at Bechstein Hall was 550.)[42] More important, Marinetti's audience had become not just the people who attended his performance in Bechstein Hall but the millions who read about it in the *Daily Chronicle,* the *Morning Leader,* and the *Times.*

Nothing could have made plainer the value of a concerted polemical onslaught, the formation of a collective identity buttressed by theatricality and publicity. Sometime in March 1912—it may have been before Marinetti's lecture, though it was certainly *after* the outbreak of publicity surrounding the Futurist exhibition—Pound sent off the manuscript for his next book of poetry, *Ripostes.* At the end of the volume he included a brief statement that has since become famous as the first public reference to Imagism: "As for the future, *Les Imagistes,* the descendants of the forgotten school of 1909, have that in their keeping." The use of French, *Les Imagistes,* to designate the new "school" is an obvious echo of the linguistic practice that had led Dorothy Shakespear to describe her plans "to hear Marinetti lecture in French, about les Futuristes," just as Dorothy's practice was probably a consequence of Marinetti's own. As Marinetti did not speak English, he delivered all his lectures in French while in England; and because he also wrote the original versions for the early Futurist manifestos in French, at least in part because French was still the lingua franca of European intellectual exchange, it was natural to speak about him in French as well. It was also the French version of new manifestos that Marinetti routinely mailed to British critics and journalists, and although mass circulation dailies translated quotations into English, the intellectual and cultural weeklies usually cited the French directly. When Pound, therefore, first announces the creation of Imagism ("As for the future, *Les Imagistes* . . . have that in their keeping"), he uses a conjunction of terms ("future" and the name of a movement in French) that plainly signals their provenance.[43]

Pound's subsequent steps toward art as public practice came in the wake of three events, all of them precipitating a collapse of the "courtly" structure of cultural production that had previously characterized Pound's milieu. In June 1912 Margaret Cravens committed suicide, leaving Pound without the financial support that had sustained him for two years and reinforced his aulic self-conception. In late October, the publishing firm that had guaranteed him one hundred pounds per year collapsed. Pound was back to where he had started, and it was not a matter he could easily forget: five hundred pounds per annum, his prospective mother-in-law advised him in September, was the minimum it would take for him to marry her daughter.[44] In late September, too, Pound learned that Edward Marsh was assembling an anthology designed to present the recent work of younger poets as a collective project, the Georgians.[45] By December it had already become clear that the volume was going to be a remarkable success. Impelled by these events, Pound began to launch Imagism in a more systematic and serious way.

On 18 August and sometime in October he sent off poems by himself and H.D. to *Poetry* magazine, characterizing them as "Imagiste."[46] In December he wrote an essay that surveyed contemporary poetry in London—the essay was published in January 1913—and contained his second public reference to Imagism, a description that ran for two brief paragraphs. Imagism was "the youngest school here that has the nerve to call itself a school."[47] The aggressive tone was at odds with the tentative definitions that followed, a contradiction already apparent in the diction. For "school" was a term that Marinetti had used in his earliest writings on Futurism, in 1909, but had subsequently rejected for its associations with the taxonomies of academic art history, instead adopting the term "movement." Indeed, Pound's presentation of "Imagism" implicitly underscored its differences from Futurism. Imagism rejected Futurism's ethos of collective identity: a school was something more informal, more casual, more individualistic, the fortuitous outcome of "two or three young men agree[ing], more or less, to call certain things good." Imagism also shunned the kind of programmatic ambitions associated with Futurism: "a school does not mean in the least that one writes poetry to a theory." (Saying this, Pound was echoing contemporary reviewers who had complained that Futurist paintings were "rather a theoretic extension than a spontaneous development.")[48] Instead Pound stressed the purely technical nature of Imagism: "Their watchword was Precision" and they sought "to produce a good single line" or just "a good short" poem. They opposed only "interminable effusions." Yet who, after all, would want to defend interminable effusions? Imagism, in short, was a movement to end movements: informal, antitheoretical, absorbed in matters of writerly technique, and averse to more global programs that linked poetry to contemporary social transformations or posed questions about the status and functions of art. Though Imagism is commonly treated as the first avant-garde in Anglo-American literature, it was really something quite different—the first anti-avant-garde. And Pound's subsequent efforts to define Imagism only accentuated these features. In an essay published two months later, in March 1913, written by Pound though printed under the signature of F. S. Flint, Pound made the opposition of Imagism and Futurism explicit: "The *imagistes* admitted that they were contemporaries of the Post Impressionists and the Futurists;

but they had nothing in common with these schools. They had not published a manifesto. They were not a revolutionary school; their only endeavor was to write in accordance with the best tradition, as they found it in the best writers of all time,—in Sappho, Catullus, Villon." Accompanying this essay was another, this one signed by Pound, "A Few Don'ts By an Imagiste," a title implicitly in opposition to the genre of the manifesto.[49] It was a timid response to the challenges raised by the Futurist presence in London, and in a moment of candor in 1927, Pound himself recalled the creation of Imagism in the most mundane terms: "The name was invented to launch H.D. and Aldington before either had enough stuff for a volume."[50] The launching and marketing of a new product—was this all that was at stake in the creation of Imagism?

Formulating the question this way fails to acknowledge the complications and unexpected consequences that were entailed in this novel use of publicity, advertising, and spectacle in connection with culture, creating new pressures that became increasingly apparent in the course of Marinetti's last two visits to England, in late 1913 and early 1914. For Pound these visits were important because Marinetti was increasingly shifting the front of his activity from the visual arts to literature: in May 1912 he published the "Technical Manifesto of Futurist Literature," in August the "Response to Objections"; in June and November 1913 he issued the "Destruction of Syntax—Radio Imagination—Words-in-Freedom," and in October "The Variety Theater."[51] English readers were kept abreast. In September 1913 the journal *Poetry and Drama,* edited by Harold Monro, devoted an entire issue to examining Futurism. (Its previous issue, notably, had devoted only a paragraph to Imagism.) The issue included a translation of "L'immaginazione senza fili," as well as almost thirty pages of poems by Aldo Palazzeschi, Paolo Buzzi, and Marinetti himself. And in a long editorial, Monro praised Marinetti warmly, hailing him for auguring a dissolution of every distinction between poetry and popular culture, art and life. Rhapsodizing about the sheer size of Futurism's audience—in Italy it had "gained the support of no less than 22,000 adherents"—Monro became positively breathless at the thought that *I poeti futuristi* (1912) had sold thirty-five thousand copies. This fact in itself, Monro said, constituted "Marinetti's most interesting attitude." Here, he declared, was poetry that was no longer written for "close and studious scrutiny by the eye," poetry "no longer . . . withheld from the people" by "educationalists," "intellectuals," or the commercial press, but poetry intended "for the ear," "for immediate and wide circulation," poetry "regaining some of its popular appeal." Single-handedly, Marinetti was restoring poetry to its status in an earlier era, an age when "the minstrel and the ballad-monger then represented our modern Northcliffe."[52] Monro's reference to Northcliffe was telling: famously, Northcliffe in 1896 had founded the *Daily Mail,* a new kind of newspaper that stressed concise writing, attractive competitions, and alluring advertisements, developing a format that effectively blurred the distinction between news and entertainment; by 1902 its circulation topped one million, then the largest in the world. (Pound, throughout his voluminous correspondence, contemptuously referred to it as "the Dilly Mile.") Northcliffe was the embodiment of mass culture, and Monro's reference to him, in the context of his celebratory remarks on Marinetti, inadvertently signaled some of the tensions latent in the collapse of life and art that he wished to celebrate: for it suggested that there was no longer a meaningful distinction between poetry and the most ephemeral of commodities, the daily newspaper. The question that had first been posed by Sir Philip Burne-Jones—where was the boundary line of art?—had reared its head again. It would be more fully explored in the course of Marinetti's last two visits to London.

Monro's remarks prefaced Marinetti's third arrival in London by two months. Once again, for six days in November 1913, Marinetti gave daily lectures and readings that attracted substantial audiences and media attention. Now, however, Marinetti began to press his attack against elite bourgeois culture to new limits, assaulting the very principles that had once grounded his own thinking—principles that still grounded Pound's own. Already in the "Founding and Manifesto of Futurism" of 1909 Marinetti had urged that contemporary art be responsive to continuous change and innovation, emphasizing contemporaneity in a way that tended to blur the distinction between art and fashion; yet he had hesitated to draw the logical conclusion that art itself was not an eternal absolute.[53] To the contrary, as late as 1911 he could still charge that his critics feared him precisely because of his defense of art as an absolute: "Perhaps they saw, shining from our eyes, the glorious passion that we nurture for Art. [The capital *A* is Marinetti's own.] To art, in fact, which merits and which demands the sacrifice of the best, we give a love that is absolute."[54] But as early as the "Technical Manifesto" of mid-May 1912 he had begun to sound a new note: "Courageously let us set about making the 'ugly' in literature, and let us kill solemnity everywhere. Go away! don't listen to me with the air of great priests! Every day it is necessary to spit on the *Altar of Art!*"[55] And now, in the new lectures that he gave in late 1913, Marinetti pursued his conclusions to their ultimate consequences. He damned the sacred conception of art: "Art is not a religion," he declaimed on 17 November at the Poets' Club, "not something to be worshipped with joined hands." Instead it "should express all the intensity of life—its beauty . . . its sordidness," and "the very complex of our life to-day." (Pound himself may have attended this lecture, as it is certain many of his friends did.)[56] Four days later, the *Daily Mail*—and no venue could have been more revealing—would publish Marinetti's manifesto "The Variety Theater," or "Le Music-Hall," with its intransigent vindication of a popular but critically despised cultural form. The music hall, wrote Marinetti, "is of course anti-academical, primitive, and ingenuous, and therefore all the more significant by reason of the unforseen nature of all its fumbling efforts and the coarse simplicity of its resources. . . . [It] destroys all that is solemn, sacred, earnest, and pure in Art—with a big *A*."[57]

When Marinetti returned to England six months later, in May and June 1914, he was given a chance to put his theories into effect. In June Marinetti was booked to appear at the Coliseum for a week, from Monday, 15 June, to Saturday, 21 June, twice daily. By now Marinetti had acquired an extraordinary stature in the life of the commercial press. Mass circulation weeklies such as the *Sketch* and the *Graphic* assiduously reported his doings and sayings. His mocking self-portrait, an assemblage of discarded pieces of wood attached to a wire brush, the bristles of which represented his hair, was featured on the front cover of the weekly *Sketch*. His views on "Futurist" clothes made headlines, and his every lecture was reported with warm good humor or respectful earnestness.[58] Major newspapers were even competing for advance news stories about the "Futurist Music," and three days before the premiere the *Pall Mall Gazette* featured a front-page story that was labeled a " 'P.M.G.' Special" about the rehearsals.[59] It was a major event indeed: Marinetti had agreed to introduce Luigi Russolo and his notorious noise-tuners, or *intonarumori*. Marinetti was crossing the boundary into a realm of cultural practice in which "traditional art" had seldom been seen.

For the Coliseum was not just a music hall in the traditional sense. Its construction and organization had epitomized a set of new developments transforming the world of Edwardian entertainment. Its site on St. Martin's Lane had been selected by Oswald Stoll, the most successful of Edwardian theatrical entrepreneurs, precisely because it was directly visible from the exit of Charing Cross station, all but addressing the crowds of respectable, prosperous people who poured into the metropolis on a day's shopping excursion. Such people might be glad for an afternoon or evening's entertainment, Stoll had reasoned. They were "middle-class people for whom a visit to a serious play might seem too ambitious and a visit to a music-hall far too racy."[60] In seeking

10. F. T. Marinetti, *Self-Portrait* (1914). From the cover of the
Sketch, 13 May 1914.

to please this audience, Stoll presented them a sanitized version of the music
hall—a "Palace of Variety" that offered, in the words of its program, "the social
advantages of the refined and elegant surroundings of a Club."[61] Marie Lloyd,
one of the greatest music hall stars, was never invited to perform at the Coliseum: her racy lyrics and double entendres were too vulgar. Stoll's theater was
part of a wider trend that was changing the music hall from a form of entertainment rooted in the culture of the working and lower middle classes and instead
assimilating it to the tastes of a middle class increasingly defined by consumerism. His Coliseum, which opened in 1904, was the biggest and most lavish
music hall in London. Its seating capacity was nearly four thousand, its stage
and proscenium were the largest ever built, and its architecture was impossible
to ignore: the centerpiece was a massive tower that soared into the air, topped by

11. F. T. Marinetti (fifth from left) and Luigi Russolo (fourth from left), rehearsing "noise-tuners" for the Futurist concert of noises at the Coliseum, London, June 1914. Photograph from the *Sketch,* 17 June 1914.

eight cupids holding a rotating globe with the name COLISEUM in electric lights. Here was something to "to catch the attention of those prosperous shoppers."[62] Here was culture as consumption, art as entertainment, and here was the place where Marinetti would complete his last performance in England.

The show, paradoxically, was not successful. And contemporary observers understood the reasons immediately. Reviewing the premiere performance, the *Times* wrote: "Signor Marinetti rather mistook his audience yesterday afternoon, when he tried to deliver an academic exposition of Futurist principles at the Coliseum, and he had, in consequence, to put up with a rude reception from a gallery which seemed fully qualified to give him a lesson in his own 'Art of Noises.'"[63] Marinetti indeed "mistook his audience," ultimately in two different yet related ways. One was historical. Marinetti had badly misunderstood the nature of the music hall itself. His sense of the music hall derived largely from his experience in Italy, where it was still a vital, turbulent genre of urban popular culture, a hybrid form addressing a public still making the

12. The Coliseum, London, designed by Frank Matcham for Oswald Stoll, 1904. Drawing by Charles W. Wyllie from the *Sphere,* 24 December 1904.

transition from a largely agrarian to a wholly urban way of life. It was a form that specifically spoke to the hybridized experience of people who had recently migrated to the metropolis, mingling motifs of the village carnival and more modern genres to treat the dislocations of urban experience. But in the more advanced industrial culture of England, where the wrenching process of urbanization had been more fully assimilated, the music hall was already a corpse that was experiencing a brief but spurious afterlife through its incorporation into the "Palace of Variety," the new institution of an advancing consumer economy. Music hall would soon be swept away by the outbreak of World War I and the arrival of Hollywood cinema. In England, in other words, the music hall was no longer a hybrid creation of popular culture but a prototype of mass commodity culture.

Marinetti's second mistake was theoretical. In the simplest terms, he failed to see that quotation and bricolage are strictly one-way streets. By this I mean that Marinetti's effort to appropriate, legitimate, and transform a still illegitimate genre such as the music hall had the effect not of delegitimating art, as he supposed, but of reaffirming its legitimacy, insofar as it fostered belief not in the value of this stake (for example, the music hall) or that stake (for example, classical theater) but in the value of the game in which all the stakes are assigned value at all.[64] More concretely, from a position within the already legitimate domain of art or high culture it was possible for Marinetti to appropriate and legitimate practices of mass culture; but from within the illegitimate domain of mass culture, the Coliseum itself, there was no theoretical ground of critical distancing by which to assimilate alien or heterogeneous cultural forms. What the *Times* reviewer termed an "academic exposition of Futurist principles" was precisely the kind of "serious" and self-reflective discourse that the Coliseum sought to exclude. And so it did. After fifteen minutes of Marinetti's first lecture the curtain was unceremoniously lowered—there was a danger, the stage manager later claimed, that "people would start throwing things." And for subsequent performances Stoll obliged Marinetti to include a gramophone playing records by Edward Elgar, the most philistine of all composers, allegedly "to bring a little melody into the act."[65] Though Marinetti finished his run of one week, the Coliseum swiftly moved to compensate for the fiasco, bringing in as its next headliner George Robey, a performer almost as popular as Marie Lloyd. Marinetti's effort to assimilate the concept of art to that of the commodity had failed.

If Imagism was an intellectual failure as an attempt to address the pressures brought to bear by the forms of cultural practice that Marinetti was introducing in England, then it must have been doubly disappointing for Pound to find that his effort to assimilate those same forms should meet with a different lack of success. For if we take it that *Blast* did indeed incorporate the Futurist attack on high art—and tellingly, among its list of those to be "blasted" was "Lord Glenconner of Glen," a name Pound surely included himself—or that it presented itself as a kind of graphic counterpart of music hall performance, then its lack of critical and public acceptance is revealing.[66] For contrary to what later critics have suggested, contemporary critics were neither angered nor provoked by *Blast*. They were simply bored, and not because *Blast* was an incomprehensible novelty, but because it was all too familiar. They said so, too, in contemporary reviews: "Almost all the pictures reproduced are (like the typesetting of the first pages), Futurist in origin, and nothing else. And as for the productions of the literary Vortices, these are not even so fresh as that. . . . All it really is is a feeble attempt at being clever. *Blast* is a flat affair. We haven't a movement here, not even a mistaken one." And in perhaps the most cutting words of all, the same reviewer remarked: "Mr. Pound used to be quite interesting when he was a remote passéist and wrote about the Provençal troubadours; but as a revolutionary I would rather have Signor Marinetti, who is at any rate a genuine hustler, whereas Mr. Pound assuming violence and ruthlessness is as unimpressive in his movements as a man who is trying to use someone else's coat as a pair of trousers."[67] *Blast* was indeed a dull affair, and the poems that Pound published in it are among the dreariest he ever produced. His attempt to address and provoke an audience through a programmatic polemical onslaught had proved a conspicuous failure. And not just in aesthetic but also in economic terms. When Wyndham Lewis later recalled the brief moment when he was the lion of London society as a result of *Blast*, he remembered how little it served him: "As a result of these sociable activities, I did not sell a single picture, it is superfluous to say."[68]

Initially, then, Marinetti's practical and theoretical activities in London during 1912–1914 had two related effects on Pound and what has subsequently come to be termed the Anglo-American avant-garde. One was to provoke a reconfiguration of the relations among the institutions in which the discourse of art and poetry had been produced until then, forcing intellectuals and artists to come to terms with the role of new institutions of mass culture and assess their bearings on the place of art in a cultural marketplace being radically transformed. The other, in so doing, was to precipitate a permanent collapse of all distinctions between art and commodity, to effect a perceptible and irreversible leveling of both within the single and amorphous category of the commodity. Further, by late 1914 it was clear that the attempts to respond to these dilemmas had proved failures, whether it was the rearguard restoration effort of Imagism or the imitative gesture of *Blast*. But if one could neither go back to reconstruct the aristocracy of the salon nor go forward to embrace the egalitarianism of the commodity, what solution was there? The answer, paradoxically, was to do a little of both at once: to reconstruct an aristocracy, but to do it within the world of the commodity—to accept, in other words, the status of art as a commodity, but simultaneously to transform it into a special kind of commodity, a rarity capable of sustaining investment value. Or, to reformulate this, the answer to the leveling effect precipitated by a consumer economy was to defer consumption into the future, to transform it into investment; which is to say, to encourage or even solicit the ephemeral seduction of the consumer economy, acknowledging the status of art as commodity, but to postpone and sublimate its consumption by turning it into an object of investment whose value will be realized only in the future. "Art," as Pound would formulate it, becomes "news that stays news."

More concretely, what had once been an aristocracy of patron-*salonniers* would now be replaced by an elite of patron-investors. For the Anglo-American avant-garde, the future lay in the new patronage provided by a small group of people such as John Quinn, Harriet Shaw Weaver, Scofield Thayer, and James Sibley Watson, Jr. The actualization of this new space within the commodity economy was achieved primarily through the new and unprecedented use of two institutions that had existed for some time but now became central to an emerging apparatus of cultural production: the little review and the limited edition, venues situated in a profoundly ambiguous social space, simultaneously sequestered and semi-withdrawn from the larger institution of publishing even while firmly embedded within the market economy. It was in the little reviews—among them the *Little Review,* the *Egoist,* and the *Dial*—that the principal masterpieces of the Anglo-American avant-garde would first be published. Likewise, their second appearance was almost uniformly in limited or deluxe editions of 200 copies (such as *Hugh Selwyn Mauberley*) or 254 copies (Eliot's *Ara Vos Prec*), or 1,000 copies (*Ulysses*)—editions at the farthest possible remove from the 35,000 copies of *I poeti futuristi*. And in this new social space, the kind of publicization that had once been aimed at a mass audience along the lines pursued by Marinetti and imitated by *Blast* were no longer of use. Asked by Margaret Anderson in 1917 how best to announce his collaboration on the *Little Review,*

Pound now replied: "IF it is any use for adv[ertising]. purposes, you may state that a single copy of my first book has just fetched £8 (forty dollars)." Similarly, seven years later, when William Bird was drafting the prospectus for the first edition of *A Draft of XVI. Cantos,* Pound would urge the same argument: "Yr. best ad is the quiet statement that at auction recently a copy of Mr. P's [first book] 'A Lume Spento' published in 1908 at $1.00 (one dollar) was sold for $52.50."[69] These remarks, far from advancing assertions of intrinsic aesthetic value based on the presupposition of Art, offer straightforward claims about the performance record of investments within a commodity economy: by 1917 *A Lume Spento* had been increasing in value at a rate of more than 50 percent a year, by 1924 at 28 percent a year. The same, by implication, should now prove true of the *Little Review* or *A Draft of XVI. Cantos.* The reason to buy these was not necessarily to read them but to be able to sell them—perhaps at a substantial profit. Readers, in short, are giving way to an uneasy mixture of patron-investors, collectors, and speculators on the rare book market, all situated within a complex and highly unstable institutional space.

What the patron-investors provided with their generous subsidies and endowments was an institutional sphere that was momentarily immune to the pressures of a market economy, partially removed from the constraints of an expansive and expanding mass culture. In this dense new space of collectors and quasi-investors, large audiences were not a help but a hindrance. Consider only the case of the Modern Gallery, which was first opened in 1916 at 500 Fifth Avenue by Marius de Zayas, a minor artist and journalist previously associated with Alfred Stieglitz and the "291" Gallery.[70] The gallery's principal clients were Eugene and Agnes Meyer, Arthur B. Davies, Walter Arensberg, and John Quinn—few but fit. In 1920 alone Quinn purchased nearly $24,000 worth of works from de Zayas, and even after returning two paintings in early 1921, the sum of his 1920 purchases totaled almost $13,000.[71] Translated into contemporary figures, this might fall somewhere between $340,000 and $390,000. Success, even survival, could depend on just such a nucleus of patron-investors, as de Zayas was told in 1919 by his French colleague, the Parisian dealer Charles Vignier, who was shaken when he learned that de Zayas was staging exhibitions that were drawing large crowds, with his gallery filled almost daily: "I feel very uneasy to learn that your Gallery is full every day. You are losing uselessly a precious strength by these vain chatterings. I would rather hear that you have seen three clients in one week, of whom one has bought something."[72] Vignier's remarks were perceptive. Ironically, de Zayas was ultimately forced to close his gallery, not because he had failed to attract a large audience, but because he had succeeded in doing so. That was the dilemma of the avant-garde.

In responding to it by creating a distinction within the world of commodity culture whereby there is one set of cultural commodities whose value is exhausted in immediate consumption and another whose worth is deferred or sublated into the future as investment, modernism gained for itself—for an evanescent moment—a breathing space within the present, a space from which it could formulate its powerful critique of commodity capitalism, even as—and at the same time as—it mortgaged that critique in the future, mirroring the very system that it critiqued. But the consequences of this precarious compromise could not be forever deferred. For it was an inevitable outcome of this situation that the avant-garde's distaste for the dictates of the marketplace should ultimately be revealed as disingenuous precisely because, and insofar as, the works of the avant-garde began to command ever more significant prices within the larger open market. After that it was only a matter of time before the emergence of forms of art that were already "precommodified," art that ironically and even nostalgically acknowledges its own exchange function, art that finds its richest moments—in several senses—in the works of Andy Warhol. These are the *tristes tropiques* of late capitalism, known in their more naive form as "postmodernism."

Chapter 2 Consuming

Investments: Joyce's *Ulysses*

Seventy-five years ago, at seven o'clock in the morning on 2 February 1922, Sylvia Beach waited at the Gare de Lyon in Paris to greet the morning express train from Dijon. As it slowed beside the platform, she later recalled, a conductor stepped down and handed her a small bundle that contained two copies of the first edition of *Ulysses*. Beach, the proprietor of Shakespeare and Company, an English-language bookshop in Paris, had just become the publisher of what would become the most celebrated novel of the century. Elated, she hastened to the hotel where Joyce was residing and handed him his copy, a present for his fortieth birthday; then she hurried back to her store and ceremoniously placed the second copy in the window. Soon a small crowd of onlookers gathered to admire the volume's handsome blue cover and celebrate the august event.[1]

This, Beach's account, confirms our most common assumptions about the publication of *Ulysses,* and hence about literary modernism. Joyce and Beach are cast as heroic figures who have succeeded despite a benighted legal system, philistine publishers, and a hostile or indifferent public; and their efforts are readily appreciated by a small yet discerning circle of readers whose insight, in the course of many years, is gradually corroborated by critics and scholars, as the book achieves canonical status. Those readers' names appear and reappear in every account of *Ulysses*'s first publication. One critic, describing a record book in which Sylvia Beach entered the names of buyers from the United Kingdom, writes: "The ledger book . . . was slowly filling with familiar names: Bennett, two Huxleys, three Sitwells, Woolf, Churchill, Wells, Walpole, and Yeats (who would receive the Nobel prize in literature in 1923)."[2] Another, commenting on the order forms that buyers had to fill out, elaborates: "André Gide was the first French subscriber. Other forms . . . are signed by W. B. Yeats, Sherwood Anderson, John McCormack, Hart Crane, Djuna Barnes, and William Carlos Williams."[3] Variations are confined to alterations of sequence or increases in catalogue length: "The many subscriptions . . . include such luminaries as André Gide, W. B. Yeats, Sherwood Anderson, Hart Crane, William Carlos Williams, Virgil Thomson, Ronald Firbank, John Dos Passos, Burton Rascoe, William van Wyck, Jo Davidson, Otto Kahn, Peggy Guggenheim, Marsden Hartley, and many others."[4] Yet there is something unsatisfying about such lists, which never extend to more than fifteen names.[5] On one hand, they conspicuously neglect to tell us who purchased the other 985 copies of the 1,000 that made up the first edition. On the other, they possess a liturgical, mantra-like quality, as if the series of names could invoke a magical power to ward off something forbidden, something to be excluded by this very act of repetitive naming. Arranged in an orderly row, like so many stylized saints standing beside one another in a Byzantine mosaic, the readers' names acquire a similar uniformity: they have been removed from the world of historical contingency and have entered a timeless realm that is free of accident, devoid of change, and impervious to the mutations of mundane life. The ritual of naming has transformed a historic event into a timeless pageant, a static sequence of grand figures. And just as the mosaic background makes each figure stand discrete and isolated against a white emptiness, so the catalogue of names furnishes a blank conceptual and historical field in which the heroism of the private individual is outlined all the more strongly for not having been explicitly mentioned. It reinforces, all the more subtly, the received narrative of *Ulysses*'s first publication, that familiar story that recounts "The Battle of *Ulysses*," lauds the "heroic efforts by Miss Beach," celebrates the "remarkable dedication of Miss Beach, [the printer] Darantiere and Joyce himself," or sings the salutary virtues that "broke the modern Odyssey into print" despite the legal obstructions and public indifference.[6] Meanwhile, the social and historical contexts are silently cast outside the purview of examination, deemed unworthy of serious attention, and rejected in favor of the generic list, an academic variant of the epic catalogue that is implicitly connected to a narrative focused on the epic efforts of grand individuals.

The first edition of *Ulysses,* it has been said, marked "not only a historic literary event but a landmark in the annals of publication history."[7] It did indeed. It signaled the decisive entry of modernism into the public sphere via an identifiable process of commodification, via its transformation into a product whose value could now be assayed within the framework of several overlapping institutions, an institutional context whose shape and structure have been left largely unexamined. My point is not to urge a revisionary account that impugns the morals or motivations of Beach or Joyce—though I suspect these were more complex than might be gleaned from our received narratives—but to situate their decisions and actions within the context of a body of institutions, a corpus of collecting, marketing, and discursive practices that constituted a composite social space. That space was intricately connected with other institutional spheres yet was also extremely malleable, responsive both to intervention from individuals and to interaction with other sectors of the public sphere. The first publication and sale of *Ulysses,* precisely because that social space was so fragile in character, happened in ways that none of the protagonists had foreseen.

In reality, individual readers played a limited role in shaping the success that greeted the first edition of *Ulysses.* Their importance was decidedly minor when compared with the influence wielded by a quite different group of buyers—the dealers and speculators in the rare book trade who bought the overwhelming majority of copies of the first edition. That was one feature that characterized publication and sale of the first edition: it brought to the fore a conflict between the interests of individual readers (viewed as a group) and professional booksellers, export agents, and dealers in rare books (viewed as another group), as both competed to obtain the same scarce resource, the one thousand copies of the limited edition. But more than simple conflict was involved. In part the marketing of the first edition became an unintended experiment in the transformation of the common reader, an experiment in which readers were solicited to take on a mélange of functions—to assume the roles of collectors, patrons, or even investors—that overlapped in complex ways with their function as consumers. The first edition of *Ulysses* should be viewed, in part, as an attempt to realize an ideal mode of cultural production of the same sort that was being theorized in the contemporaneous Bel Esprit project launched by Ezra Pound, which proposed that thirty people agree to guarantee ten pounds per year to T. S. Eliot. Both projects, however, were ultimately troubled by unresolved ambiguities in their assumptions about art, the assessment of value, and their respective roles in a market economy and the public sphere, questions that passed unnoticed in both contemporary and subsequent assessments of the *Ulysses* edition. Although most observers have viewed the first edition as an unqualified success, the issues it left unanswered may have turned it into something that more nearly resembles a Pyrrhic victory. To recognize this can tell us much about some of the crucial ironies of the modernist enterprise, ironies that continue to vex our debates about the arts and their audiences, culture and its consumption, even today.

Although the events that culminated in the book publication of *Ulysses* on 2 February 1922 have been recounted in numerous biographies and specialized studies of Joyce, most of them have offered anecdotal narratives that avoid analytical and critical evaluation.[8] I rehearse them here partly to help readers bring them to mind and, more important, to situate them within a contextual description that differs sharply from received accounts. Before Joyce's agreement with Beach, three very different plans had been considered for the book publication of *Ulysses*—plans developed by Harriet Shaw Weaver, John Rodker, and Ben Huebsch. Though all were ultimately rejected, the dynamics that had been set in motion when they were under consideration continued to influence the way Beach's edition was conceived and executed.

Plans for the book publication of *Ulysses* began to take shape almost as soon as Joyce had completed his famous move from Trieste to Paris, where he arrived on 9 July 1920. Until then it had been tacitly assumed that the completed work would be published in the same way as Joyce's previous novel. *A Portrait of the Artist as a Young Man* had first been issued in December 1916 by the American publisher Huebsch, who then sent overseas the unbound sheets for the English edition that was issued a few weeks later by Weaver, owner and director of the Egoist Press. (The Egoist Ltd. had published the *Egoist,* a monthly journal, from 1913 through December 1919 and in 1916 had created a book-publishing wing, the Egoist Press.) No one had especially worried over the question of precedence, whether the English or American edition would appear first; that was a pragmatic issue to be resolved in the light of circumstances. From the English viewpoint, it depended on finding a printer, for British law holds not just the publisher but also the printer liable for legal actions arising from publication, and on those grounds several printers had previously objected to specific passages and refused to print them without alterations when *Ulysses* was being published serially in the *Egoist* (from March 1918 on). In the spring of 1919, however, Weaver finally found the Pelican Press, a firm that would soon print the concluding issues of the *Egoist* (from July to December 1919). The firm's manager, she reported, was "a Roman Catholic Irishman" who "had been much interested" by *A Portrait*. He now read the first ten episodes of *Ulysses* and pronounced himself "willing" to undertake the novel.[9] Weaver, after bringing the *Egoist* to a close with the final issue of December 1919, thought that she had finally resolved the problem of *Ulysses*. She had not calculated on Joyce's move to Paris.

This move was executed under the aegis of Pound, who stayed in the city with Joyce for some two weeks (9 July to 21 July, from the day of Joyce's arrival to the date of his own return to London) in order to help him get settled. It was a hectic period during which Joyce was introduced to nearly everyone whom Pound knew. Among them was Rodker, a minor poet whose poems, prose sketches, and criticism—including an essay on Joyce's *Exiles*—had appeared in the *Little Review* during Pound's tenure as foreign editor from 1917 to 1919.[10] When Pound resigned in early 1919, Rodker succeeded him; a few months later, he launched a private press and publishing firm, the Ovid Press.[11] When he left London for Paris in May 1922, Rodker told Wallace Stevens that he was "going to France for two or three months' holiday. I've been sweating very hard at the press, doing all the printing myself."[12] There he was introduced to Joyce, undoubtedly by Pound. On 27 July, he and his wife, the author Mary Butts, took Joyce and his family to dinner.[13] The next morning Rodker hastened back to London to check on his business affairs. He was greeted by a disaster. Writing a brief note to accompany a copy of *Hugh Selwyn Mauberley* for Stevens, one of his best clients and a well-known book collector, he explained his situation: "These last books are I think the Swan Song of the Press. I have come back to find more bills than I could possibly have imagined to exist."[14]

Rodker returned two days later to Paris, where he continued to see Joyce on an occasional basis. By mid-August, despite his increasingly straitened financial circumstances, he presented Joyce with a plan to publish *Ulysses*. On 16 August, Joyce wrote to Weaver, who by now had assumed the role of his agent and factotum, asking her to confirm her prior report that the Pelican Press was willing to print all of *Ulysses*, so that he could know how to reply to Rodker. Weaver promptly checked with the firm, then informed Joyce that it had reluctantly but firmly declined to print the novel.[15] Joyce now assumed that

Rodker would undertake the book, perhaps publishing it from Paris.[16] But when Rodker finally saw "Nausicaa" and "Oxen of the Sun," which were still only episodes 13 and 14 of a work that promised to grow much longer, he realized that his artisanal handpress was no match for so vast a project and that his lack of capital probably ruled out the question altogether.[17] Though Rodker's plan came to nothing, it is important because it was the first to raise the possibility of a limited and deluxe edition; in doing so, it planted a seed that would come to fruition in the famous first edition issued by Beach—but only after it had been assimilated to a quite different project.

In September 1920, when an unsolicited copy of the *Little Review* that contained the infamous "Nausicaa" episode was sent to the daughter of a prominent New York attorney, it set off a chain of events that led John Sumner, secretary of the New York Society for the Suppression of Vice, to file an official complaint. A warrant was sworn out against the Washington Square Bookshop, where Sumner had purchased several copies, and American postal authorities, now alerted to the case, announced that they would hold up mailing of the issue pending the outcome of a hearing scheduled for 4 October.[18] The defense was entrusted to John Quinn, a prominent corporate attorney and noted cultural patron who had earlier organized much of the financing that supported the *Little Review,* largely because of his loyalties to Joyce and Pound. Quinn managed to get the case against the Washington Square Bookshop dropped, then to postpone the hearing for the *Little Review* until 18 October. At that hearing (finally held on 21 October), the magistrate decided to hold the defendants over for trial in Special Sessions, where the case would be heard by three judges. From the start, Quinn was convinced that Special Sessions would rule against the *Little Review;* therefore, he aimed not at winning the case but at adjourning it as long as he could. He planned to follow two strategies: first, to obtain a series of modest postponements by pleading the press of previous engagements in court; then, to move that the trial's venue be changed from Special Sessions, where "conviction would be certain," to the Court of General Sessions, where it would be tried by jury.[19] Even if he still lost the case before a jury, he would have gained enough time to get the book in print.

Quinn was also certain just what kind of edition was required—a private edition. He even cited specific examples of the sort that he had in mind: James Huneker's novel, *Painted Veils,* which had been published a few months earlier by the American firm Boni and Liveright; two novels by George Moore, *The Story-Teller's Holiday* and *Avowals,* issued several years earlier by the British publisher William Heinemann; and D. H. Lawrence's *Women in Love,* released by the American house Thomas Seltzer, also in 1920.[20] "Private edition," as used here by Quinn, was a technical term that had recently acquired a highly particular meaning. It did not refer, as it usually did then and still does today, to an edition that was privately printed in an extremely small print run (one hundred to two hundred copies), with the intention that copies circulate as gifts among friends and acquaintances of the author. Instead it was a ploy that several publishers had recently devised to evade the laws on obscenity that prevailed in both the United States and England. The first firm to use it had been William Heinemann, which published all of Moore's later novels with the simple phrase "privately printed" displayed on the title page. Instead of distributing the volume through normal retail outlets, Heinemann announced that it was available only "by subscription" directly from the publisher. In this way, it could argue that the book was not for sale in the public realm, hence could not be charged with harming public morals. It also hoped to increase earnings. Prices for the "private edition" were raised to five times the average price for a new novel; by selling the book directly to readers, thereby eliminating the 30 to 35 percent of the price that would normally go to the bookseller, the firm earned still more. Indeed, the publisher could even increase its royalties to the author and still have better than average profits. Heinemann's practice was noticed almost immediately by Thomas R. Smith, an omnivorous collector of erotica, who was also the chief editor at the firm of Boni and Liveright. It was at Smith's instigation that Liveright published Huneker's *Painted Veils,* the story of a Wagnerian soprano named Ishtar who deliberately debauches a student of theology. The price was $10.00 (at a time when the average book cost between $1.50 and $2.50), and the book was available only "by subscription." Quinn was only too familiar with the novel; he had read it in manuscript form at the beginning of 1920 when Huneker had given it to him to solicit his legal advice.[21] Huebsch, Joyce's American publisher, was, no doubt, familiar with it as well.

Quinn, then, planned to have *Ulysses* published as a "private edition" in the strict sense that this term had acquired in the United States in 1920. If he could defer the trial long enough for this to occur, he believed, the work as a whole would amply demonstrate that Joyce's intentions were neither obscene nor pornographic, while Joyce might earn income enough to bridge the gap until an ordinary edition could be published. But Joyce was far from having completed the novel, and Huebsch was frightened by the potential legal imbroglio. He temporized, as did Quinn, who succeeded in postponing the trial first to December, then to February. On 14 and 21 February 1921, the case finally went to court: the three judges of Special Sessions rejected Quinn's motion for a trial by jury, ruled that *Ulysses* was obscene, and pronounced the editors of the *Little Review* guilty of publishing obscenity. They were fined fifty dollars each, and it was understood that they would publish no further episodes of *Ulysses*. These events precipitated the collapse of all plans for an American edition. Five weeks later, on 24 March, Huebsch informed Quinn, who was also acting as Joyce's counsel and representative in the United States, that he would be unable to publish *Ulysses* without excisions and alterations in the text. Quinn refused, on Joyce's behalf, and on 5 April Huebsch formally declined the manuscript, sending a letter to Weaver, Joyce's patron and unofficial agent in London.

Joyce, residing in Paris, was left uninformed about the trial's outcome or its implications for *Ulysses*. When the *Little Review* trial was still pending, Quinn was suddenly overwhelmed by work resulting from the stock market crash that struck in November 1920. He had been unable to find time to write "any book or art letters or letters to personal friends" for seven months, as he explained to Pound in May 1921.[22] Thus, Joyce was left to discover news about the trial on his own. On Thursday, 31 March 1921, Joyce stopped by Beach's bookstore and was given a press cutting from the *New York Tribune* that reported the trial's outcome. Shocked, he hurried to an "American bank" where he "bribed the porter to let me look up the files of all the papers they had." He returned "the next day" as well and "copied out another from the *Sun* and the Boston *Transcript*." Two days later on Sunday, 3 April 1921, he wrote to report the news to Weaver.[23] Despite what might have seemed an unprecedented disaster, Joyce was not disconsolate, for between his discovery of Thursday and his letter of Sunday, another event had intervened.

Joyce, it can be safely inferred, stopped for his daily visit to Shakespeare and Company on Friday, 1 April, for when Beach wrote a letter to her mother on the same date, she described the prospects for her store thus: "Mother dear its more of a success every day and soon you may hear of us as a reglar [*sic*] Publishers and of the most important book of the age . . . . . . shuuuuuuuu . . . it's a secret, all to be revealed to you in my next letter and it's going to make us famous rah rah!" (Beach's ellipses). Evidently Beach did not post her letter immediately but continued to add a paragraph here and there as time permitted. Perhaps as much as a week later (8 April?), she concluded with a triumphant postscript: "P.S. Its decided. I'm going to publish 'Ulysses' . . . in October . . . . !!! Ulysses means thousands of dollars of publicity for me. Subscriptions to be sent to Shakespeare and Company at once."[24] Joyce and Beach had reached their fateful agreement. On 10 April, Joyce announced their arrangement to Weaver. Referring to his having definitively ended discussions with Huebsch, Joyce went on:

> The next day I arranged for a Paris publication to replace the American one—or rather I accepted a proposal made to me by *Shakespeare and Co,* a bookseller's here, at the instance of Mr Larbaud.
>
> The proposal is to publish here in October an edition (complete) of the book so made up:
>
> 100 copies on Holland handmade paper at 350 frs
> > (signed)
>
> 150 copies on vergé d'arches at 250 frs
>
> 750 copies on linen at 150 frs
>
> that is, 1000 copies with 20 copies extra for libraries and press. A prospectus will be sent out next week inviting subscriptions. There are many already in advance with shops here, I am told. They offer me 66% of the net profit. . . . The actual printing will begin as soon as the number of orders covers approximately the cost of printing.[25]

Within a week, as he had anticipated, Beach and Joyce devised a four-page prospectus that was sent to potential subscribers.

Joyce's agreement with Beach marked a radical change in the kind of edition that was now proposed, a change that was largely due to the influence of Adrienne Monnier, the proprietor of a French bookstore located near Beach's. Monnier, who saw her shop as "half convent" and herself as a "nun of other times," had already acquired experience in publishing several deluxe editions, and it was she, as Beach later recalled, who now "initiated me into the mysteries of limited editions."[26] The "special" or "private" edition that had been previously discussed by Quinn and Huebsch was essentially an ordinary edition in disguise; it was still addressed to a relatively wide readership and was described as "private" only to reduce the risk of prosecution and to mask an increase in prices and profits. What Beach proposed was something quite different—a genuine deluxe edition. The difference was apparent in every feature: price, royalties, discount structure, audience, and authorial control. The Huebsch-Quinn private edition had been expected to sell at £2; Beach's edition would sell at three different prices, the lowest of which stood at £3 3s. (nearly 60 percent higher), the highest at £7 7s. (more than 350 percent higher).[27] No less marked were changes in royalties. An ordinary edition would have given Joyce royalties of 15 to 20 percent on gross sales; the Huebsch-Quinn edition would have given him a higher figure, perhaps 25 to 30 percent, with the increase coming largely

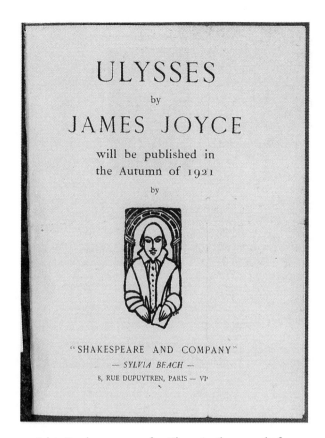

13. Sylvia Beach, prospectus for *Ulysses,* April 1921; 1st leaf.
22 × 16.3 cm. Courtesy of the Yale Collection of American
Literature, Beinecke Rare Book and Manuscript Library, Yale
University.

from alterations in the discount structure as described below. The royalties on a
deluxe edition, though, were much bigger, typically 50 percent, and Beach
herself proposed that Joyce receive 66 percent of the net profits. Equally marked
were differences in the discount structure and venues of sale. An ordinary
edition was normally offered to booksellers at a discount of roughly 33 percent.
The American "private edition" eliminated the discount structure altogether,
requiring individual readers to purchase the book directly from the publisher as
"subscribers." A deluxe edition, in contrast, had an extremely modest discount,
typically around 10 percent. The small discount was a direct function of another, much more important difference—a change in audience. An ordinary

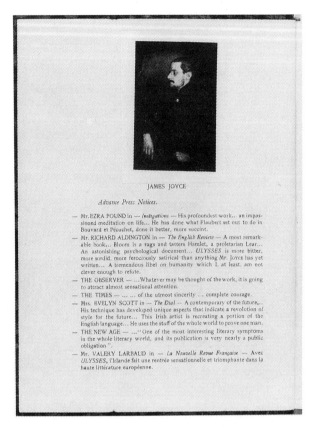

JAMES JOYCE

Advance Press Notices.

— Mr. EZRA POUND in — *Instigations* — His profoundest work... an impassioned meditation on life... He has done what Flaubert set out to do in Bouvard et Pécuchet, done it better, more succint.

— Mr. RICHARD ALDINGTON in — *The English Review* — A most remarkable book... Bloom is a rags and tatters Hamlet, a proletarian Lear... An astonishing psychological document... *ULYSSES* is more bitter, more sordid, more ferociously satirical than anything Mr. Joyce has yet written... A tremendous libel on humanity which I, at least, am not clever enough to refute.

— THE OBSERVER — ...Whatever may be thought of the work, it is going to attract almost sensational attention.

— THE TIMES — ... ... of the utmost sincerity . . complete courage.

— Mrs. EVELYN SCOTT in — *The Dial* — A contemporary of the future... His technique has developed unique aspects that indicate a revolution of style for the future... This Irish artist is recreating a portion of the English language... He uses the stuff of the whole world to prove one man.

— THE NEW AGE — ..." One of the most interesting literary symptoms in the whole literary world, and its publication is very nearly a public obligation ".

— Mr. VALERY LARBAUD in — *La Nouvelle Revue Française* — Avec *ULYSSES*, l'Irlande fait une rentrée sensationnelle et triomphante dans la haute littérature européenne.

14. Prospectus for *Ulysses,* 2d leaf. 22 × 16.3 cm. Courtesy of the Yale Collection of American Literature, Beinecke Rare Book and Manuscript Library, Yale University.

edition, or even a "private edition" of the American sort, was addressed primarily to individual readers. A deluxe edition, instead, was directed partly to a small corpus of well-to-do collectors but principally to the dealers and speculators who sold to collectors—which is to say, to dealers themselves, who alternated between selling some copies to clients and holding others until the edition was exhausted and its value on the collectors' market had doubled or tripled. Thus, when Joyce informed Weaver that Beach's edition would "replace the American one," he was describing the project only as seen from his viewpoint; for him the Beach edition would indeed "replace the American one," or so he hoped. But his remarks concealed the extent of the change that was taking place. It was a decision to reconceive the very notion of audience and readership: to transform

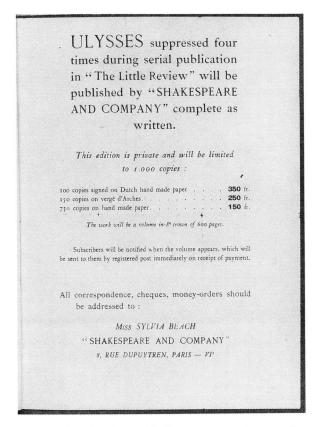

ULYSSES suppressed four
times during serial publication
in "The Little Review" will be
published by "SHAKESPEARE
AND COMPANY" complete as
written.

*This edition is private and will be limited
to 1.000 copies :*

100 copies signed on Dutch hand made paper	**350**	fr.
150 copies on vergé d'Arches.	**250**	fr.
750 copies on hand made paper.	**150**	fr.

The work will be a volume in-8° crown of 600 pages.

Subscribers will be notified when the volume appears, which will
be sent to them by registered post immediately on receipt of payment.

All correspondence, cheques, money-orders should
be addressed to :

Miss SYLVIA BEACH

"SHAKESPEARE AND COMPANY"

8, RUE DUPUYTREN, PARIS — VI

15. Prospectus for *Ulysses,* 3d leaf. 22 × 16.3 cm. Courtesy of the Yale Collection of American Literature, Beinecke Rare Book and Manuscript Library, Yale University.

the reader into a collector, an investor, or even a speculator. Moreover, the particular royalty structure of Beach's edition, which guaranteed Joyce the unprecedented figure of 66 percent of net sales, had the effect of turning every purchaser of the edition into a quasi-patron, someone directly supporting the artist himself.

The full extent of the change that took place with the agreement between Joyce and Beach may also have gone unnoticed because of Weaver's continued belief that she was going to publish the ordinary English edition that she had been planning since 1919. True, Weaver had been disappointed when the Pelican Press declined to print the novel in August 1920, but the subsequent withdrawal of Rodker had left her free to assume that she would publish *Ulysses*

ORDER FORM

Please send me ULYSSES by JAMES JOYCE

NUMBER
OF COPIES *

Edition on Dutch hand made paper with signature of the Author . . . **350** fr.

Edition on vergé d'Arches . . . . **250** fr.

Edition on hand made paper . . . . **150** fr.

I will pay on receipt of notice announcing that the volume has appeared.

Name 　　　　　　　　　　　　　　　　*Signature :*

Address

* Please cancel editions not required.

16. Prospectus for *Ulysses,* 4th leaf. 22 × 16.3 cm. Courtesy of the Yale Collection of American Literature, Beinecke Rare Book and Manuscript Library, Yale University.

anyway, proceeding as she had previously done with *A Portrait,* when she purchased extra sheets from the American publisher Huebsch and then had them bound herself. The Huebsch-Quinn plan for a "private edition"—and it is unlikely that Weaver even understood what the term meant—had left this assumption unaltered. Indeed, so firm were Weaver's plans that already in late 1920 she had sent out announcements of her ordinary English edition, and by January 1921, she had received preliminary orders for some 150 copies. The new project formulated by Joyce and Beach would also have no effect on her plans, she assumed, for the Beach edition was meant only to "replace the American one" that had been abandoned by Huebsch, as Joyce had put it. As late as 12 May 1921, therefore, when Weaver generously assembled "a list . . . of book-shops to whom I shall send the circulars" that would announce Beach's edition, she still excluded English shops from the list, "as I take it that you would not be sending to them."[28] She would soon be disabused of that notion.

Weaver's continued belief in the imminent publication of an ordinary English edition was also a function of her inexperience; she had no idea what a deluxe or limited edition was. Yet the tensions between the incompatible conceptions that animated these two projects could only be deferred, not evaded, as soon became apparent in the correspondence between Weaver and Beach about the question of the bookseller's discounts. Weaver, we should recall, was herself a publisher. She had begun in 1915 with the *Poets' Translations* series, six small pamphlets priced at not more than sixpence each, published between September 1915 and February 1916, and over the next four years, she issued seven books: Joyce's *A Portrait* (February 1917), Eliot's *Prufrock and Other Observations* (June 1917), Pound's *Dialogues of Fontanelle* (October 1917), Wyndham Lewis's *Tarr* (July 1918), Pound's *Quia Pauper Amavi* (October 1919), Lewis's *The Caliph's Design* (October 1919), and Richard Aldington's *Images* (November 1919). These she issued in relatively small editions ranging from five hundred (*Prufrock*) to one thousand copies (*Tarr* and *The Caliph's Design*).[29] Despite their modest print runs, all had been conceived as ordinary editions— available for sale to a general public of common readers. Weaver, as one might expect, was quite conversant with the standard discount offered to shops—her own was ordinarily 33 percent—and her extensive experience with the marketing of her own books had made her acquainted with a goodly number of booksellers. Further, since American bookshops had shown a steady interest in several of her titles, she had also become familiar with exporting agents who catered to the American market. On 21 April, eleven days after Joyce had informed her of the new plans, Weaver wrote to Beach to discuss the question of bookshops: "I have had a number of orders from shops, English and American. Will you kindly tell me whether you propose to give any discount to shops; and, if so, how much? Of course the shops ordering from us were expecting an ordinary edition, but some of them might probably obtain orders for your special edition." The reply from Beach left her deeply disconcerted, and on 27 April she registered her consternation: "I have had no experience of limited expensive editions and it had not occurred to me that booksellers make a practice of buying copies to hold up and sell at double or treble the original price. In these circumstances I quite agree with you that a discount of 10 per cent is sufficient for them."[30] Weaver's consternation is telling, for it indicates that the distinction between the ordinary and the limited edition resided not in the number of copies but in the institutional structure into which the copies were integrated, the channels of distribution through which they passed. Weaver herself had published three editions that were substantially smaller (500, 600, and 750 copies) than Beach's, but they had all been directed toward a general public, however indifferent it may have proved. Beach's edition was directed primarily toward dealers, toward speculators. The reason to buy a book published by Weaver was to read it; the reason to buy the edition proposed by Beach was quite different—to be able to sell it again, perhaps at a significant profit if all went well. Here was the final and consummate paradox of modernism. Though we tend to associate modernism with the emergence of the New Criticism and the triumph of close reading, the effect of modernism was not so much to encourage reading as to render it superfluous. What modernism required was not the individual reader but a new and uneasy amalgam of the investor, the collector, and the patron.

The ordinary edition and the limited edition entailed antithetical and incompatible understandings of production, audience, and market dynamics. They could not coexist. The persistence of Weaver's plan for an ordinary edition posed an insuperable problem for Beach's project. No one, after all, would want to pay the hefty price of the deluxe edition when a few months' wait would procure the same book at one-fifth the price. To resolve this question, Beach and Weaver had to reach agreement—a sticky question, since Weaver was also Joyce's patron, furnishing him with his only steady income. It was Robert McAlmon, the young American writer who resided in Paris but regularly traveled to London to visit his wife's wealthy family, whom Beach entrusted with the delicate task of persuading Weaver to announce that the English edition would be deferred indefinitely. McAlmon's visit to Weaver was followed by a letter from Beach. On 8 July, Weaver told Beach exactly what she wanted to hear: "I am much concerned at hearing, first from Mr. McAlmon and then from you, that the announcement of the cheaper English ordinary edition of *Ulysses* has been affecting adversely the chances of the Paris limited edition." "The cheaper prospective edition," Weaver now conceded, "is doing harm," and to redress it she would "send out to all shops on our lists (and to any people I hear of who are waiting for the cheaper edition) the notice" that the English edition was postponed "indefinitely."[31] Beach promptly thanked her—and well she might have. The deluxe edition was inherently monopolistic; it presupposed that one could exploit a market by manipulating the ratio of supply and demand; to succeed, it required that supply be issued from only one source. Having eliminated the Weaver project, Beach could now turn to the other side of the equation, increasing demand.

To generate demand required publicity. Beach, in fact, was fascinated by the operations of modern public relations: her sister Cyprian was planning to become a film actress, and as Beach explained to her other sister, Holly, their mother had "had a great deal of expenses getting Cyprian equipped as a rising star." A month later, she reported to Holly: "Cyprian did some filming in the city the other day and there were crowds of star-gazers you may believe."[32] In the case of Joyce, much of Beach's task had already been accomplished for her by newspaper coverage of the *Ulysses* trial, which had been unusually extensive, including stories in the *New York Times, Chicago Herald Examiner, New York Tribune, Boston Transcript, New York Sun, New York World, New York Herald, New York Daily News,* and *New Age* in London.[33] Beach was deeply interested in the question of publicizing the novel, both for Joyce's sake and for her own. When she announced her agreement with Joyce to her mother, she wrote (as previously noted), "it's going to make us famous rah rah! . . . . Ulysses means thousands of dollars of publicity for me." Writing to Holly Beach several weeks later, she stressed the same motif: "Ulysses is going to make my place famous. Already the publicity is beginning and swarms of people visit the shop on hearing the news."[34] In a letter to Holly the next month, she reiterated the theme: "It's all owing to your help and publicity work for Shakespeare and Company that I've been able to make such a success out of the thing! And YOU know it. The Tribune sent around their Miss Rosemary Carr to interview me for a writeup which will appear ere very long."[35] The "writeup" appeared two weeks later, covering nearly a full column and including a photograph of Beach with a caption that described her as "a Maecenas for Paris writers, poets, and bookworms."[36] No less important was another brief notice that had appeared a few weeks earlier in a London newspaper, the *Observer.* Although it consisted of only a single paragraph, it encapsulated motifs that would prove central to the publication of *Ulysses.*

For Britons, the *Observer* is still a part of everyday culture, but for most Americans it remains little known. Although founded in 1791, its modern history begins in 1905, when it was purchased by Alfred Harmsworth, Baron Northcliffe, the newspaper magnate who in 1896 had created the *Daily Mail,* often considered the first newspaper for a mass public. Three years later, Harmsworth appointed as the *Observer*'s chief editor James L. Garvin, who would hold the post until 1942. Within a year, Garvin had increased weekly circulation from 20,000 to 57,000 readers; by 1914, the figure had risen to 170,000 and by 1915 to nearly 200,000, the level at which it would remain throughout 1915–1930. The newspaper's success was due partly to Garvin's genuine writing and editorial gifts, partly to a larger change in British society and culture. As one writer shrewdly expressed it, "The Victorian Sabbath was giving place to the Edwardian weekend."[37] The *Observer* was a Sunday newspaper, and in the years before the rise of radio or television it became a focus for relaxation and reflection. Garvin devoted pages 4 and 5 of the newspaper to books, music, and the countryside, and he oversaw a staff of gifted journalists. Not least among these was Sisley Huddleston, who became the *Observer*'s Paris correspondent, covering both diplomatic and cultural affairs, the latter in his "Paris Week by Week." Only seven days after Joyce wrote to Weaver announcing his agreement with Beach, Huddleston included a notice under the subtitle "James Joyce." It reported the result of the New York trial in February, then concluded:

> James Joyce was almost in despair when an American girl, Sylvia Beach, who courageously founded a little library of English books in the Quartier Latin, at the sign of Shakespeare and Company, came to the rescue. She has undertaken to have printed in France and to publish privately the big and strange volume. Whatever may be thought of the work, it is going to attract almost sensational attention.[38]

Two points need to be made concerning Huddleston's feature. One concerns its rhetoric: Huddleston was plainly using the language of cinematic melodrama (the author was "in despair," until "an American girl . . . came to the rescue"), and yet this vocabulary has furnished the lexicon that recurs in discussions of the first edition down to the present. In her 1959 memoir, *Shakespeare and Company*, Beach recounted her decision to publish the first edition, naming the chapter "Shakespeare and Company to the Rescue"; when a scholarly critic narrated the same event in 1988, he concurred: "Miss Beach . . . came immediately to the rescue."[39] Even before the book was published, the narrative of its publication had been established. The other point concerns the notice's practical consequences. In May, Weaver advised Beach: "The enterprising manager of Messrs. Jones and Evans [a prominent bookstore] wrote to me for your address after seeing a notice in the *Observer*. I am glad to hear he has ordered three copies of each edition."[40] Weaver's report testifies to the power of the newspaper as a medium, and that of the *Observer* in particular. When the *Observer* later published Huddleston's review of *Ulysses* on 5 March 1922, four weeks after the book's release, it was only two days later that Beach received almost 150 orders for the book. Yet when ordinary readers responded to Huddleston's review, they were inevitably brought into an uneasy relationship with more professional booksellers and speculators. Or to put it in more practical terms, when they read Huddleston's review and attempted to purchase *Ulysses*, they discovered that many copies were already in the hands of the anonymous but "enterprising manager of Messrs. Jones and Evans." The anonymous manager, or the type that he represents, never figures among the lists of heroic readers that scholars have traditionally offered in discussing the first edition of

Ulysses—but he may have been the most significant protagonist of them all.

Briefly appeased by Beach's explanation about the discount proposed for bookshops, Weaver soon pressed for a larger discount for export agents and wholesalers. Citing the American firm Stevens and Brown, she wrote:

> They are not the kind of firm which would be likely to buy copies to hold up and sell at an advanced price. For wholesale and export agents such as this firm I think it will be necessary to offer 12 1/2% or 15% to induce them to try to get orders. Would you agree to 15% in cases such as this? This firm said that it was scarcely worth their while to take any trouble over the book at a discount of 10% because their customers, being booksellers, they will themselves have to allow some discount.[41]

Two months later, Weaver raised the point anew: "Some of the shops here (Messrs. Jones and Evans for one) say that even 15% is not sufficient inducement to them to order more than a very few copies." All bookshops, she added sympathetically, were "suffering from the general trade depression in this country."[42] Her letter arrived in late July when the first surge of orders that had greeted announcement of the edition was beginning to flag. Partly in the hope of inducing more sales, partly in response to Weaver's pleas, Beach decided to offer a discount of 20 percent to all bookstores, export agents, and rare book dealers.[43] (She also extended the discount to members of the trade or other publishers and to members of the press, the latter in a bid for favorable reportage.) Her decision had a paradoxical effect: it made the edition more accessible to a wider audience, enabling a modest number of bookstores to place orders on behalf of individual readers, but it also made the edition more attractive to speculative booksellers, who could now rest assured of a small profit even if they charged only the published price, rather than holding the edition in the hope of greater profits.

Orders from dealers and agents soon mounted, and the London firm of William Jackson is highly representative of the trend that emerged. On 7 July 1921, the firm ordered eight copies.[44] On 16 August, its order was increased to twenty copies, with a note from Jackson adding, "I shall probably want more yet." On 21 September the order was increased again to thirty-five copies, and on 3 January 1922 it was changed to seventy copies. As more than six months had elapsed since the firm first placed its order, Jackson wrote on 19 January to inquire "when the book will be ready." Four days later, having been advised that copies would be available in a matter of weeks, he increased his order to eighty copies. Finally, on 1 February, he raised his order to one hundred copies. It is an astounding figure, accounting for 10 percent of the entire edition and for 13 percent of the issue at 150 francs. Of the cheaper copies that were most likely to be purchased by ordinary readers, more than one in seven was bought by one dealer alone. To be sure, the size of Jackson's purchase was unusual, and it constituted the largest single order that Beach received. But it suggests the influence that the dealers wielded as a group. If we glance only at the purchases (in francs) of the eighteen shops, dealers, and agents who placed orders that totaled more than 1,000 francs, we can sense the extent of their role in the first edition.

The Galignani Library	1,080
224, rue de Rivoli, Paris	
Hodges & Figgis	1,160
20 Naussau Street, Dublin	
Mitchell Kennerly	1,200
489 Park Avenue, New York	
Brentano's	1,600
37, avenue de l'Opéra, Paris	
Mitchell's Bookstore	1,600
Buenos Aires	
Washington Square Bookshop	1,620
28 West Eighth Street, New York	
T. S. Mercer	1,680
4 Tufton Street, Westminster, London SW1	
Birrell & Garnett	1,880
19 Taviston Street, Gordon Square, London	
The Irish Book Shop	2,240
45 Dawson Street, Dublin	
W. H. Smith & Son	2,760
248, rue de Rivoli, Paris	
Gordon & Gotch	3,000
10 St. Bride Street, London EC4	
B. F. Stevens & Brown	3,040
4 Trafalgar Square, London WC2	
The Sunwise Turn	3,040
51 East Forty-fourth Street, New York	
John Clark, Exporter	3,200
12 Ludgate Square, Ludgate Hill, London EC4	
Librairie Emile Terquem	4,680
1, rue Scribe, Paris	

Agence Générale de Librairie	5,160
7, rue de Lille, Paris	
The Chelsea Book Club	5,280
65 Cheyne Walk, London SW3	
William Jackson, Export Bookseller	11,600
16 Tooks Court, Cursitor Street, Chancery Lane, London	

Taken together, these dealers alone accounted for 55,280 francs, nearly 40 percent of the 142,000 francs in gross sales that Beach took in for *Ulysses*.[45] When shops and dealers that placed smaller orders are also taken into account, excluding those who placed orders on behalf of individual readers—and in their correspondence they took pains to cite their clients' names when doing so—the total comes to nearly 60 percent of the gross sales. (Individual readers, in contrast, account for slightly more than 40 percent, though this figure shrinks to 36 percent if we exclude the journalists and reviewers who received press discounts.)

Dealers, shops, and export agents consumed a surprisingly large share of the edition, but not all of it. If one were obliged to identify a single moment at which the first edition can be said to have entered the public sphere, becoming genuinely available to a substantial public, it would be Sunday, 5 March 1922, when Huddleston's review of *Ulysses* appeared in the *Observer,* reaching its readership of roughly two hundred thousand people. Huddleston firmly expressed his admiration for the book, declaring it a work of genius. Joyce's style(s) he praised without reserve, saying that his phrases were "as perfect as these things can be" and that "a single just-right sentence" could concentrate "a great sweep of meaning." He even offered a brief primer in how to read what was then being called "the interior monologue," and by addressing the educated reader in a frank and easygoing manner, he effectively communicated his regard for Joyce's achievement.[46] The response was immediate. Two days later, on 7 March, as Pound explained to his father, "Observer review brought in orders for 136 copies of Ulysses, last Tuesday; 136 in one day at 15 bones the copy."[47] Nine days later, the last of the 150-franc copies had been sold, and Beach was advising buyers that they would have to purchase the more expensive issues. Many, quite simply, could not afford them.[48]

The plight of the ordinary reader is epitomized in a letter written by R. C. Armilt, a resident of Kilmarnock, who, in response to Huddleston's review, wrote directly to Joyce himself. He had, he explained, deeply admired *A Portrait.*

Some time ago I read your "Portrait of the Artist." I admired it. I recognized it as a fine, unusual piece of work. It was a new note in our literature with I know not what incalculable influence in the future.

I desired to read more of you, to hear more of you. Now I see that you have published another book privately. . . . Doubtless there is good reason for this procedure. Possibly you are not to blame. It may be no right of people like myself to have the fine and beautiful literature of our day. But what am I to do?

I am not a rich man.

Armilt concluded, almost pleading, "am I to be denied the joy of reading one more work which is not for this time alone?" Armilt turned out to be lucky: his letter arrived on the last day that cheaper copies were still available. Others were less fortunate.

Yet to pose a straightforward opposition between common readers and speculative dealers is to lose sight of the multiplicity of functions that accrued to the role of the reader-buyer as a consequence of the deluxe edition, especially as it had evolved under Beach's direction. To understand this better, however, we must briefly consider the question of the edition's cost: what did it mean, in everyday terms, to buy a copy of the first edition of *Ulysses* in 1921–1922? Answering that question requires a glance at prevailing exchange rates. Because purchasers of *Ulysses* paid for their copies when they were ready from the printer, the relevant period is a span of five months, from 2 February 1922, when the first copies reached Beach, to roughly 1 July, when the edition was exhausted. Throughout this time, the franc was fairly stable. On 2 February, the dollar stood at 11.925 francs on the Paris Bourse, while on 30 June, it stood at 11.995 francs, and in the intervening months it fluctuated little. The situation was no different on other exchanges: in New York, on 1 February, the dollar was trading at 11.97 francs, while on 1 July it was trading at 11.94 francs. Similar stability prevailed in the ratio of the franc to the pound, which stood at 52.725 on 2 February and 51.395 on 1 July.[49] The book's prices in each currency were as follows:

Copies 1–100	350 francs	£7 7s.	$30
Copies 101–250	250 francs	£5 5s.	$22
Copies 251–1,000	150 francs	£3 3s.	$14

To compare the cost of living from one era to another is a notoriously hazardous undertaking, and it would be unwise to lay claim to more than a rough approximation. Still, anecdotal evidence can give at least some indication of what such sums could buy in Paris, London, or New York. For example,

Morrill Cody, a young American journalist who moved to Paris in 1921, later recalled:

> Living in Paris in the early twenties was cheap. . . . Then one could manage to live in Paris for less than twenty-five dollars a month. Soon after my return [in 1921] I got a job on the European edition of Colonel McCormick's *Chicago Tribune.* It paid only fifteen dollars a week, but it was enough for a small hotel room and food and occasional drink at the Select or one of the other popular cafés in the neighborhood. Some of my friends with incomes of one hundred dollars a month lived very well, indeed, with their wife or partner.[50]

Cody was young, single, and without responsibilities, and quite plainly he was tolerant of spartan conditions. More typical was the case of Ezra Pound and his wife, Dorothy. They moved to Paris in early April of 1921, and in October, they rented a fairly spacious studio at 70, bis rue Notre-Dame-des-Champs. The rent was three hundred francs a month.[51] Pound's salary at this time was an average of twenty-five dollars per month, though his income was supplemented by occasional royalties, payments for publications, and gifts of ten to twenty dollars from his parents. Altogether he earned some forty dollars a month, somewhat more than the twenty-five recommended by Cody, yet Pound also found it difficult to make ends meet.

Pound was fortunate, however, in one respect. His British wife had her own income, receiving from her parents two hundred pounds per year, or just under four pounds per week.[52] Her family evidently preferred not to support Pound, and their estimate of her needs was meant to correspond with a modest living wage in England. In 1924, "the average man at full work . . . obtained 60s. a week," or three pounds. In 1924, it was also estimated that the annual "income from wages per house" was "£210 [$1,050] if there was no unemployment or absence owing to sickness during the year," a figure that amounts to just over four pounds a week.[53] Anecdotal evidence reinforces that figure. In May 1922, the future mystery writer Dorothy L. Sayers, who was twenty-nine years old and a graduate of Oxford, took a job as a copywriter with the advertising firm of S. H. Benson: her salary was four pounds (twenty dollars) a week.[54]

The cost of living was slightly higher in the United States at this time. Cody thought his weekly salary of fifteen dollars rather low in 1921, but in 1919, Robert Sherwood was hired for twenty-five dollars a week to be on the staff of *Vanity Fair* in New York, and a year later, when Jeanne Ballot became executive secretary to the magazine's editor, she received twenty-two dollars a week. Margaret Case Harriman, who also worked on the editorial staff of *Vanity Fair,* received thirty-five dollars a week in 1922.⁵⁵ While such figures give only an approximate idea of how much the first edition of *Ulysses* cost, they make clear that even the cheapest issue, priced at 150 francs (£3 3s., or $14.00), was not inexpensive. In Paris, it represented almost half a month's rent for a studio in a moderately priced part of the city; in England, it approached or exceeded the average weekly wage for a normal adult; and in New York, it was 50 to 67 percent of the weekly salary for editorial staff of the city's most prestigious magazine. To buy a copy of the first edition of *Ulysses,* in other words, was not an action that can be readily compared with the everyday purchase of a book; for those who were not wealthy, it required at least some deliberation, some consideration about disposable income and its allocation.

When private readers purchased copies of the first edition, they did not just buy a book, they also assumed some of the functions of patrons. Several features of the deluxe edition worked toward establishing a patron-client relationship. One was the contract between Joyce and Beach, which stipulated that he receive 66 percent of the net profits. To an extent that was without precedent in ordinary editions and unusual even among deluxe editions, money from individual readers went directly to the author. But this economic structure merely reflected a broader effort to restore a more direct, less mediated relationship between author and reader. The book was no longer an industrial product, a mere commodity shaped by the conventions of the publishing industry and produced by the machinery of the large publishing house. Every facet of its production was now associated with the author: he was asked to approve the paper, typeface, and page layout for each issue, as well as to choose the color for the cover and even to authorize the inks that would reproduce the color. The logic of this drive toward a more direct rapport between author and reader also shaped the edition's pricing structure, which culminated in the issue priced at 350 francs (copies numbered 1–100), with each copy signed and dated by Joyce. Still, it may give pause that it should be only and precisely the highest-priced issue that to the greatest degree "restored" unmediated relations among author, work, and reader, for it suggests that this restoration was partly fictional, if not factitious: the deluxe edition could *seem to restore* those more direct relations insofar as it bracketed from consideration the larger world of industrial and financial relations that sustained the incomes of those who could afford it.

To ask that readers become patrons, that consumers become at least passive producers, that the artist work for an identifiable audience rather than a mass public, was a leitmotif of early-twentieth-century discussion about the social structure of the arts. Roger Fry's hope, expressed in 1912, that the new professional classes would become a significant force of patronage was typical of a broad movement that also included the German Expressionist artists gathered around die Brücke in Dresden, sustained by a group of "passive members"— professionals, businesspeople, and intellectuals who contributed a monthly sum for which they received a yearly graphics portfolio.[56] It is not an accident that another attempt of this sort was conceived in March 1922, just when sales of the first edition of *Ulysses* were at their height: Ezra Pound's Bel Esprit project, his proposal that thirty individuals each guarantee ten pounds (fifty dollars) per year to Eliot, providing him with an income of three hundred pounds. Bel Esprit, Pound explained in a contemporary essay, was needed "because the individual patron is nearly extinct." In effect, the Bel Esprit project would create a practical organizational structure that would institutionalize the community forged by the deluxe edition of *Ulysses*. It would be a deluxe edition in perpetuity, but now, instead of retrospective consumption, Pound urged, the "geographically scattered association" would engage in prospective patronage.[57]

The strands of patronage, consumption, collecting, and speculation were intricately interwoven in the emerging fabric of modernism. But perhaps nowhere can their complex interaction be better discerned than in an account of the Sunwise Turn, a New York bookstore that purchased eighteen copies of *Ulysses* for more than three thousand francs, enough to make it the sixth largest buyer of the first edition.[58] The firm's existence virtually coincided with the rise, triumph, and assimilation of modernism (founded in 1916, it was sold to the Doubleday chain in 1927).[59] The shop was first opened by Madge Jenison and Mary Mowbray Clarke, and their plans for it combined an uneasy mixture of modernizing professionalism and primitivist vitalism. The store would offer "all that is related to modern life," doing so with "the professional spirit which puts its knowledge and integrity at the disposal of the community." But the store's name derived from an Irish agrarian expression describing farmers who prefer to "do everything daesal (sunwise)," a phrase that they thought expressed "one of the deepest feelings of primitive life, that when you go with the sun you get all the beneficent and creative powers of the earth."[60] "The sunwise turn" suggested movement in a direction that would harmonize with primitive feeling and yet synchronize with modernity.[61] By "selling books in a more modern and civilized way," the shop would "carry them . . . into the stream of creative life of our generation."[62] The store's full name was "The Sunwise Turn: A Modern Bookshop."

The bookstore opened in 1916 on Thirty-first Street just east of Fifth Avenue, where it remained until 1919. "We were to conduct it like life, and it was to look like life," the owners felt. The decor was designed by Arthur Davies, a close friend of Quinn, who had been a principal organizer of the famous Armory Show in 1913. Davies colored the walls "a burning orange" and worked the other colors of the prism into the woodwork and detailing, and he entrusted the shop sign to Henry Fitch Taylor, another prominent organizer of the Armory Show. The shop was lavish in displaying "beautiful pieces of sculpture and textiles and paintings"; Mowbray Clarke's husband was a sculptor, and she hoped that the store might serve to attract patrons for him.[63] But the emphasis on display and exhibition also stemmed from less personal considerations. When planning the store, Jenison and Mowbray Clarke had borne in mind "that an art dealer needs only five patrons buying $2,000 a year to keep him afloat, and that if we could have fifty patrons who bought $500 worth of books a year, we would be safe." (They had originally planned to locate in some vacant rooms available in the building that still housed Alfred Stieglitz's studio and gallery at 291 Fifth Avenue.) But this attempt to assimilate the bookstore to the art gallery, to operate it on principles derived from art dealers, proved difficult in actual practice, for the two owners soon discovered "how few people there are, *except collectors,* who buy $500 worth of books a year."[64] The shop turned out to be a paradox: a store could not survive if it relied on only "fifty patrons," and yet it also could not survive by selling to a mass of undifferentiated buyers, since the profit margin on books was simply too small (roughly 30 percent at this time). To survive and succeed, the store had to sell other wares (such as stationery), goods with higher profit margins that would offset the low returns on books. "So you survive at bookselling by selling something else," as Jenison summarized her discovery. "You may sell old and rare books. Profits are always large on collector's items."[65] Thus Jenison discovered through experience that only collectors spend five hundred dollars on books each year and that rare books bring in larger profits; these larger margins were critical to a store's survival and success. The Sunwise Turn, in short, exhibited paintings, textiles, and sculptures for the same reason that it pursued an extensive trade in rare books and signed editions: profit margins on them supplemented the meager returns on ordinary books, and they attracted an elite of cultured and well-to-do clients whose every purchase was not only larger but more profitable.[66] To thrive, a bookstore needed not just readers but a core group of collector-patrons.

There was a second reason as well. The display of textiles and artworks also fostered a distinctive marketing profile: "Only give the world something with character to talk about and it will carry your name to the sunset. . . . It is the cachet of an imaginative personality that sells it." Every feature of the store—the decor, the stationery, even the bookwrappings—was marshaled to this end. "The sale of thousands of books strayed into our shop because we wrapped them in curious brilliant packages. Some artists who worked on the designs made them so deliriously lovely that it was difficult to make up one's mind ever to open them."[67] Yet the unremitting emphasis on display and image, as such remarks suggest, could lead to a paradoxical state of affairs, one in which active readers were slowly replaced with passive consumers, mere buyers who were less engaged with a book's contents and more bedazzled by its wrappings. The attention given to rare books and artworks, the insistence on exhibition, display, ambience, packaging—all originally conceived as supplements to the core activity of bookselling—inexorably altered the relations among the store's functions. Buying was no longer a means to the experience of reading but an experience in its own right, an autonomous activity that threatened to overshadow and replace the reading event that it was meant to facilitate.

After a lackluster beginning (in 1916, sales totaled $12,192; in 1917, $12,874), the store began to thrive (in 1918, sales reached $18,259; in 1919, $37,782). In autumn 1919, armed with more capital from a new partner, Harold Loeb, the shop moved into new quarters at 51 East Forty-fourth Street (part of the Yale Club building), where the decor of the previous location was painstakingly reconstructed. The next year, 1920, it posted more than $70,000 in sales. The new location was directly across from Grand Central Station, and the immediate vicinity housed four hotels and ten of the city's more prominent clubs. The space was more than double and the foot traffic triple that of the earlier location. The store launched a series of lectures and readings in combination with book signings; authors included Robert Frost, Amy Lowell, Lola Ridge, and Alfred Kreymborg. It also became a publisher, issuing volumes by Witter Bynner, Rainer Maria Rilke, Ananda Coomaraswamy, and Lord Edward John Dunsany, among others.[68]

The Sunwise Turn, it can be argued, also furnished consumers and personnel with training in the modernist culture of collecting and patronage. One example will suffice. The father of Loeb, the third partner, was a Wall Street broker in the influential house of Kuhn-Loeb, while his mother was a member of the prominent Guggenheim family. When Loeb's twenty-one-year-old cousin Peggy Guggenheim was looking for something to do, he suggested that she join the store's group of unpaid assistants for a while. As Jenison later recalled:

They sold thousands of dollars worth of books for us. They filed invoices. They swept floors. They ran errands. I have sometimes secreted a smile behind a monograph to see . . . Peggy Guggenheim, in a moleskin coat to her heels and lined with pink chiffon, going out for electric-light bulbs and tacks and pickup orders at the publishers, and returning with a package large enough to make any footman shudder and a careful statement of moneys disbursed.[69]

Yet Loeb, who knew Guggenheim far better than Jenison, was more perceptive in assessing her experience at the Sunwise Turn. She "was one of the young people whom Mary Clarke affected," and it was this influence that later led her to "collect . . . the latest in experimental painting and [give] money and meals to poor artists and writers."[70] When Guggenheim left the store, she sailed to Europe, eventually settling in Paris; her first step as a patron-collector was taken a little later, on 15 February 1922, when she stopped in Beach's store and purchased, with "cash" as Beach duly recorded, a copy of the first edition of *Ulysses* numbered 339.[71] (Guggenheim may have overestimated the attendant privileges: a few weeks later when Joyce found himself invited to a party celebrating her marriage to Laurence Vail, he confessed his bewilderment. "I scarcely know him," he wrote, speculating that someone in his family had "met him or her somewhere.")[72]

The Sunwise Turn, quite plainly, encouraged an ambiguous atmosphere, one in which motifs of advancing consumerism and cultural patronage joined in a brief, uneasy, and unstable embrace. The store itself was caught in the ambiguity. As Loeb recalled:

For me, the "profit system" existed whether I liked it or not; and since it did, I accepted the first rule of business: to operate without loss. Other shops carried on without a subsidy, and I felt that ours should too. Mary, however, was against capitalism itself. To her the word "profit" had an evil connotation. She would have been willing to operate in the red, if someone would have picked up the tab and made up the loss. . . . I insisted that the shop be run so that it could continue without outside help.[73]

There was to be no resolution. Loeb finally sold his share of the shop in early 1921, and Mowbray Clarke struggled on until the store was purchased by a larger rival.

Guggenheim's subsequent career—her lifelong patronage of Djuna Barnes, her famous collection of paintings now in Venice—is readily understandable in light of her experiences at the Sunwise Turn. Many of the store's clients were collectors. Perhaps the most prominent was Alfred Knopf, the young publisher who had issued Pound's *Pavannes and Divisions* in 1918 and Eliot's *Poems* in 1920, both at the urging of Quinn. Knopf "used to come occasionally and buy royally"; he purchased two copies of *Ulysses* directly from Beach, availing himself of the 20 percent discount allowed to publishers, and added them to what eventually became one of the finest private book collections in the United States.[74] Another was Huebsch, the publisher whose plan to bring out *Ulysses* had collapsed in the aftermath of the *Little Review* trial; during especially busy evenings in the Christmas season, Huebsch "stopped in about eight and put on labels" for packages to be delivered the next day. Huebsch purchased three copies of *Ulysses* directly from Beach, also availing himself of the trade discount.[75] Yet another buyer was Leon Fleischmann, a senior editor for the publishing firm of Boni and Liveright, who had first met Loeb and Guggenheim when they were working at the Sunwise Turn. Fleischmann moved to Paris in 1921, where on 8 February 1922 he acquired numbered copy 254 of *Ulysses*.[76] (His wife, Helen, whose liaisons with other men he reportedly encouraged, would later marry Joyce's son, Giorgio.) Although they were not prominent collectors, Jane Heap and Margaret Anderson (the two editors of the *Little Review*) also frequented the Sunwise Turn, and evidently they even had discussions with Mowbray Clarke and Jenison about what to do with *Ulysses*. The Sunwise Turn was another agent within the same institutional space that housed Beach's Shakespeare and Company. As Mowbray Clarke informed Beach in a letter that accompanied the store's order for eighteen copies of *Ulysses*, "We thought of publishing it here but didn't have the money."[77]

Buyers of the first edition, by virtue of their participation in the economy of collecting, now became investors. This was plain enough to most contemporaries; hostile reviewers called its price "excessive" and "exaggerated."[78] One commented more extensively: "The volume is to be had by those who take the trouble to seek it out for about £3 10s., and most of those who are troubling to seek it out are buying it as an investment—they flatter themselves that a first edition of this remarkable author will bring them a handsome profit within a few years."[79] It took much less time than that. By September, when another reviewer noted that "the edition is limited and the price is rapidly ascending in the 'curious' market," he was guilty only of understatement.[80] Already on 27 March, scarcely seven weeks after the first copies had reached Beach in Paris, Quinn reported that copies of the lowest-priced issue of *Ulysses* were generally circulating in New York for $20 (£4, or 200 francs) with one having reached $50, almost 350 percent more than the original asking price.[81] In late June in

Paris, only eight days after the edition had sold out, copies of the 150-franc issue were going for 500 francs (£10, or $50).[82] On 5 August, six weeks later, Mitchell Kennerley heard that copies in London were bringing £10 each, but a week later, on the basis of firsthand observation, he reported that copies in London were fetching £20.[83] In October, Joyce informed his aunt Josephine Murray: "The market price of the book now in London is £40 and copies signed are worth more. . . . In a few years copies of the first edition will probably be worth £100 each, so book experts say, and hence my remark."[84]

Participants followed the vertiginous success of the first edition with the intensity of stockbrokers, and everyone hastened to pronounce it a triumph. In the aftermath of Huddleston's review in March, Weaver hastened to offer Beach her congratulations: "I had a card from Mr. Joyce yesterday saying that the 150 franc edition is out of print already—much sooner than I had imagined it would be. Many congratulations on your success as a publisher!"[85] Pound was no less insistent in announcing the same news to Alice Corbin Henderson, the former associate editor at *Poetry* magazine: "'Ulysses' is as you probably know 'out' triumphantly and the edition probably sold by now. . . . Record sale for one day was 136 on last Tuesday. So thaaat's that."[86] Indeed, the edition's success seems almost to have blinded people to changes that it was bringing about in their own perceptions and conduct. By May 1922, Weaver, who had once found it inconceivable "that booksellers make a practice of buying copies to hold up and sell," was urging Beach to do just that: "In any case I should think it would be well worth your while to hold back a number of copies to sell at a fancy price when the edition becomes a collector's curiosity as it is certain to do."[87] The rhetoric of investment was so tenacious that even in the 1950s, when Beach was writing her memoirs, she remarked of Joyce, "As soon as *Ulysses* was off his hands, he lost interest in it as a book if not as an investment."[88]

Conservative critics who lamented the rise in the first edition's price may have been too literal-minded in their understanding of the investment being asked of readers. For readers less fortunate than Peggy Guggenheim, the substantial price of the first edition inevitably dictated a certain psychic investment, demanding assent to strong claims about the work's aesthetic or literary value, claims that could then, legitimately or not, be justified by being translated back into economic terms. That thinking, in turn, bore witness to a much broader social phenomenon, the collapse of shared confidence in the notion of aesthetic autonomy and the independent coherence of aesthetic value—a collapse precipitated partly by the theoretical and institutional onslaught of the avant-garde as codified in the writings of Futurists, Dadaists, and Surrealists, or perhaps as best epitomized in Marcel Duchamp's famous "Fountain"; and partly by the relentless and ever increasing penetration of capitalist relations into every dimension of life, including the aesthetic, penetration that increasingly eroded the boundaries between art and commerce. Readers, no longer confident that they could appeal to the public sphere in support of their assertions about the aesthetic value of *Ulysses,* turned to the workings of the market itself, taking its outcomes to be confirmations, even justifications, of their claims.

One sees this logic at work in Pound's remark written to his mother and father in mid-1921, just as they were approaching retirement and looking for good investments: "I don't, en passant, know any sounder investment (even commercially) than the first edition of Ulysses."[89] Pound's comment epitomizes what might be called the double order of values that was at stake in the first edition. When he first urges that the edition is a "sound investment," he is merely using the term in a weak sense as a metaphor for something else; "sound investment" can be translated as "genuine literary achievement," and his comment acquires a sardonic undertone from the knowledge, shared by his parents, that that is not the kind of investment they are seeking. But when he hastens to add "even commercially," he invokes a second order of values associated with investment in the more common or literal sense, as an outlaying of money for profit or gain; here the first edition is a sound investment because it will increase in monetary value. Pound does not articulate the nature of the connection between these two orders of value, between his aesthetic claim and his assertion about monetary value, but their juxtaposition works to elide the two into a single category or to suggest that the second justifies the first, that an increase in the monetary value of the first edition works to justify claims about the artistic or literary value of *Ulysses.* Pound was not, I think, being naive about the philosophical difficulties inherent in mediating between these orders; more likely, he was taking for granted that those difficulties were of no interest to his parents, whose everyday outlook assumed that the workings of the marketplace were essentially just and self-justifying, serving as a homogeneous guarantor of value. For his parents, as for society at large, an increase in monetary value would validate or justify claims about artistic value. Pound, in acceding to their assumptions, bore witness to the same crisis of aesthetic value that prompted participants in the first edition to think its success would also justify claims about the work's aesthetic value, that its fortunes would ratify assertions of cultural worth. "Where is the value?" asked one early reviewer after listing many traits of *Ulysses* that he thought would prove trying to readers. "Better to

wait a few generations," he answered himself.[90] For the modernists, there was
no time to wait.

At stake in the intensity of discussion about the first edition's investment
value was a gnawing anxiety about the nature of value and its justification in
a market economy and an increasingly democratic society. For what set the
avant-garde art market apart from other markets, after all, was precisely "an
extreme ambiguity in the value of the objects that are sold."[91] Instead of being
attributed on the basis of production costs, or even merchandising costs, value
in this kind of market is largely discursive in nature, based on evaluations by
experts, critical and journalistic opinion. Yet for a work such as *Ulysses*, little
hope appeared in those quarters. That explains why participants in the planning of the edition pursued two strategies in attempting to market the edition.
On one hand, they especially sought out purchasers with prominent and
distinguished names, such as William Butler Yeats and George Bernard Shaw,
in the same way that gallery owners attempt to place new paintings or sculptures with eminent collectors. Here was one alternative to critical and journalistic opinion, a potential source of discursive capital that would ratify the work's
value. On the other hand, they turned to the workings of the market itself,
taking its outcomes to be confirmations, even justifications, of their claims.

The modernists had already witnessed, within their lifetimes, the deepening
penetration of capitalist relations into every feature of everyday life, including
its increasing extension in the realm of cultural production. They were not
especially optimistic about utopian alternatives to a market economy (and the
history of the twentieth century seems to have confirmed their skepticism), and
they were certainly not going to wait until such alternatives were realized to test
the validity of their claims. They were eager to demonstrate that their work
could be successful now and to construe market success as a justification for
their aesthetic and cultural claims.

In forfeiting demands for public sanction to the operations of the marketplace, the participants in the first edition of *Ulysses* encouraged a misunder-
standing that has continued to reverberate in debate about the avant-garde and
its public, art and its audience. For the marketplace is not, and never can be,
free from systemic distortions of power, and its outcomes cannot be equated
with undistorted participation in practices of justification, or with norms of
equal and universal participation in discussions about cultural and aesthetic
value. The operations of the market are not an adequate substitute for free
agreement; indeed, they are not a substitute at all, insofar as they are operations
of an entirely different order. (How different an order is fully evident at nearly

every step in the proceedings that attended the first edition of *Ulysses;* for if we are to be honest and set aside our abiding affection for *Ulysses,* we will admit that the marketing practices for the first edition were essentially monopolistic manipulations of supply and demand, actions characteristic not of a free market, if such a thing exists, but of unconstrained cartels.) The invisible hand of Adam Smith is not a moral or rational agent, nor can it be an aesthetic agent. And it can never be a substitute for processes of mutual intelligibility and critical justification. Insofar as the first edition of *Ulysses* became the exemplary case for a substitution of exactly this sort, while simultaneously remaining an archetype of the modern encounter between difficult art and its public, its "success" served only to obscure the immense loss of faith in the integrity of the aesthetic that it entailed. The echoes of that success can still be heard today in arguments that museums should receive our support because they attract tourism, stimulate business, or expand the tax base, or that the National Endowment for the Arts should be encouraged on similar and equally dubious grounds.

Strangely, and yet appropriately, it was the person who first "initiated" Beach "into the mysteries of limited editions," Monnier, who alone among the original participants in the first edition of *Ulysses* came to perceive the immense tragedy that had occurred. Monnier was writing in 1938 and reflecting on the causes of what she now called "the scourge," the devastation that had followed when the fragile economy of patron-investors lay in ruins and the modernist experiment was past:

> I have said that the scourge was just and it is true that for several years, even the ones called the years of "prosperity," we all behaved ourselves rather badly. We made books objects of speculation; we made or let be made a *stock exchange* for books. . . . Myself, did I not often propose books, saying that in a month the price would have at least doubled? And it was so easy to sell under those conditions. Now, repentance! Ah, it was well done![92]

Monnier's tone was perhaps unduly apocalyptic, derived from the religious vocabulary that so deeply appealed to her, but she was accurate in identifying characteristics that had helped shape the economy of literary modernism. It is a commonplace of cultural history that literary patronage gradually vanished in the eighteenth century due to changes in copyright laws, the spread of literacy, and the steady emergence of a popular market. Yet it is a fact that much of the literature that we now designate "modernist" was produced under the aegis of a revived patronage that flourished on a remarkable scale. For several reasons, however, the patronage of literary modernism was rarely the pure or disinterested support that we typically associate with patronage. The increasing penetration of capitalist relations into every facet of life, into the mind itself, meant that both writers and patrons were uneasy about an institution so clearly at odds with the work ethic, the meritocratic ethos that subtends market relations. As Robert Louis Stevenson had put it in 1881, he would agree to forgo writing popular fiction provided that someone "give me £1,000 . . . and at the same time effect such a change in my nature that I shall be content to take it from them instead of earning it."[93] John Quinn, to cite one example, quite plainly served as patron to Pound; yet he always arranged it so that Pound was receiving a salary for some editorial function, whether as foreign editor of the *Little Review* or correspondent and agent for the *Dial.* Patronage, as an essentially premodern form of social exchange, had to be disguised as something else if it were not to seem too at odds with the modern world.

One mask that it adopted was the concept of "investment." Patrons were not just giving away money in misguided sentimentalism about the arts, they were investing in something that would increase in value in the future. But for literature, the question remained: what *was* that something? In March 1922, only days after learning of the success that was greeting the first edition of *Ulysses,* Pound devised his Bel Esprit proposal to guarantee a healthy income to Eliot, "because the individual patron is nearly extinct." But although it was conceived as a replacement for patronage, Bel Esprit was not merely patronage in a new form, a point that Pound stressed to John Quinn:

> I can't come back too STRONGLY to the point that I do NOT consider this Eliot subsidy a pension. I am puke sick of the idea of pensions, taking care of old crocks.
> For me my £10 a year on Eliot is an investment. . . . I put this money into him as I would put it into a shoe factory if I wanted shoes. Better simile, into a shipping company, of say small pearl-fishing ships, some scheme where there was a great deal of risk but a chance of infinite profit.[94]

Yet the metaphor of investment was only partially applicable to literature: normally one's return on a successful investment results in an increase in one's own wealth or property; but because literary property remains the author's, investment could hardly characterize the process Pound wished to describe. To achieve more congruity between the metaphor of investment and the dilemmas posed by intellectual property, it was necessary to concretize the literary, to turn it into an object. Which is why the deluxe or limited edition acquired such prominence: it transformed literary property into a unique and fungible object, something that more nearly resembled a painting or an objet d'art, a "something" that could genuinely rise in value, at least on the collector's market.

Literary modernism constitutes a strange and perhaps unprecedented withdrawal from the public sphere of cultural production and debate, a retreat into a divided world of patronage, investment, and collecting. Uneasiness concerning the ethical legitimacy of patronage, corresponding efforts to assimilate patronage to concepts of investment and profit, and the concomitant attempt to objectify literary value in the form of the rare book or deluxe edition—all these trace a profound change in the relations among authors, publishers, critics, and readerships. To a remarkable degree, modernist literature was an experiment in adopting exchange and market structures typical of the visual arts, a realm in which patronage and collecting can thrive because its artisanal mode of production is compatible with a limited submarket for luxury goods. (Perhaps it is no accident that paintings repeatedly figure as metaphors for the literary work in this period, from *A Portrait of the Artist* to Lily Brisco's abstract portrait of Mrs. Ramsay in *To the Lighthouse*.) A submarket of this sort is extremely responsive to pressures from a small nucleus of patron-collectors: even a single figure or

17. Sylvia Beach and James Joyce in Shakespeare and Company, with poster "The Scandal of Ulysses," 1922. Photo courtesy Firestone Library, Special Collections, Princeton University.

institution can alter its dynamics, as attested by the power of the J. Paul Getty Museum in the market for old masters. Modernism required not a mass of readers but just such a corps of patron-collectors, or patron-investors.

A famous photograph of Sylvia Beach and James Joyce, taken in mid-1922, shows them seated beneath a poster announcing "The Scandal of Ulysses," the title of a hostile review that appeared in the *Sporting Times*. Beach is seen turning toward Joyce, with the poster just above his head, while Joyce casts a distracted glance at some papers on the table. Their actions suggest Olympian indifference, evincing only contempt for the specter of mass culture lurking behind them. But as Harriet Shaw Weaver noted when she sent the placard to Beach in Paris: "I don't know how widely it figured in London. I should not have known of it had I not happened to go to the office of the paper."[95] The scandal of *Ulysses*, or at least of the first edition, did not consist in the philistine hostility of mass culture, as opposed to the discerning judgment of elite readers. The real scandal lay elsewhere, in that intangible yet perceptible social space where aesthetic value became confused with speculation, collecting, investment, and dealing, a space in which modernism and commodity culture were not implacable enemies but fraternal rivals.

Chapter 3 The Price of Modernism: Publishing *The Waste Land*

"History is a nightmare," wrote James Joyce. "History has cunning passages, contrived corridors / And issues," murmured T. S. Eliot. It characterizes the epic, declared Ezra Pound, in a transparent reference to his own life's work, *The Cantos*.[1] The modernists were obsessed with history. They mourned it and damned it, contested it as tenaciously as Jacob wrestling with the image of God: "I will not let thee go, except thou bless me." Yet if the deity of history had ever deigned to reply to them, it might have said: "Behold, I set before you this day a blessing and a curse." Modernism, scholars announced in 1965, had "passed into history." The comment appeared in the preface to a textbook; it was in part a historical description and in part a speech act enacting what it appeared to describe, a key moment in modernism's passage to academic respectability.[2] Today, of course, we confess that we live on the hither side of that moment. We take for granted modernism's place in the canon or even equate its progress among the professors with its trajectory through history. Yet in doing so, we forget that modernism flourished long before 1965, that it had erupted into the public consciousness at least forty years earlier, and that its status as a cultural resource had been secured by an array of institutions quite removed from the tepid confines of the academy. The event that epitomized this process was the publication of *The Waste Land* in late 1922, which announced modernism's unprecedented triumph. It generated an avalanche of publicity that marked a crucial moment in its critical fortunes, establishing the poem as a reference point for the assessment of modernism by a wider public. Long before textbooks about it were written, popular and critical understanding of modernism had already been configured by the specific dynamics of transmission that characterized modernism's productive processes and grounded its extraordinary success. The complex events that culminated in the publication of *The Waste Land* articulated both its essential features and its contradictions. It behooves us to reconsider that earlier, more fractured moment, to reconnoiter the problematic terrain suggested by the preposition *into* in the phrase *into history.* For *into* evokes transition, a liminal moment attended by the possibility of failure, a risk that modernism's passage through the "contrived corridors" might have miscarried.

A core of basic facts about the publication of *The Waste Land* has long been known. In October 1922 it was simultaneously published in two journals: the *Criterion* in England, on 16 October, and the *Dial* in the United States, around 20 October (though in the November issue). In December it appeared in a third form as an independent volume that for the first time included Eliot's explanatory notes, published by the American firm of Boni and Liveright.[3] Together these constituted an event that has become a staple in the legend of modernism's emergence and triumph. Yet a reconsideration of that event might begin by exploring not where the poem was ultimately published but where it was *not* published: in the witty, sophisticated pages of *Vanity Fair,* or the intransigent leaves of the *Little Review.* Though neither has been discussed in connection with the release of *The Waste Land,* both were considered as potential publishers at various points in 1922 as negotiations for the poem followed their unpredictable course. And together these possibilities, with the untold stories that lie behind them, hint at the variety of possibilities of modernist publishing—how modernism negotiated its way among the "contrived corridors" of its own production.

One might begin by examining an unnoticed occasion in early August 1922, when John Peale Bishop visited the Paris studio of Ezra Pound. Two weeks earlier Bishop had resigned his post as managing editor of *Vanity Fair,* and ostensibly he was traveling on an extended honeymoon after his recent marriage. Unofficially, however, Bishop had come to visit the savage god of modern experimentalism—and to talk business.[4] The topic was the publication of *The Waste Land,* a work that Bishop had never read but whose vicissitudes he had been following for five months. In early March, while still in New York and laboring for *Vanity Fair,* he had received an article for publication from Aldous Huxley that reported the poem's composition and announced—mistakenly, it would turn out—its imminent publication in the *Dial.* An astute and conscientious editor, Bishop had phoned to confirm the report with his colleague and counterpart at the *Dial,* Gilbert Seldes. Seldes was puzzled, having heard nothing about the poem; on 6 March he cabled *Dial* co-owner and chief editor Scofield Thayer, who was then residing in Vienna: CABLE WHETHER ELIOT POETRY COMING SELDES. Three days later Thayer replied: ELIOT REFUSA THAYER. Seldes immediately contacted Bishop and urged him to alter Huxley's article to indicate that the poem's appearance in the *Dial*

18. Passport photo of Scofield Thayer, co-owner and co-editor of *The Dial,* 1921. Courtesy of the Yale Collection of American Literature, Beinecke Rare Book and Manuscript Library, Yale University.

was, as Seldes expressed it, "problematical but probable."[5] More important, Bishop had now glimpsed the growing rift between Eliot and the *Dial*.

By late April 1922, in fact, relations between Eliot and Thayer had completely broken down, and in the wake of their collapse Pound had begun to intervene actively in the search for a publisher. On 6 May 1922 he wrote to Jeanne Foster, beloved companion of New York lawyer and patron John Quinn, occasional contributor to *Vanity Fair,* and friend of Bishop.[6] Pound was soliciting an offer of publication for the poem in the bluntest possible terms: "What wd. Vanity Fair pay Eliot for 'Waste Land.' Cd. yr. friend there [Bishop] get in touch with T. S. E., address 12 Wigmore St., London W.1." By August, when he visited Pound, Bishop was clearly apprised of the situation—indeed, was responding to a suggestion advanced by Pound himself. The two met on 3 August, and two days later Bishop reported their conversation to Edmund Wilson, his closest friend and his successor as managing editor at *Vanity Fair:*

> Pound I met the other afternoon. I found him extended on a bright green couch, swathed in a hieratic bathrobe made of a maiden aunt's shit-brown blanket. His head is quite fine, but his voice is offensively soft, almost effeminate and [illegible word], and his body is rather disagreeably soft. However, he was quite gracious, and the twinkle of his eyes whenever he makes a point is worth something. He held forth for two hours on the intellectual moribundity of England—the old stuff. Here's the thing however—Eliot is starting a quarterly review: he is to run 'Waste Land,' the new series of lyrics in the first number: he and Thayer have split and the *Dial* will not publish it. Perhaps you might want to arrange for the American publication. Pound says they are as fine as anything written in English since 1900. I'm lunching with EP tomorrow [6 August] and will report further.

Whether Bishop wrote again to Wilson as he promised is unknown. On 7 August he left for Vienna, and by the time his letter could have reached Wilson in New York (around 16 August) and Wilson could have replied, his proposal had already been overtaken by events previously set in motion.[7] Yet the seriousness with which it was advanced by both Bishop and Pound should indicate that *Vanity Fair* was considered a serious contender to publish the poem. How serious, indeed, we shall see later.

Bishop's meeting in August also indicates the centrality of Pound's role in prompting and facilitating this abortive plan, recapitulating a story that grows increasingly familiar: Pound was the cultural impresario and entrepreneur who, precisely by virtue of these roles, occupied a critical position at the heart of modernism.[8] It is this position, in fact, that informs the rhetoric in which he articulated his advocacy of *The Waste Land*'s publication: "Pound says they are as fine as anything written in English since 1900," wrote Bishop, evidently quoting him verbatim. A month earlier Pound had written to Felix Schelling, his former professor at the University of Pennsylvania: "Eliot's *Waste Land* is I think the justification of the 'movement,' of our modern experiment, since 1900."[9] Bishop had clearly been subjected to a variant of the same argument: the poem was important precisely for its representative quality, and publishing it was not necessarily a matter of appreciating its literary quality or sympathizing with its substantive components—whatever those were—but of one's eagerness to position oneself as the spokesperson for a field of cultural production, the voice of an array of institutions ("the justification of the 'movement,' of our modern experiment, since 1900"). How much this animated Bishop's interest in the poem is underscored by a curious anomaly in the nature of his enthusiasm, for Bishop was praising a poem that he had yet to read—indeed, whose exact title was still a bit obscure to him ("'Waste Land,' the new series of lyrics").[10]

Bishop's imperfect knowledge was not unique. Indeed, insofar as he knew the title of the poem at all, he knew more than Horace Liveright had known when he first advanced his own offer of publication for the poem on 3 January 1922—the date being notable because it was before the poem had been completed, before it had even acquired its present title. Liveright's interest, like Bishop's, was the consequence not of an aesthetic encounter with a work he had read and admired but of an eagerness to buy a product that promised to meet a series of minimum conditions. Yet what were these conditions?

Liveright's access to Eliot's poem, like Bishop's, had been mediated by Pound. It was he who assumed the function of stage director cuing the characters in their parts: the shy, reserved poet played by T. S. Eliot, the brash young publisher acted by Horace Liveright. Eliot had arrived in Paris on 2 January 1922 and would stay for two weeks, until 16 January. He had come from Lausanne, bearing the disorderly sheaf of manuscripts that he and Pound began to edit and revise, producing a quasi-final version of *The Waste Land.*[11] His arrival coincided with the visit of Liveright, the partner who was guiding editorial policy at Boni and Liveright. Liveright was touring Europe to acquire new works of literature, and his visit to Pound was designed to set their relations on firmer ground. In 1919 he had published Pound's *Instigations,* in 1920 he had undertaken *Poems, 1918–1921,* a volume released only three weeks before his arrival in Paris, and in the summer of 1921 he had paid Pound for a translation of Remy de Gourmont's *Physique de l'amour,* an engagement that had helped Pound avert financial disaster. Now Liveright hoped to establish more stable relations; he trusted Pound's capacity to recognize new talent, saw him as a valuable link to other authors whose work interested him, and even entertained the idea that Pound's work might prove commercially viable at some point in the future.[12] In turn, Pound thought that he might make Liveright into the principal publisher of modernism and hoped to secure a long-term agreement guaranteeing financial security and time for work.

Poet and publisher courted one another actively. During the six days of Liveright's stay in Paris (30 December 1921–4 January 1922), they saw each other daily.[13] Pound treated Liveright to visits with Paul Morand and Constantin Brancusi, and the young publisher left "a good impression" on Pound, who felt that he was "going toward the light[,] not from it." He was "much more of a man than publishers usually are," and indeed "perhaps the only man in the business."[14] He was "a pearl among publishers."[15] The masculine publisher had arrived at an opportune moment. Joyce was seeking an American publisher for *Ulysses,* and Eliot would need a publisher for his unfinished poem. On 3 January 1922, Liveright had an extraordinary dinner with Joyce, Eliot, and Pound to discuss a milestone publishing program. The encounter was productive. With Joyce he agreed to publish *Ulysses* and to give $1,000 against royalties. To Pound he offered a contract guaranteeing $500 annually for two years in addition to translator's fees for any work from French agreed upon by both parties. To Eliot he offered $150 advance against 15 percent royalties and promised publication in the fall list. Liveright was nervous only about length; in a brief note dated 11 January, a week before Eliot had even left Paris, he worried that the poem might not be long enough. "I'm disappointed that Eliot's material is as short. Can't he add anything?" he pleaded with Pound.[16]

Pound, it is clear, was eager to gather under one roof the principal authors and works of modernism, including Yeats, whom he encouraged to abandon a long-standing contract with Macmillan in favor of Liveright.[17] At stake in these efforts was an attempt to present modernist writings as the articulation of an idiom, a serviceable language that was shared (and in this sense collective in character) yet amenable to a high degree of individuation: the voice of a "'movement,' of our modern experiment since 1900." In short, his activity was characterized by programmatic ambitions and a coherent sense of their interaction with market conditions.

The same traits surface in his dealings with Scofield Thayer, the editor of the *Dial* who was eventually to purchase *The Waste Land.* Pound lobbied forcefully for the poem's publication from the outset, invoking a rhetoric by now familiar.

On 18 February 1922, when Thayer and Eliot were still at a preliminary stage of discussion, Pound wrote to Thayer: "Eliot's poem is very important, almost enough to make everyone else shut up shop." When Thayer replied (5 March) that he could not comment on the poem's merits, since Eliot had not yet sent him the text, Pound persisted: "His poem is as good in its way as *Ulysses* in its way, and there is so DAMN little genius, so DAMN little work that one can take hold of and say, 'This at any rate stands, makes a definite part of litera-ture.'" *The Waste Land* was represented as a verse equivalent of *Ulysses*, a work that epitomized not just the experiences of an individual, whether author or protagonist, but the modernist claim to a hegemonic position in the institution of "literature," an ambiguous entity that was distinct yet inseparable from the commercial production of reading matter and discourse. Its merits resided not in a specific set of words or text but in its capacity to articulate this collective aspiration of an elite.

Pound's letter of 9–10 March also outlined practical suggestions that would prove pivotal both for *The Waste Land* and for subsequent literature: "I wish to Christ he had had the December award," he hinted. But other solutions were also available. Eliot might be granted "a professorship," as Robert Frost had recently been. Or he might be given a job on the *Century* or the *Atlantic,* since "he is not an alarming revolutionary, and he don't, as I at moments, get mistaken for a labour-leader or bolshy bomb-thrower."[18] Yet it was the hint of "the December award," the Dial Award for services in the cause of letters (granted for the first time four months earlier), that would bear fruit both for Eliot and for modernism.

Pound's suggestions were advanced just when communications between Eliot and Thayer were breaking down. On 8 March Eliot had telegraphed Thayer that he could not accept less than £50 ($250). Unfortunately, the message was distorted in transmission, and Thayer had received a shocking request for an unprecedented sum: "cannot accept under !8!56 pounds = eliot + [*sic*]." In reply, on 12 March Thayer reiterated his offer of $150 for the poem, a figure that was advanced without sight of the manuscript and was 25 percent higher than the $110 to $120 he would normally have paid.[19] (One should recall that income per capita in the United States at this time was about $750 per annum; by contrast, the 1986 income per capita was $14,166. Viewed as a percentage of these figures, Thayer's offer was the equivalent of roughly $2,850 in 1986 dollars.)[20] Not unreasonably, Thayer also asked to receive a copy of the manuscript. In addition, he pointed out the staggering deficits the *Dial* was

incurring and argued that it could not alter its policy of "pay[ing] all contributors famous and unknown at the same rates." In reply Eliot was curt and frankly
insulting, and he proceeded to withdraw the poem entirely:

> Please excuse my not replying sooner to your letter, except by my wire; but I have had
> a good deal of trouble over letting my flat furnished and moving here, where I shall be
> till the 20th June. In addition, there have been engrossing personal affairs, and I have
> been prevented from dealing with any correspondence.
>
> I also took some days to think about your offer, during which time I happened to
> hear on good authority that you paid £. 100 to George Moore for a short story, and I
> must confess that this influenced me in declining $150 [£30] for a poem which has
> taken me a year to write and which is my biggest work. To have it published in a
> journal was not in any case the way I should choose for bringing it out; and certainly
> if I am to be offered only 30 to 35 pounds for such a publication it is out of the
> question.
>
> I have written to Ezra Pound to explain my reasons for refusing to dispose of the
> poem to the Dial at that price and he concurs with me. . . .
>
> You have asked me several times to give you the right of first refusal of any new
> work of mine, and I gave you the first refusal of this poem.

Opposite Eliot's charge about George Moore, Thayer noted in pencil: "nov-
ellette length / serially." At the bottom of the letter he also noted: "Seen Moore
work[,] exception for him[;] and because review had offended[,] Moore had
already sacrificed several hundred dollars." True, the *Dial* had paid Moore a
higher than usual fee, but in part this was because of the work's length, in part
because the *Dial* had been remiss in fulfilling earlier obligations to Moore
("had offended"), thereby forcing him to sacrifice "several hundred dollars," for
which the larger payment had been a form of compensation. But more important was Thayer's remark opposite Eliot's last sentence withdrawing the offer to
publish. Thayer vented his tart indignation: "Not submitted."[21]

Eliot's allegations about Moore appeared to invoke a principle of equal pay
for all contributors. In fact, it was precisely the opposite principle that interested him, as he had explained a few days earlier to Pound: "I think these people
should learn to recognize Merit instead of Senility, and I think it is an outrage
that we should be paid less merely because Thayer thinks we will take less and
be thankful for it, and I thought that somebody ought to take steps to point this
out."[22] At first sight Eliot's argument may strike us as sympathetic, if only
because it seems so familiar. But the issues were rather more complicated: in an
important sense the question of aesthetic value is inseparable from commercial
success in a market economy, a difficulty that beset every argument for the

intrinsic merit of literary modernism. By 1922 literary modernism desperately required a financial-critical success that would seem comparable to the stunning achievement of modernist painting, yet every step in this direction was hampered by market constraints less amenable to the kinds of pressure from elite patronage and investment that had secured the fortunes of Cubism and modern painting. The legal definition of intellectual property—which continued to belong to the author after its purchase by the consumer, in contrast to a painting or a statue, which became the property of the purchaser—posed a series of intractable dilemmas. Patronage could nurture literary modernism only to the threshold of its confrontation with a wider public; beyond that point it would require commercial success to ratify its viability as a significant idiom. That was the question that permeated discussion about publication of *The Waste Land:* assuming that the poem epitomized the investment of twenty years in the creation of a collective idiom—"our modern experiment, since 1900"—the protagonists were obliged to find a return on their investment in modernity.

Thayer was shocked and insulted by Eliot's letter of 16 March and refused to engage in further communications with him. Instead he turned to Pound, who was more vulnerable to the threat of losing his job with the *Dial* and might be reproached for having encouraged Eliot's intransigence. On 10 April Thayer demanded that he explain himself: "Perhaps you will be able to enlighten me as to why you concur with Eliot in his refusal to let The Dial have his poem."[23] In reply Pound rehearsed the same charge (which Eliot had communicated to him), that George Moore was "getting special rates from *The Dial* (also Sherwood Anderson)," and he concluded: "That being the case I can hardly reprove Eliot—if you have put the thing on a commercial basis, for holding out for as high a price as he can get. [Added in autograph in margin:] (i.e. if The Dial is a business house, it gets business treatment. If The Dial is a patron of literature T. contends it should not pay extra rates for 'mere senility,' all of which is extreme theory-ism, perhaps, on his part.)" But in passing, Pound added another point. He could hardly attest to the veracity of Eliot's or Thayer's claims, but in general he preferred that the poem be published in the *Dial:* "I shd. perhaps prefer one good review to several less good ones. I have, as I think you know, always wanted to see a concentration of the authors I believe in, in one review. The Dial perhaps looks better to me than it does to Eliot. (Life in general does.)" As always, Pound displayed a keen understanding of the nexus between cultural ambitions and their institutional actualization.[24] Implicit in his remarks to Thayer was his view that literary modernism could best present itself as a shared

language through a centralization suggesting the coherence of its ambitions—
the same project that animated his endeavor to unite the works of Joyce, Eliot,
Yeats, and himself under the umbrella of a single publisher. Such a project
would facilitate the perception of modernism as an idiom both collective and
capable of individuation: an identifiable, distinctive, and serviceable language.
Yet with equal acuteness Pound also articulated a central dilemma that characterized the *Dial* and the role it might play in any such project. Was the *Dial* a
form of patronage, or was it a commercial venture? Unlike the traditional
journals that were organs of publishing houses, the *Dial* could shun the increasing diversity and heterogeneity that typified the ordinary journals, presenting itself as a benign and "disinterested" patron. Its owners, by contrast,
were actively engaged in purchasing works of modern painting and sculpture
and in this sense were investors in a market commodity whose value was rapidly
rising, in part through the efforts of the publicity apparatus that they themselves owned and controlled. Literary modernism, by analogy, was now court-
ing the risk of becoming "smart art," an investment that would pay and pay big
if successful in an expanding market. But pay whom?

The contradictions were irreconcilable. Driven by conflicting imperatives,
the participants muddled through the summer of 1922. On 30 April Thayer
summarized the state of his relations with Eliot: "We now correspond only
through Pound with whom my relations are also strained, but who seems to
desire to keep his job." Pound himself was more cavalier. On 6 May, while
traveling through Italy, he paused to send Thayer a postcard: "My present
impression of the case is 'Oh you two Bostonians.'"[25] The surface gaiety,
however, was a pose. The same day he also posted his letter inquiring about the
price that might be offered by *Vanity Fair.*

Discussions remained stalled throughout the rest of May and June as the
participants reconsidered their strategies. On 2 June Pound and Eliot met in
Verona, a meeting recorded a few weeks later by Pound in a series of drafts and
draft fragments suggesting the substance of their conversations. One of these
(later incorporated into *The Cantos*) makes clear that they considered the
editorial program of Eliot's new review (still untitled, but soon to be named the
Criterion), a topic that probably led to another: where to publish *The Waste
Land.*[26] From the outset of his undertaking the *Criterion,* Eliot had entertained
the idea that it might collaborate with American reviews in simultaneous
publication; his first letter announcing the new journal to Pound, written on 12
March, had proposed exactly this: "I also see no reason why some things should
not appear in this and in the Little Review concurrently."[27] The timing of this

suggestion should be noted: it was four days after Eliot had sent his provocative telegram to Thayer and four days before he withdrew his offer of publication to the *Dial*. It was a curious proposal: Eliot had not published in the *Little Review* since 1918 and had never evinced particular interest in its fortunes. Yet if Eliot was already assuming that *The Waste Land* would be published by his own journal in England, then his 12 March reference to the *Little Review*—addressed to Pound, a primary force behind its editorial activity—was probably an effort to suggest a replacement for the *Dial*. The same idea, we may suppose, arose in their discussions at Verona. And quite naturally so, since the editors of the *Little Review* were now in Paris and often in touch with Pound, who had recently assembled a special Brancusi issue for them. Like *Vanity Fair*, the *Little Review* was also a possible candidate for what had now become a project of simultaneous publication.

In the wake of the Verona meeting, the decisive episodes in the story unfolded quickly. Pound returned to Paris on 2 July 1922 and two weeks later received a personal visit from James Sibley Watson, Jr., the co-owner and co-editor of the *Dial* and the partner of Thayer. Two days later Pound reported the meeting to his wife, Dorothy, who was away in London: "Usual flood [of people visiting]: Lunch with Watson of Dial, on Wed. [19 July], amiable . . . wants T's poem for Dial, etc." The report leaves no doubt about the purpose of Watson's visit: he had come to purchase *The Waste Land*.[28] No doubt he was treated to a variant of Pound's argument that the poem was "as good in its way as Ulysses in its way"—resonant, even haunting terms to Watson now that he was in Paris. When he had gone to Beach's bookstore to pick up his own copy (number 33, at 350 francs) of *Ulysses*, he had learned that the last of the 150-franc copies had already soared to 500 francs. Watson and Thayer, after all, had ordered nine copies of the first edition for themselves, the *Dial*, and various staff members (Thayer purchased copy number 73). And Thayer understood the kind of publicity such a work could generate: he had been called as a witness at the *Little Review* trial and seen at first hand its sensational newspaper coverage. Influenced by these events and the assumption that the poem vindicated the project of modern experimentalism, Watson was seized with anxiety that the *Dial* would suffer an ignominious defeat in its effort to position itself as *the* representative of advanced cultural life. What if the poem were published in the *Little Review* or even *Vanity Fair*? The day after his meeting with Pound, Watson flew to Berlin and met with Thayer.[29]

The chief subject of discussion in Berlin was *The Waste Land* and the *Dial's* prospects for publishing it. Increasingly fearful and excited, the two editors

reached an unprecedented decision: they would offer Eliot the second annual
Dial Award with its $2,000 prize as payment for the poem, in confidence, but
officially they would pay only the $150 that had been their original offer.[30]
Literary history records few spectacles so curious or so touching as two editors
of a major review offering a figure nearly three times the national income per
capita—in 1986 terms, the payment would exceed $40,000—for a poem
neither of them had seen or read. What they had decided to purchase was less a
specific poem, more a bid for discursive hegemony. Moreover, their strategy for
reaching their goal was exquisitely self-fulfilling: since news of the Dial Award
would attract media attention, it would augment the sales of the work and
further redound to the credit of the *Dial.*

Seven days after his encounter with Thayer, Watson returned to Paris and
met with Pound a second time. Two accounts of the meeting survive, one by
Pound addressed to his wife, Dorothy: "Watson in Thursday [27 July] with
Cummings . . . Wat. troubled at not having T. S.'s poem for Dial."[31] More
revealing is Watson's account, addressed to Thayer:

> Pound has written a [autograph addition:] *very* veiled hint to Eliot. He took me to see
> Brancusi, who [illegible word] appears very anxious not to be reproduced anymore. I
> gather this is mostly a pose. Such chittering and apologizing and kowtowing as
> Pound indulged in I have never before seen. It was disgusting. I pointed out several
> things I thought you would like, but no, I must take what the master will give. "You
> win the victory," says Brancusi, as though I had been beseeching him for a week. A
> dam' Pyrrhic victory, by me! . . . He will, of course, be furious if we don't take any;
> and Pound will say that we have destroyed his only remaining Parisian friendship. I
> hope you will write Brancusi rather than have me go to see him again; if I go, I shan't
> take Pound, that's sure. . . . Pound looks pretty unhealthy. He handed me two
> lemons which he recommends very highly and which I send to you on the [canceled:
> hope] chance you may like one of them.[32]

Pound's letter to Eliot, which has not survived, was written immediately after
Watson's visit on 27 July. And though his "hint" had been "*very* veiled" when
issued from Paris, a certain rending evidently took place as it crossed the channel.
Eliot understood fully the implications of his request for a typescript: "I will let
you have a copy of the Waste Land for confidential use as soon as I can make
one. . . . I infer from your remarks that Watson is at present in Paris. I have no
objection to either his or Thayer's seeing the manuscript."[33] Evidently it took
Eliot some two weeks to arrange (or type himself) a copy of the typescript, and it
was not until 12 or 13 August that he sent it to Watson in Paris. When it arrived,
Watson hastily read it and reported the news to Thayer in Vienna:

In response to Pound's letter Eliot has assumed a more conciliatory attitude and has sent on a copy of Wasteland for our perusal. I am forwarding it to you. . . . Anyway I wrote him more plainly about the prize and await his answer. I found the poem disappointing on first reading but after a third shot I think it up to his usual—all the styles are there, somewhat toned down in language [autograph addition:] *adjectives!* and theatricalized in sentiment—at least I thought.[34]

Here again, one is struck by the discrepancy between Watson's initial assessment of the poem and views of it enshrined in later criticism. "On first reading" Watson found the poem "disappointing," and after perusing it three times he considered it merely "up to [Eliot's] usual." Indeed, in some respects it was below his usual: the diction seemed flat ("somewhat toned down"), the tone "theatricalized." Yet all this makes only more remarkable Watson's decision to advance a publication proposal that entailed an unprecedented scale of payment, which he presented to Eliot in a letter of 13 or 14 August.

Eliot responded on 15 August: "Subject to Mr. Liveright's consent, I would let the *Dial* publish the poem for $150, not before November 1st. In this event I would forego the $150 advance from Mr. Liveright, and he would delay publication as a book until the new year. Possibly he would be glad to do this, on the possibility of the book's getting the prize, which might increase the sales."[35] His proposal reached Watson late in the afternoon of 16 August. The next day, however, he was seized with panic at the audacity of his proposal and sent a telegram reporting that he could not make up his mind. On 19 August Watson reported both events to Thayer:

Got a letter from Eliot [received 16 August] regretting his haste in thinking we were trying to rob him, and offering us the right of publishing his poem simultaneously in Dial with its pub. in the Criterion. I find from Pound that Bel Esprit hasn't enough yet for one year, that it goes to Eliot only when he leaves his bank and engages in writing exclusively. He gets only a nominal salary from Lady Rothermere. In other words I don't see why we shouldn't be doing something moderately popular in giving him the award. But the next day [17 August] I got a [canceled: cable] telegram saying "don't act till you receive a second letter." Haven't received it yet, though it may come on board tonight when we touch at Plymouth. So the matter is still in the air. Please don't do anything definitive without letting me know first. I reach New York probably August 26, and there is also the telegraphie sans fil.[36]

Pound, clearly, had informed him about the difficult state of Eliot's personal finances. Watson, in turn, hoped that this might be exploited to the advantage of the *Dial,* that it might be viewed as "doing something moderately popular in giving him the award." Eliot's actual services to letters (the ostensible justification for the award) and the merits of *The Waste Land* were issues that never appeared in his discussion of the Dial Award. Instead, Watson cheerily admitted his view that the proposal was a device intended to garner goodwill for the *Dial*, a tactic in its struggle to consolidate its position as the dominant journal of advanced culture.

Meanwhile, on 21 August Eliot sent his own letter to Quinn, apprising him of the recent developments and leaving open the possibility for action: "A few days ago I had an attractive proposal from Mr. Watson of the *Dial* who are very anxious to publish the poem. . . . They suggested getting Liveright to say postpone the date of publication as a book, but I have written to them to say that it seemed to me too late to be proper to make any change now and that I should not care to trouble either Mr. Liveright or yourself with any questions of alterations in the contract."[37] Nine days later Eliot wrote to Pound and reported his letters to Watson and Quinn:

> I received a letter from your friend Watson most amiable in tone . . . offering $150 for the "Waste Land" (not "Waste Land," please, but "*The* Waste Land," and (in the strictest confidence) the award for virtue also. Unfortunately, it seemed considerably too late, as I had the preceding day [14 August] got contract, signed by Liveright and Quinn, book to be out by Nov. 1st, etc.) I can't bother Quinn any more about it, I don't see why Liveright should find it to his advantage to postpone publication in order to let the Dial kill the sale by printing it first, and there has been so much fluster and business about this contract that I don't want to start the whole thing up again, so I see nothing but to hope that the Dial will be more businesslike with other people. Watson's manner was charming, if Thayer had behaved in the same way the Dial might have published it long ago, instead of pretending that I had given him the lie as if he was *ehrenfähig* anyhow. Anyway, it's my loss, I suppose; if Watson wants to try to fix it up with Liveright I suppose he can, that's his affair. I suppose the move was entirely due to your beneficent and pacific efforts, which are appreciated. Dam but [why] don't they give the prize to you? More presently.[38]

Notwithstanding the disingenuous demurral by Eliot, the issue was already all but settled. The suggestion he had advanced—that the *Dial* undertake to arrange terms with Liveright—was rapidly realized through the agency of Watson. On 29 August his ship arrived in New York; the next day he received Eliot's letter of 21 August broaching the new arrangement. He set to work immediately, as Gilbert Seldes duly reported to Thayer: "Watson has just come back and the Eliot affair is taking up much of our time."[39] A week later he and Seldes met with Liveright in the New York office of the lawyer John Quinn, and there the deal was concluded. Liveright required that the *Dial* purchase 350 copies of the volume at standard discounts, assuring himself an advance sale and adding $315 to the *Dial's* costs for procuring the poem. But the *Dial* had achieved its victory, and the outcome was a remarkable success.

Liveright reported on the later events in a letter to Pound written on 5 February 1923, eleven weeks after the poem's publication in the *Dial,* seven weeks after his own release of the book-cum-notes: "God bless you and Cantos IX to XII. If we can get as much publicity from them as The Waste Land has received, you will be a millionaire. The Waste Land has sold 1000 copies to date and who knows, it may go up to 2000 or 3000 copies. Just think, Eliot may make almost $500 on the book rights of this poem. And Gene Stratton Porter makes $40,000.00 to $60,000 a year out of her books. Well, it's all in a life time, so who cares."[40]

Liveright's sales estimate was remarkably accurate. Yet more important was the tenor of his comments, insofar as it tended to echo Watson's rationale in urging Thayer to take on the poem: the argument that the *Dial* would "be doing something moderately popular in giving him the award." Liveright's stress on how much publicity the award-and-publication package received is telling. For by now it should be clear that the publication of *The Waste Land* marked the crucial moment in the transition of modernism from a minority culture to one supported by an important institutional and financial apparatus.

The contours of this transition can best be understood by a rapid survey of the three journals that were considered for simultaneous publication in the United States—the *Little Review,* the *Dial,* and *Vanity Fair.* Each represented a moment in the growth and triumph of modernism. When Eliot suggested in March 1922 that the *Criterion* engage in simultaneous publication with the *Little Review,* his proposal looked back to the world of modernism's past, to its origins in a *littérature de cénacle,* to the heady days of 1917–1918 when his own poems and articles had appeared in the rebellious journal. When Pound suggested in May and August that the poem be published by *Vanity Fair,* his proposal looked forward to modernism's future, to the ease and speed with which a market economy could purchase, assimilate, commodify, and reclaim as its own the works of a literature whose ideological premises were bitterly inimical toward its ethos and cultural operations. These distinct moments were mediated by what, in the early 1920s, was modernism's present: the sensibility epitomized by the *Dial,* a form of production supported by massive and unprecedented patronage that facilitated modernism's transition from a literature of an exiguous elite to a position of prestigious dominance.

The velocity of this process is illustrated by the fate of Eliot's own work shortly after the publication of *The Waste Land.* Only seven months later, in June 1923, *Vanity Fair* devoted an entire page to reprinting earlier poems by

Eliot; among them were "Sweeney Among the Nightingales" (first published in the *Little Review* in 1918), "A Cooking Egg" (first published in a tiny journal named *Coterie* in 1919), and "Burbank with a Baedeker" (first published in the short-lived *Art and Letters* in 1919). Linking the poems was an editorial box in the center of the page, presumably composed by managing editor Edmund Wilson, that lucidly articulated the journal's assumptions and aims: "Since the publication of *The Waste Land,* Mr. T. S. Eliot has become the most hotly contested issue in American poetry. He has been frequently attacked for his unconventional form and what many readers consider his obscurity. But if one has read Mr. Eliot's earlier poems . . . from which the present selection is made, one gets the key to both his technique and his ideas." In subsequent months of 1923–1924 *Vanity Fair* conducted an intense campaign, printing articles by Eliot in July, November, and February, and a study of Eliot's work by Clive Bell in September 1923. Eliot had indeed become "the most hotly contested issue in American poetry"—in part because the *Dial* and *Vanity Fair* had said so themselves.[41]

It was a long way from the world of the *Little Review,* a distance that can be measured more accurately if we recall some of the journal's principal features. (Because information on the *Little Review* is notoriously sparse, I shall also use data from the *Egoist,* which Eliot edited during 1918 and which occupied a similar position within the economic structure of modernism.)[42] The *Little Review* had existed in a special space that was insulated from the direct demands of larger market structures by the beneficent hand of a modest yet influential patronage (such as the syndicate organized by Quinn or Harriet Weaver's support of the *Egoist*). The scale of such operations was tiny; circulation of the *Little Review* was roughly three thousand, and for the *Egoist* it typically hovered near two hundred.[43] Both maintained a low ratio of advertising to circulation revenues, something like 1:10, indicating that they survived by a direct rapport with a restricted group of readers.[44] They rejected the strategy of the mass circulation journals that had been the dominant market force since the late 1890s and instead returned to the kind of direct relationship with readers that had typified literary magazines in the genteel tradition. This relationship was also reflected in their form of sales: neither enjoyed newsstand sales (distributing agencies were not interested), and both were associated with a meager set of specific retail outlets (the Washington Square Bookshop, the Sunwise Turn, and Brentano's in New York for the *Little Review;* the stores of Friedrich Neumaier, Elkin Mathews, and Harold Monro in London for the *Egoist;* and Sylvia Beach's Shakespeare and Company in Paris for both). At its height the *Egoist* sold only

132 copies to readers who were not already subscribers, the *Little Review* only 600 (19.4 percent of total circulation). Advertising, too, played a minimal role in the *Little Review*. Its issue for September 1918 contained sixty-four pages and three covers (inside front, inside back, and back) that could potentially carry ads, but the journal used only one and a half of those pages (2.25 percent). In its issue for spring 1922, which was exactly the same length, paid ads more than doubled to three and a quarter pages—but that still amounted to only 4.8 percent of the journal. Advertising, following a convention of the genteel tradition, was segregated at the beginning and end of an issue.

The *Dial* operated quite differently. Its subscription list was some two and a half times larger than the *Little Review*'s: 6,374 in 1922 (compared with the

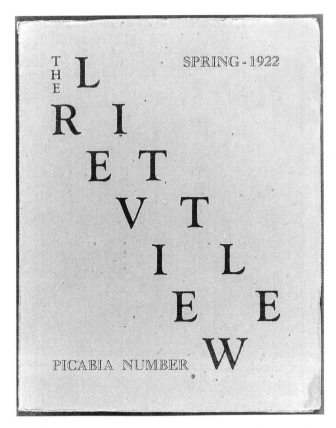

19. The *Little Review*, Spring 1922; 24.4 × 19.3 cm. Courtesy of the Yale Collection of American Literature, Beinecke Rare Book and Manuscript Library, Yale University.

average of 2,500 for the *Little Review* in 1917). Its ratio of advertising to circulation revenues was not 1:10, but 1:3 (specifically, $9,100 to $31,400)—much lower than those of more commercial journals, to be sure, but much higher than those of the *Little Review* or the *Egoist*. But above all, the *Dial* was supported by massive patronage: its deficits for the three years from 1920 to 1922 were, respectively, $100,000, $54,000, and $65,000, a cumulative deficit of $220,000 that was paid for directly by Thayer and Watson at the rate of $4,000 per month from each.[45] Nothing is more revealing than comparable figures for the *Little Review,* which in 1918 was supported by a syndicate of four donors whose contributions totaled $2,350 per year, or for the *Egoist,* which from 1917 to 1920 was supported by donations from Harriet Weaver averaging £253 ($1,265) per year.[46]

THE

D I A L

NOVEMBER 1922

VOLUME LXXIII   NUMBER 5

50 cents a copy

20. The *Dial,* November 1922; 25 × 16.6 cm. Courtesy of the Yale Collection of American Literature, Beinecke Rare Book and Manuscript Library, Yale University.

How the *Dial* mediated a transition between the *Little Review* and *Vanity Fair* is also apparent in its editorial practices. The *Dial,* for example, repeatedly published materials that had previously appeared in the *Little Review,* such as Wyndham Lewis's "Starry Sky" or a photo of Ossip Zadkine's sculpture "Holy Family."[47] Indeed, at times all three journals were publishing the same material: the spring 1922 issue of the *Little Review* was devoted to works by Brancusi, the May number of *Vanity Fair* showed photographs of the same works, and the November issue of the *Dial* reproduced Brancusi's *Golden Bird* for a third time in the same year. Its mediating role was also apparent in editorial policy. The *Little Review* boasted its intransigent aestheticism on the masthead: it would brook "no compromise with the public taste." But the *Dial* was more cautious; in a letter of November 1922 Thayer told his managing editor that he wished to publish works that "have *aesthetic value* and are not *commercially suicidal.*"[48] The litotes "not commercially suicidal" is noteworthy, and translated into ordinary prose it means *might be successful.* The journal's official policy was also a compromise; it invoked an uneasy translation of Crocean idealism to justify eclectic aestheticism, a tone of patrician urbanity, and the conviction that "one must confine one's self to works of art" independent of social or moral considerations.[49] The *Dial,* in other words, differed from the *Little Review* and *Vanity Fair* in its tone of high seriousness and gravity, not in substantive ideology.

Yet the *Dial* did not borrow only from the *Little Review;* in some respects it strove to imitate *Vanity Fair.* Editorially it copied *Vanity Fair*'s practice of offering a regular "London Letter" and "Paris Letter," and it imitated *Vanity Fair*'s institution of so-called service departments that offered advice and arrangements for the purchase of books and travel. Its layout and design were also conspicuously similar, and by 1922 the two magazines were even using the same printing operations. The *Dial* also attempted to integrate editorial and advertising functions in ways reminiscent of *Vanity Fair:* its monthly listing of gallery exhibitions took pains to praise its own advertisers. And like *Vanity Fair,* too, its management stressed publicity, advertising revenues, and street sales (as opposed to subscriptions). It developed displays to be set up at newsstands, and it aggressively cultivated a larger metropolitan public. When its editors contemplated penetrating the British market in 1921, Eliot urged them to pursue the same course abroad: "you must have your future manager here arrange for the paper to be visible and handy on every bookstall, at every tube station."[50] When the *Dial* published *The Waste Land* and announced its award, Thayer ordered the staff to keep a minute record of every reference to these events in the press—an early form of market testing.[51] Above all, the *Dial* imitated the central principle behind the success of *Vanity Fair* and its sister journal *Vogue:* in an era when most publishers were attempting to produce magazines aimed at a mass market, Condé Nast, publisher of *Vanity Fair* and *Vogue,* and Thayer deliberately appealed to a select, restricted audience.[52]

The *Dial* was acutely conscious of its competition with *Vanity Fair,* a theme that recurs in letter after letter by Thayer. On 16 December 1922 he complained to his mother that contributors and staff members of the *Dial* were frequently writing for *Vanity Fair.* Ten days later he lamented to Seldes: "If we have no aesthetic standards whatever in what respect are we superior to Vanity Fair which in other respects gives more for the money?" A month later he urged Seldes to hasten the printing of a new photograph "lest 'Vanity Fair' get ahead of us on this point too." And four months later he ordered him to secure rights to a new painting by Pablo Picasso: "Otherwise Vanity Fair will be getting it." How closely the market for the two journals overlapped became clear when the *Dial* issued its special art folio in June 1923. Desperate to stimulate sales, Thayer begged Seldes to intervene: "Cannot you get Rosenfeld to write the thing up for Vanity Fair, which is our most important selling possibility?"[53]

To be sure, the *Dial* and *Vanity Fair* were not twins. By comparison the *Dial* was a modest operation. Its $9,100 in advertising revenue was tiny compared with the $500,000 per annum generated by *Vanity Fair.* Paid advertising occupied less space; in the November 1922 issue that included *The Waste Land,* 27.5 of 156 pages (or 18 percent) were taken up by advertising. Compare this with the July 1923 issue of *Vanity Fair,* which contained Eliot's poems: of 140 pages, 76 were devoted to paid advertising (54 percent), and many articles offered fashion and automobile reviews that were advertising thinly disguised. The *Dial,* like the *Little Review,* segregated its paid ads in sections placed only at the beginning and end of the journal; most of its ads came from publishers, all were printed in black and white, and few made conspicuous use of visual imagery. *Vanity Fair,* in contrast, handsomely displayed its arresting and splashy ads, many in color and set among the editorial contents. In 1922 the *Dial*'s circulation stood at 9,500 copies per month; in the same year *Vanity Fair*'s reached 96,500 (see table).[54] (Other monthlies boasted still larger circulations, such as *McClure's Magazine* with 365,000, or *National Geographic* with 734,000; monthlies classed as "women's publications" had the largest circulations: *McCall's Magazine,* 1,340,000, and *Woman's Home Companion,* 1,468,000.)

Despite their diversity, one set of interests did bind together the *Little Review,* the *Dial,* and *Vanity Fair*—their involvement with the visual arts. All three journals were copious in publishing photographs of contemporary painting

21. *Vanity Fair,* August 1923; 32.5 × 24.8 cm. Courtesy of the Yale
Collection of American Literature, Beinecke Rare Book and
Manuscript Library, Yale University.

and sculpture. More important, however, was another affiliation that this
signaled, one with the world of contemporary art collecting. John Quinn, who
was patron of the *Little Review,* Scofield Thayer, who was co-owner, patron, and
editor of the *Dial,* and Frank Crowninshield, who was the editor of *Vanity Fair,*
were all major buyers of contemporary art. Quinn's purchases, as we have seen,
totaled $24,000 in 1920 alone. In 1923 he purchased Paul Cézanne's portrait of
his father; a huge still-life interior by Henri Matisse, six by eight feet; *The Jungle*
by Henri Rousseau; five Picassos, including the magnificent *Portrait of William
Uhde;* two small works by Georges Braque; and three major works by Brancusi.[55] Thayer was almost as active: after residing in Paris, Vienna, and Berlin,
and acting under the influence of Herwarth Walden, owner of the famous Der

Journal Circulation and Revenues, 1922

	Little Review	Dial	Vanity Fair
Total circulation	3,100	9,500	96,500
Subscriptions	2,500	6,374	—
Retail sales	600	3,100	—
Advertising revenue	$500	$9,100	$500,000
Circulation revenue	$5,000	$31,400	$357,000*
Ratio, ad revenue:			
circulation revenue	1:10	1:3	1:0.7
Paid ads (% of pages)	4.8	18	54
Yearly patronage	$2,350	$73,300	0
Price per copy	$1.00	$0.50	$0.35
Subscription per year	$4.00	$5.00	$3.50

*Based on assumption of 66,000 subscribers and 30,000 street sales

Sturm gallery, Thayer gathered a judicious collection of pre–World War I German Expressionists, including Oskar Kokoschka, along with a substantial number of works by Picasso, Matisse, and others, and at his instigation the *Dial* published a lavish collection of contemporary art reproductions titled *Living Art*.[56] Frank Crowninshield was also a collector: his penthouse flat housed eighteen paintings by André Segonzac, five by Amedeo Modigliani, seven by Jules Pascin, a large collection of African art, and one work by virtually every major painter in Paris.[57] Often he drew upon his own collection for works to be reproduced in the magazine, and at times he wrote captions for photographic art features. In 1929 he became one of the original seven members of the board of the Museum of Modern Art, and when Alfred Barr first announced the formation of the museum in 1929, he did so, revealingly, with an essay in *Vanity Fair*.[58] Quinn also published two essays in *Vanity Fair*, one on the sculptor Jacob Epstein and another on Joyce, a pairing that suggests the extent to which contemporary art and literature might be counterpoised. And when Quinn held a private party in 1923 to unveil his new Georges Seurat painting, the great *Le Cirque*, he invited only his immediate family and Frederick James Gregg, the lead writer on art for *Vanity Fair* and an old friend.[59]

Much can be learned from the interaction among the three journals and their common role as potential publishers of *The Waste Land*. For these journals, it is clear, are best viewed not as antagonists who represented alien or incompatible ideologies but as protagonists who shared a common terrain, whose fields of activity overlapped and converged at crucial points within a shared spectrum of marketing and consumption. Their activity suggests that there was no single or essential feature that distinguished the avant-garde from modernism. These were not irreconcilable poles of a dichotomy, as has been argued by scholars such as Peter Bürger, Andreas Huyssen, or Marjorie Perloff, who have urged that a set of formal devices (montage, for example) constituted a vague yet potent ideology that challenged dominant cultural norms, assaulted the bourgeois concept of art, or anticipated the concerns of postmodernism.[60] Such arguments are sustained only by confining one's attention to formal values viewed in isolation from their social actualization. When seen in institutional terms, the avant-garde was neither more nor less than a structural feature in the institutional configuration of modernism. It played no special role by virtue solely of its form, and it possessed no ideological privilege; instead it was constituted by a specific array of marketing and publicity structures that were integrated in varying degrees with the larger economic apparatus of its time. Its typical endeavor was to develop an idiom, and that, indeed, is how the editors who purchased *The Waste Land* perceived it: they were buying "the justification of the 'movement,' of our modern experiment, since 1900." They were purchasing a work whose scope and pretensions could vindicate an emerging idiom— vindication that could, in a market economy, be ratified only in the conspicuous expenditure of money: whence the Dial Award with its lavish expenditure for a single poem; whence Liveright's decision to double his normal per copy expenditure on advertising for *The Waste Land;*[61] whence Thayer's concern to register every reference to the *Dial*'s announcement of the award and publication of the poem. They were organizing an event that might be "moderately popular" (Watson), an occasion to generate "much publicity" (Liveright)— itself the surest commodity of the modernist economy.

The three journals that were considered as candidates for *The Waste Land* formed a tripartite structure within the productive apparatus of modernism. But a similar structure, with analogous kinds of relations, also informed modernism's larger productive economy. In particular, a modernist work was typically published in three forms: first, in a little review or journal; second, in a limited edition of recently collected poems (or as an individual volume if the work was large enough); and third, in a more frankly commercial or public edition issued by a mainstream publisher and addressed to a wider audience. Especially important were the two forms of book publication, the limited and the public editions. These were part of a protocol that had become normative in the course of a complex fusion of heterogeneous and to some degree conflicting traditions of publishing. On one hand, there was the program of multiple publication itself, with its origins in practices that had been developed by Alfred, Lord Tennyson as part of his effort to be a truly national poet: in 1878, to cite only one instance, Tennyson had issued his collected works in both a thirteen-volume Shilling Edition and a single-volume Crown Edition printed in three bindings (plain, gilt, and Roxburgh), a program that effectively addressed a diverse and heterogeneous audience (first-year sales of roughly thirty thousand and sixty thousand, respectively).[62] On the other hand, there was the limited edition, with its origins in the publishing practices of William Morris and the Kelmscott Press. Originally the limited edition had realized a programmatic rejection of the capitalist production of texts. In its production, for example, the role of the publisher was minimized and authorial control was maximized, the standardized design and formatting that had become publishing norms were replaced with special typography and layout, and the altered author-publisher relations were embodied in differing contractual arrangements: instead of a small advance against 15 percent royalties, the author usually received a guaranteed advance against 50 percent profits and a right to republish in another (more commercial) form within a specified amount of time. But the rebellious impulses of the Morris enterprise were Janus-faced: Though Morris had at first intended to produce books solely for his own interest, the sheer cost of his experiments had obliged him to issue them as limited editions that might recoup at least a share of the expenses. The limited editions, in turn, had been rapidly assimilated by the rare and antiquarian book markets that had matured in the nineteenth century, turning them into commodities and potential investments. Thus, while the book increasingly resembled the work of art, as indeed its producers hoped, the work of art itself had already become subject to a commodity economy. Inevitably the limited edition was rapidly appropriated by other constituencies that were not merely indifferent but even hostile to the socialist impulses that had animated Morris.

One constituency was represented by William Butler Yeats, whose sisters founded the Dun Emer (later the Cuala) Press in 1902 with advice and help in typographical design from Emery Walker, a close associate of Morris at the Kelmscott Press.[63] Beginning with *In the Seven Woods* in 1903, all of Yeats's works were published first in a limited edition at the Dun Emer/Cuala, then in a public-commercial edition with Macmillan. In turn, through Yeats's influence on his young admirer Ezra Pound, the practice of publishing books in two forms was adopted by the emerging English avant-garde, for which it became an indispensable instrument. The limited edition established a kind of special productive space insulated from the harsh exigencies of the larger marketplace. It bypassed a broad public receptive to standardized products (such as the six-shilling novel) and suspicious of novelty, and instead addressed a prosperous minority with a luxury good that emphasized innovation and was produced in small quantities (though with high profit margins per sale). It enacted, in other words, a return to an essentially precapitalist economic structure, an artisanal economy producing luxury goods in limited quantities for aristocratic consumption. By the early 1920s it had become a routine step in a tripartite publishing program—journal, limited edition, and public or commercial edition—that was now normative for the avant-garde.

Yeats did not represent the only constituency that appropriated and adapted the ways of Morris. In the United States, similar forms of book production were soon adopted by the ensemble of figures and institutions often labeled the genteel tradition and associated with Boston and Harvard University. The entire process is epitomized in the career of the typographer Bruce Rogers.[64] After working briefly in Indianapolis for a journal called *Modern Art,* Rogers moved to Boston in 1895, where he was soon frequenting circles that evinced a growing interest in fine books and the experiments of Morris. Among them were the Grolier Club, a society founded in 1884 to promote the collecting of fine books, *The Knight Errant,* a review that devoted extensive discussion to William Morris, established in 1892, and the Tavern Club, founded the same year, headed by Professor Charles Eliot Norton, and devoted to fine books. From 1895 to 1912 Rogers worked for the Riverside Press, which acted as Harvard's printer, during which time he assimilated Morris's interest in the well-made book to his anachronistic and classicizing style of typography. After several other jobs, Rogers settled down. Between 1920 and 1928 he was serving as typographical adviser to Cambridge University Press and working for the printing firm of William Edwin Rudge, for which he issued a series of limited editions published by Maurice Firuski, owner of the Cambridge, Massachusetts, bookstore known as Dunster House. Which, strangely, brings us back to T. S. Eliot.

The Waste Land, as is well known, was not published in book form solely by Horace Liveright; nearly ten months later (12 September 1923) it appeared a second time, issued by Virginia Woolf's Hogarth Press in a limited edition of about 460 copies. The date suggests it was an afterthought, as if Eliot had been seeking to retrace a missed step in the normal process of avant-garde publishing. Yet the idea of a limited edition was anything but tardy. Eliot had begun to worry about the precarious implications of his agreement with Liveright almost immediately after their encounter in January 1922. It was a precipitous move that bypassed the normal rhythms of avant-garde production, in which a work was transmitted from a small elite to an ever wider yet presumably less discriminating audience, and therefore a move that threatened the status of his work. Like anyone who works within a specific institution, Eliot had internalized an array of unwritten protocols considered normal and appropriate. No sooner had he completed the poem in its final version (probably in the first week of February 1922) than he began to seek a publisher who would issue a limited edition. On 14 February he lunched with Conrad Aiken and discussed his dilemma. Aiken, the next day, reported their conversation to Maurice Firuski, the Cambridge bookseller and publisher who was issuing Aiken's own book of poetry *The Pool of Priapus:*

> Brief is this note, and chiefly occasioned by a talk with Tom Eliot at lunch yesterday. He has a poem, 450 lines long, wh. I haven't seen. He seeks a publisher who will produce it nicely, and in America, and in a small edition. Firuski! cried I, and there you are. When I elucidated, mentioning [Bruce] Rogers and 450 copies and two years exclusive right and a possible hundred dollars and a beautifully produced book, his eyes glowed with a tawny golden light like fierce doubloons, his hands took on singularly the aspect of claws, his nails tore the table-cloth, and he took your address. . . . As I say, I have not seen the poem. It may or may not be good, or intelligible. But, reflect: Eliot has a real reputation; a poem of that length by him will be a real curiosity, even perhaps an event; and he assumes that you will have of course, the English as well as the American market. He may have to get Knopf's permission, as I did, to make the arrangement: he doesn't remember how his contract stands. But that, I fancy, will present no difficulty, for the book is too small for Knopf, and besides Knopf doesn't regard Eliot as a golconda . . . Address: 9 Clarence Gate Gardens, London, W. W. 1.[65]

Eleven days later, on 26 February, Eliot himself also wrote to Firuski, pursuing the same question more fully in a letter that has not previously been published.

> Your name has been given me by Mr. Conrad Aiken, who has also shown me a volume of poems by Mr. John Freeman, recently published by you, with the appearance of which I was very much pleased.
>
> I have now ready a poem for which that form of publication seems to me the most suitable. I understand that you issue these books in limited editions, and that for the volumes you take in this series you give a sum down in advance royalty.
>
> My poem is of 435 lines; with certain spacings essential to the sense, 475 book lines; furthermore, it consists of five parts, which would increase the space necessary; and

with title pages, some notes that I intend to add, etc., I guess that it would run to from 28 to 32 pages.

I have had a good offer for the publication of it in a periodical. But it is, I think, much the best poem I have ever written, and I think it would make a much more distinct impression and attract much more attention if published as a book.

If you are interested in this, I should be glad to hear from you what terms you would be prepared to offer for it, at your earliest convenience, as the other offers for it cannot be held in suspence very long.

Eliot's letter, of course, is fascinating.[66] Among other things, it affects the long-standing debate about the poem's notes, suggesting that they were not merely a late and arbitrary addition imposed by the publishing exigencies of Horace Liveright, as often argued, but an integral part of the work as Eliot himself wished to have it published—a nod to the eighteenth-century tradition of poetry (Alexander Pope's notes to *The Dunciad,* for instance) that had so informed some of the poem's earliest drafts. But more important for our purpose, the letter demonstrates how fully Eliot understood the protocols of avant-garde publishing, as well as how easily those procedures could be assimilated to features already long established in a genteel tradition of private and limited editions. The book of poems by John Freeman (1880–1929) that Eliot had admired was *The Red Path, a Narrative, and the Wounded Bird,* a slender volume of poems issued in 425 copies that were printed for Firuski's Dunster House at the press of William Edwin Rudge, its design executed by Bruce Rogers. The volume was handsome and, like all of Rogers's work, inspired by classical models of typography and design; it suggested a tone of genteel decorum, a distinctly Harvardian note, and yet it sounded that tone with even greater subtlety, as if to hint at an elite within the elite, a more reflective minority with discriminating taste opposed to that of a broader elite that unreflectively assumed its privileges solely on the basis of class, money, and inherited status.

Despite having already received "a good offer" of $150 for the poem from Thayer and the *Dial,* and despite his preliminary agreement with Liveright in Paris, Eliot preferred to see the work issued in a limited edition: "I think it would make a much more distinct impression and attract much more attention if published as a book." To be sure, Liveright had also offered to publish the poem as a book, but a different kind of book: a public and more commercial edition that would directly address a wider audience and not be preceded by the limited edition typical of the avant-garde. That proposal violated the institutional logic of avant-garde production, so much so that Eliot instinctively sought a form of publication that would set matters right. Firuski, however, was slow to respond. Moreover, by 12 March (only two weeks after his letter to Firuski), Eliot had received another note from Liveright reaffirming his interest in publishing the poem. As Eliot promptly informed Pound: "Liveright wrote to say he wanted it, and I have written asking what he wants to give and telling him the exact length," adding cryptically, "and I have other plans also if Thayer doesn't cough out."[67] The other plans, of course, were those with Firuski, plans presented as an acceptable alternative to publication in the *Dial*. The plans underscore a common procedure of publication: just as the *Dial* occupied the middle position in the tripartite structure of journal publication (between the *Little Review* and *Vanity Fair*), so the limited edition occupied the middle position within the larger tripartite structure of avant-garde and modernist publishing (between journal and commercial edition). Indeed, it was the violation of this logic that distinguished the actual publication of *The Waste Land*, its first appearance in book form being the commercial edition by Liveright, and it was a late and retrospective effort to "correct" this anomaly that prompted Eliot to issue a limited edition with the Hogarth Press in 1923.

Eliot, it is clear, wanted his poem to be successful, yet not too successful. For the prospect of immediate publication by a commercial firm raised prospects that were largely unimaginable within the logic of modernism. And similar considerations must also have influenced the discussions concerning *Vanity Fair* as a possible venue for the poem. Pound, after first raising the issue on 6 May 1922, presumably reported his action to Eliot during their meeting in Verona a month later, though how they viewed this prospect cannot be stated with any degree of certainty. Still, it is clear enough not only that Pound and Eliot considered *Vanity Fair* a potential publisher but also that *Vanity Fair* considered itself a serious candidate. The journal not only sent John Peale Bishop to discuss the project with Pound in Paris, it even advanced an explicit offer of publication. The proposal appeared in a letter written by Edmund Wilson to Eliot on 1 August 1922. Eliot, in another letter that has not been previously published, replied on 14 August: "Thank you for your letter of the 1st inst., I should be very glad to do for you such an article as you suggest. For the next two months I shall be far too busy to attempt such a thing, but I think that I should be able to provide one during October or November if that is satisfactory to you. As for a poem, I am afraid that is quite impossible at present as I have only one for which I have already contracted."[68] Eliot, plainly, was not being straightforward; as yet he had not "contracted" for *The Waste Land* in a journal at all. Only a day or two before his letter to Wilson, in fact, Eliot had sent off the typescript of *The Waste Land* to Pound and James Sibley Watson, Jr., in Paris, and only the day *after* his letter to Wilson did he write to Watson announcing his terms for the poem: the Dial Award plus $150, provided he publish the poem not much before the book issued by Liveright. Eliot, it is clear, rejected the offer from *Vanity Fair* not because he had "already contracted" for its serial publication but because *Vanity Fair* represented a degree of commercial success and popular acceptance that would have undermined the status that he was trying to establish for the work. That status, however, was not simply intrinsic or implanted in the poem's text, it was a function of the institutional structures that had informed its production at every step in the poem's life.

In retrospect, we can see that the proposal for a limited edition by Firuski looked not only back to the Cambridge and Harvard environment of Eliot's college days but also forward to modernism's future, to the moment when Eliot would make his triumphant return to Harvard in 1932 and seal the fateful association between modernism and the academy. Yet that association, which has been so much commented on, did not occur naturally or without relations to other changes in the wider culture. By the early 1930s, in fact, all the magazines that Eliot had once considered for *The Waste Land* were dead or dying. The *Little Review* and the *Dial* had both closed in 1929, and *Vanity Fair* would expire in 1936. The Great Depression effectively eliminated the structures of private patronage that had sustained modernism's growth and its emergence as a significant idiom within the languages of the twentieth century. Thereafter, modernism would be slowly but inexorably absorbed into the university, as it had also been appropriated by the marketing and publicity apparatus of *Vanity Fair*.

The price of modernism, in this sense, was a double one. In part, it was a specific and concrete figure epitomized in the sums paid to Eliot for publication of *The Waste Land*: $150 as the price of the poem proper, $2,000 for the Dial Award, a subsequent $580 in royalties on the sales of the Liveright edition, and perhaps another $100 from the Hogarth Press edition—altogether about $2,800, a figure that in modern terms would surely be somewhere between $45,000 and $55,000. (It was two and a half times the $1,150 earned annually by the executive secretary to the editor of *Vanity Fair*.)[69] But hidden among such figures was another, more important price: an obscuring of a determinate productive space, the elision of boundaries between specific institutions and wider zones of cultural activity, the illusion that "art" or "the poem" or "the text" had been the central concern of participants whose decisions were consistently made when as yet they had not read a word of the work in question. And not without reason, for the text was largely irrelevant. *The Waste Land* was transmitted not through a conduit that received and reproduced a neutral image of its original but through a multiplicity of social structures driven by conflicting imperatives: it became part of a social event in a discontinuous yet coherent process, an unprecedented effort to affirm the output of a specific marketing-publicity apparatus through the enactment of a triumphal and triumphant occasion. It was not simply the institutions that were the vehicle of the poem; the poem also became the vehicle of the institutions. Like any cultural work, it was more than a sum of meanings implanted or intended by its author; it was inseparable, finally, from the contradictory network of uses in which it was historically constituted.

If nothing else, reconsidering the publication history of *The Waste Land* might prompt us to question the dominant methodology of modern literary studies since roughly the end of World War II. Generations of students have been exhorted to look closely at the poem, to examine only the text, to indulge in a scholastic scrutiny of linguistic minutiae. Yet if we consider more fully the experience of those who actually engaged in modern textual production, assuming that the case of *The Waste Land* tells us anything, we might elect a rather different procedure. Indeed, if we named it in their honor, we could call it the modernist principle of reading and formulate it thus: The best reading of a work may, on some occasions, be one that does not read it at all. Such an extreme formulation would doubtless be misleading. Yet it might remind us that close reading is itself a historical form of activity that appears at a precise moment in the development of professional literary studies and that other kinds of reading are and have been practiced—not least among them the not-reading that was practiced by the editors of the *Dial,* itself a trenchant "reading" of *The Waste Land*'s place in the structural logic and development of literary modernism. We might learn from them. Reading as we do, instead of as they did, we leave the ambiguous heritage of modernism in history just as desocialized and unexplored as it was before. History may be a nightmare, as the modernists often claimed, but when they entered what Eliot called the "contrived corridors" of its making, at least they never failed to "protract the profit of their chilled delirium."

Chapter 4 From the Patron

to *il Duce:* Ezra Pound's Odyssey

Historians of Anglo-American literature often view 1922 as the *annus mirabilis,* the miraculous year in which first *Ulysses* and then *The Waste Land* were published, both events made possible in great part because of massive patronage. Since 1919 Joyce had been receiving an annual income of £250 from interest earned on a gift of £5,000 bestowed by Harriet Shaw Weaver; by 1922 her gifts had mounted to £9,000 in principal and were earning £450 per year; and in June 1923 she added another £12,000, making a total of £21,000 that furnished Joyce with an annual income slightly above £1,000.[1] Eliot, in addition to publishing in magazines subsidized by patronage, had received the Dial Award as payment for *The Waste Land,* a payment funded by the lavish patronage of Scofield Thayer and James Sibley Watson, Jr. Even when modernist authors appeared to earn royalties, they often proved to be merely patronage in disguise. The advances and royalties that Joyce received from the *Egoist* and its book-publishing wing were not the result of profits: Weaver subsidized both operations, and when she closed the press in 1924 her net loss on Joyce's books, even after several editions had sold out, totaled nearly £900. Patronage was the foundation of the institutional structure known as the avant-garde.

Yet patronage was also an essentially premodern form of social exchange, and however much it might be disguised as royalties, payments for editorial work, or prizes, it lacked the ideological and social sanction widely accorded to the impersonal mechanisms of the market and, more important, the identifiable criteria and stable norms that characterize modern expert and professional systems. Patronage thrived, in part, because of a loss of faith in the efficacy and fairness that the abstract mechanisms of the market could bring to bear on cultural production; it was a response to the belief that much of what happens in the market is not reasonable but arbitrary and out of anyone's control, and an attempt to reintroduce a dimension of personal participation and trust into the increasingly abstract and bureaucratized system of cultural production. Yet it also courted the risk of being too personal, too dependent on the goodwill and good fortune of a tiny elite, too subject to mere caprice in the dispensation of its largesse, too lacking in the reliability and rationality that secures trust in the functioning of an institution. When Ezra Pound in March 1922 proposed and publicized the famous Bel Esprit project—thirty people were each to pledge £10 per year to T. S. Eliot, furnishing him with a guaranteed income of £300— it was partly an attempt to normalize, to regularize, the workings of an otherwise capricious institution, patronage. By year's end the scheme had collapsed. Its failure marked the end of efforts to transform patronage into a public activity, to create a public sphere, however numerically limited, around the institution of the avant-garde. Its demise also ended the possibility of reintroducing elements of reliability, predictability, or trust into the institutional logic of the avant-garde. Pound now turned elsewhere, back to the figure of the patron. Yet patronage, paradoxically, could become a mirror image of the workings of the market, arbitrary in its choices and operations, fickle in its distribution of rewards. To believe in its operations demanded not just reasoned assent or conditional trust, but something more—faith.

It should come as no surprise that the motif of patronage is explicitly taken up in Pound's principal composition of this period, the so-called Malatesta Cantos, or Cantos 8–11. To oversimplify, they depict the life and times of Sigismondo Malatesta, the quattrocento ruler of Rimini, a small town just south of Ravenna on the Adriatic coast of Italy. Sigismondo sponsored the reconstruction of the church of San Francesco, a building long regarded as a landmark in architectural history. In the idealizing lens of late-nineteenth-century historiography, he was the ideal patron, discerning in his selection of an architect (the great Leon Battista Alberti), discriminating in his choice of artists (the magnificent painter Piero della Francesca and the talented sculptor Agostino di Duccio), and generous in giving them latitude to work as they wished. He was also, in the lexicon favored by nineteenth-century writers, a despot, a ruler whose authority was unchecked and arbitrary, his decisions ratified by no one, his choices subject to no identifiable norms or criteria. Sigismondo, in short, epitomized all the issues embedded in the institution of patronage, the questions of art and authority, power and public assent.

Pound saw the church of San Francesco for the first time in May 1922 while touring with his wife through central Italy; it was three months after the publication of *Ulysses,* two months after his first announcement of Bel Esprit, and five months before the publication of *The Waste Land.* Two weeks after he first saw the church, he met with Eliot in Verona to discuss the poem's publication and plans for Eliot's new review (supported by patronage from Lady Rothermere, wife of the newspaper magnate). In the spring of 1923 Pound returned to Italy to conduct further research into the life and times of Sigismondo Malatesta, gathering more materials to be used in writing the Malatesta Cantos. This time, while staying in Rimini, Pound had his first significant experience with members of the Fascist Party. The experience related directly to his writing about Sigismondo and later sparked his favorable view of Benito Mussolini and Fascism's effects in everyday life—the most fateful choice of his career. Only five months later, in the late summer of 1923, Pound was already engaged in efforts (which have been discovered only recently) to persuade Mussolini to adopt a program of cultural patronage outlined and to be directed by Pound himself. Pound, in short, had found his imaginary patron and the resolution to the question of art, authority, and public consensus. The thread that links together this intricate complex of events and motifs is the figure of the great patron, Sigismondo Malatesta, and the question of faith in his judgment: through him, the modernist culture of patronage was assimilated to the emerging culture of Fascism.

Although the Malatesta Cantos have been widely discussed in studies of Pound, in part because of the massive shift in Pound's poetics that they embody, little notice has been given to two lines that appear in the closing passage of Canto 10. The passage itself is curious and seemingly out of place in *The Cantos,* for it offers a narrative that makes use of plot and suspense, devices that otherwise appear rarely in Pound's work. It depicts a battle that took place in 1461, focusing on the scene just as the protagonist Sigismondo Malatesta is about to address his troops. The narrator, evidently an old soldier who has fought alongside Sigismondo, seems to be reliving the sense of impending conflict, and his tone is taut with anticipation. Sigismondo's forces are badly outnumbered: thirteen hundred cavalry and five hundred infantry are arrayed against the enemy's four thousand cavalry and one thousand infantry. The battle has already begun; the enemy troops are approaching:

> And they came at us with their ecclesiastical legates
> Until the eagle lit on his tent pole.
> And he said: The Romans would have called that an augury
> *E gradment li antichi cavaler romanj*
>   *davano fed a quisti annutii,*
> All I want you to do is to follow the orders,
> They've got a bigger army,
>   but there are more men in this camp.[2]

The language of Sigismondo's brief speech designed to rouse his troops has a soldierly simplicity ("All I want you to do is to follow the orders"), and it makes a direct appeal to manly pride and camaraderie ("but there are more men in this camp"). Its opening gambit, however, is more complex: Sigismondo observes an eagle that has just landed on the top of his tent and, seizing the occasion, he interprets it as a presage of victory, a sign that his troops will win: "The Romans would have called that an augury," he says, then adding, "And the ancient Romans placed great faith in such annunciations." To the reader outside the text, Sigismondo's invocation of antiquity signals his familiarity with the culture of early Renaissance humanism, with its appeal to ancient practice as a guide to present conduct; to the common soldier who is the immediate audience within the text it remains simple enough to convey its general force. Quite abruptly, at this point, the canto breaks off, ending like a serial film on a note of suspense. Will the speech succeed? Will Sigismondo prevail or go down in defeat? To learn the answer, we must turn the page.

Canto 11 begins with a flashback to the action of the previous episode. Once more we hear the phrase "And the ancient Romans placed great faith in such annunciations," followed by fifteen lines that further delay the conclusion and build up suspense: we receive a lengthy list of Sigismondo's commanders (a miniature variant of the epic catalogue), we are told about the size of the respective armies, and then we learn the battle's outcome:

> And we beat the papishes and fought
> them back through the tents
> And he came up to the dyke again

And fought through the dyke-gate
And it went on from dawn to sunset
And we broke them and took their baggage

Sigismondo has won, at least for the moment, and from the outcome we can infer that his speech proved effective.

Yet however much the device of narrative suspense has been highlighted, more than the outcome of a single battle is at stake in this passage. For here the theatrical trappings of war serve as the platform for a very different drama, a restaging of interpretation. Sigismondo achieves his victory by virtue of his capacity to interpret an event as an augury, a sign. He himself becomes an augur, a diviner whose task is to determine whether the gods approve a proposed action—in a more extensive sense, to foretell the future. He takes on the functions of the poet and becomes "the antenna of the race." His actions, in effect, epitomize some of the deepest structures governing the relations among text, reading, and history within *The Cantos* itself. Confronted with an unexpected event in the face of a cataclysm that threatens his destruction, Sigismondo reads it through the prism of history, interprets its significance for the present, and transforms it into a guide for conduct in the future, so lending interpretation a performative dimension within "the present" of the text, turning it into an exhortation to action in the face of an overwhelmingly hostile reality. Sigismondo offers more than just a reading of a single event; his actions constitute a reading of reading. They recapitulate the interpretive processes that are also being enacted within the text by the author, processes that are then to be assimilated by the "real" reader who is outside the text. Within the text, the reader of *The Cantos* is likewise confronted with apparently random events that occur in an environment hostile to everyday reading, inimical to conventions of narrative and sequence, just as he is likewise invited to assess them in the light of history, whether given by the text itself or secured in a shared background of knowledge, beliefs, and cultural practices. In the world outside the text, the reader is also solicited to transform that interpretive knowledge into action, be it the action of interpretation itself or the action of living differently in the light of imaginative experience. At the heart of this paradigm is a reference to interpretive practices from the past, the auguries of ancient Rome, protocols in which the governing term is *faith*—for it is faith that the Romans once gave to such annunciations, and faith that Sigismondo now demands of his men. Faith is the term that mediates a transition from an apparently historical discourse that rests on everyday notions of referentiality and representation to another discourse that invokes a notion of experience and brings it to bear on the future. But faith in what?

We might call this the "Sigismondo paradigm" of interpretation—an ideal configuration of event and text, reading and history—which constitutes one of the principal protocols offered by *The Cantos,* a paradigm of its own interpretive activity and a model of how that activity should be assimilated by readers. And yet, as readers will have already noticed, our initial summary of this passage has glossed over several cruces entailed in its interpretation, local difficulties that bear upon similar questions of event and reading, history and understanding. The presence of these questions at both micro and macro levels is not surprising. The question of how one was to interpret history, both past and contemporary, was one that was acquiring a special urgency in the wake of the Great War, which had utterly transformed the political surface of European culture. The monarchies that had ruled Germany, Austria, and Russia for centuries had vanished, replaced by new democracies and an intransigent form of socialism. Still, these were all political orders that had been in existence long before the Great War. What made the question of history so pressing in late 1922 and early 1923, when Pound was working on the Malatesta Cantos, was the interpretive challenge posed by the brusque arrival of Fascism at the center stage of Europe with Mussolini's accession to power. How to read history—especially recent history, contemporary history?

Sigismondo Malatesta (1417–1468) is known to posterity for a single mission that he pursued for more than a decade: his sponsorship of the reconstruction of the church of San Francesco, often called the Tempio Malatestiano, in the town of Rimini.[3] The building is considered a landmark in Western architectural history because it was the first ecclesiastical edifice to incorporate the Roman triumphal arch into its structural vocabulary.[4] The massive central doorway, flanked by two blind arches, plainly owes much to the Arch of Augustus, the oldest triumphal arch in Italy, which is also in Rimini. The interior, too, is striking: it teems with an elaborate series of sculptures and bas-reliefs by Agostino di Duccio, and the sacristy for the Chapel of San Sigismondo houses a fine fresco by Piero della Francesca. The church's reconstruction, initially undertaken as the refurbishing of a single chapel within an extant church that dated from the thirteenth century, assumed new dimensions in 1449–1450 when Sigismondo entrusted the project to Leon Battista Alberti, one of Alberti's earliest and most important commissions. Alberti redesigned the building's entire facade, added the central doorway, and adorned the sides with a series of seven deep arches divided by massive piers. He also planned to add a transept and to crown the intersection of nave and transept with a soaring dome, but a precipitous decline in Sigismondo's political fortunes left him unable to bear the costs of construction. By 1460 work on the project had stopped and the church was left incomplete.

Sigismondo's political career was shaped by the shifting balance of power that prevailed in the Italian peninsula, divided among the five major states: Venice and Milan in the north, Florence in central Italy, and Rome (or the papacy) and Naples in the south. In the course of his lifetime Sigismondo served each of them as a condottiere, though by the later 1450s the major states increasingly regarded him with suspicion, either because his conduct of various campaigns had lacked sufficient vigor or because he was reported to have engaged in duplicitous dealings with his opponents.[5] In 1459 he joined another condottiere, Giacomo Piccinino, in an imprudent attempt to unseat the Aragonese dynasty that ruled Naples and replace it with the Angevin dynasty of southern France. For Milan the scheme raised the specter of invasion from France, and Francesco Sforza, ruler of the Milanese duchy, reacted sharply. So did papal Rome, partly because it too wished to prevent the establishment of a French presence in the peninsula, partly because Sigismondo's actions offered a pretext for the church to reassert its claims over territories long lost to its control. The territories were those of Sigismondo. By law the Malatestas were not the rulers of Rimini and the surrounding countryside but vicars of the church who, in return for an annual fee, were granted absolute control over all taxation and legal matters. By the late 1440s, however, the papacy was beginning to change, increasingly assuming the institutional traits of the Italian *casato*, or extended family enterprise, and acquiring its elastic corporate and dynastic structure as well as its ambitious expansionism.[6] Hoping to regain control over territories it had lost in the past, the papacy was taking its first steps toward the formation of the modern papal state that would rule over central Italy until 1860. Sigismondo's was among the first of many minor states that would disappear in the next half century. That, of course, was no consolation for him. In 1461 he managed to survive a ferocious campaign launched against him, defeating a superior ecclesiastical army at the battle of Nidastore on 2 July—the battle that is the subject of Pound's lines quoted above. The next season his luck ran out. On 12 August 1462 his troops were routed at the battle of Senigallia, and less than a week later those of his ally Piccinino were annihilated at the battle of Troia. When peace terms were drafted, Sigismondo lost everything except the city of Rimini and a few nearby towns.

Already during Sigismondo's lifetime the church of San Francesco aroused discussion, and in the centuries that followed it elicited a growing body of scholarly and antiquarian commentary.[7] But it was in the eighteenth century that new and related arguments about the church's significance began to appear. It was urged, for example, that the church was not a church at all, at least not in the ordinary sense; nor was it just a monument to the Malatesta dynasty or Sigismondo's exemplary status as its preeminent representative. Instead, the building had been designed to commemorate Sigismondo's love for Isotta degli Atti, his mistress and later (after 1456) his third wife. The crucial evidence adduced in support of this view was the entwined cipher, made up of the letters *S* and *I*, that is sculpted everywhere among the church's interior and exterior decorations. The sign, in the new view, referred to the first letters in the names of Sigismondo and Isotta. This interpretation was first broached in 1718, debated inconclusively in 1756, then raised a third time in 1789, after which it was embraced without argument.[8]

The figure most responsible for diffusing a new understanding of Sigismondo and his career outside Italy was the great historian Jakob Burckhardt. His *Civilization of the Renaissance in Italy,* first published in 1860, largely created the modern notion of the Renaissance as a distinct historical period that signals the emergence of modern individualism. Burckhardt assigned Sigismondo an exemplary status, presenting him as the crowning figure among "the furtherers of humanism." His court had epitomized "the highest spiritual things" and had been a stage "where life and manners . . . must have been a singular spectacle." His greatest achievement had been the reconstruction of the church of San Francesco, a project inspired by "his *amour* with the fair Isotta, in whose honour and as whose monument the famous rebuilding of S. Francesco at Rimini took place."[9] Burckhardt turned Sigismondo into the epitome of "the whole man," a new human "type" who represented a form of historical existence crucial for the course of civilization, the type that had ushered in the age of modernity, a figure equally capable in war and art, in action and contemplation, one whose unfettered individuality united ruthless realism with lofty ideals: "Unscrupulousness, impiety, military skill, and high culture have been seldom so combined in one individual as in Sigismondo Malatesta."[10] The "whole man" embodied in Sigismondo became the repository of an immense paradox: he was both the figure who had given birth to modernity and a symbol of all that modernity had later lost and betrayed, a rebuke to modernity itself. Translated into French (1876), Italian (1877), and English (1886), Burckhardt's work placed Sigismondo at the center of European intellectual debates about the nature of modernity—its origins, meaning, and prospects—and so about the very meaning of civilization.

Burckhardt's vision was recapitulated and transformed in myriad ways. The popular English historian John Addington Symonds viewed the church of San Francesco as "a monument of . . . the revived Paganism of the fifteenth century" and "one of the earliest buildings in which the Neopaganism of the Renaissance showed itself in full force." Though ostensibly a church, it had "no room left for God." Symonds noted the many outrages allegedly committed by Sigismondo (including the murder of several wives), but he tempered their opprobriousness by integrating them within a liberal view of history that saw the violence of early individualism as a transient stage within the otherwise benign formation of modernity.[11] Much bolder was a French journalist and art historian named Charles Yriarte, whose lengthy biography of Sigismondo was published in 1882. Yriarte claimed to have discovered a love poem "written by Sigismondo in honor of Isotta." He called it "the most characteristic of Sigismondo's works" and urged that its zodiacal references provided "the key to the enigma" of the elaborate bas-reliefs found inside the church of San Francesco. "It is not God who is worshiped here; instead it is for her that the incense and the myrrh are burned."[12] His study formed the foundation of a consensus that was uncontested for decades, from its publication to roughly 1920. Encyclopedias, travel guides, novels, plays, and scholarly monographs repeated his claims again and again. From 1886 to 1929, every edition of the *Encyclopaedia Britannica* reported that the church of San Francesco was built "to celebrate the tyrant's love for Isotta" and "dedicated . . . to the glorification of an unhallowed attachment"; its sculptural decorations "derived . . . from a poem in which Sigismondo had invoked the gods and the signs of the zodiac to soften Isotta's heart."[13] Baedeker travel guides repeated the same claims, and popular novelists such as the British author Edward Hutton elaborated these motifs yet again.[14]

The consensus forged by Yriarte began to come under attack around 1910, in the work of two scholars in Rimini who collaborated in research examining the many original and as yet unpublished documents housed in the city's archives and library. In 1909 one of them, Giovanni Soranzo (1881–1963), published "The Cipher SI of Sigismondo Pandolfo Malatesta," which reconsidered the meaning of the much discussed sign. There was not a single contemporary document suggesting that the sign referred to both Sigismondo and Isotta. Indeed, the only document to discuss the sign, a chronicle by one of Sigismondo's closest collaborators within the court, specifically stated that it referred to Sigismondo alone. It was common practice, moreover, among the courts of northern Italy to use the first two letters of someone's name as an abbreviation: Niccolò d'Este was frequently cited as NI, and Sigismondo's son, Roberto, was commemorated on numerous ceramics and other artifacts by the cipher RO. Even more damaging to Yriarte's thesis, the most common spelling of Isotta's name during her lifetime was "Ysotta" or "Yxotta," a spelling that appeared in nearly all the contemporary legal documents concerning her. One year later, Soranzo's colleague Aldo Francesco Massèra issued a detailed examination of all the poems and poets allegedly connected with Isotta. The notorious poem that Yriarte claimed to have discovered, the work that he had termed "the key to the enigma" of the church's sculptural decorations, had been written not by Sigismondo but by Simone Serdini, a poet from Siena who had communicated with the court of Rimini during the decade after 1410. Serdini had died in 1419 or 1420, some twelve years before Isotta degli Atti was born. It was unlikely that his poem referred to her or her relations with Sigismondo, which began in 1446.[15]

Yet the work of Soranzo and Massèra scarcely affected the legend of Sigismondo and the church of San Francesco. Soranzo's essay was published in a journal of provincial history devoted to Romagna, of which Rimini is a part, and Massèra's appeared in a journal for professors of Italian literature. But the more important reason for neglect of their work was a form of ideological resistance. Burckhardt had placed Sigismondo and the romantic reading of the church at the center of a much wider debate about the culture of modernity, a debate only partially responsive to issues of evidence and historical documentation. Some writers chose to ignore the research of Soranzo and Massèra; Edward Hutton, for example, in his 1913 guidebook to the province of Romagna, simply repeated the claims of his earlier novel. Others turned the historical claims into symbolic ones; Luigi Orsini's 1915 guidebook to Romagna transformed Yriarte's argument about the poems into metaphor: the church of San Francesco was "a poem of indestructible beauty, uniting all the tenderest harmonies of art and feeling."[16]

But the most important attempt to address the arguments advanced by Soranzo did not appear until 1924, when Corrado Ricci (1858–1934), a gifted art historian, published his monumental study of the church of San Francesco. While it was true, as Soranzo had shown, that every known document indicated that the sign SI had been understood during Sigismondo's lifetime to refer solely to Sigismondo himself, this had been only the sign's "official meaning." Behind it had stood an "equivocal meaning" known only to Sigismondo, Isotta, and perhaps a few of their intimates. Sigismondo himself, in fact, had designed the sign precisely in order to create this kind of ambiguity.[17] Ricci offered no evidence for this claim; his argument was a transparent evasion, untypical and unworthy of a scholar otherwise noted for historical rigor and insight. Yet Ricci himself may not have understood why it so mattered to him to argue for the sign's "romantic" interpretation, which merely epitomized the basic structure underlying the Romantic legend of the church itself: in each case the genuine meaning, the hidden yet true meaning, is not in conformity with culturally (and therefore historically) given values but is achieved only by the shedding of historical attributes (habits, conventions) and meanings of the cultural system, a laying bare of something other—a hidden meaning that stands apart from everyday language and institutional discourse, a privileged site in which the sign and the church express sheer authenticity, their grounding in pure self-hood. Here, in other words, is semiosis that has been disembedded from local and temporal contexts of interaction and restructured in a conceptual time-space that is more indefinite, autonomous, and universal. Sigismondo acts in conformity not with historically determinate conventions of religious piety or dynastic self-aggrandizement but with an experiential impulse deemed univer-sal—just as the meaning of the sign SI is located not in the geographically determinate practices of northern Italy or the temporal context of the mid-quattrocento but in an impulse that is largely disembedded of time and space. It is a process that recapitulates the so-called disembedding mechanisms that some sociologists consider one of the fundamental features of modernity.[18] And Sigismondo was nothing, in the Burckhardtian understanding, if not the epitome of modernity itself.

While liberal historiography sought to account for Sigismondo by situating him within a progressive account of modernity, others emphasized the more rebellious implications lodged in the Burckhardtian interpretation. Friedrich Nietzsche accentuated them to the point of turning the entire Renaissance into the promise of a modernity that had been subsequently thwarted, a modernity not yet realized: "The Italian Renaissance contained within it all the positive forces to which we owe modern civilization: liberation of thought, disrespect for authorities, victory of culture over the darkness of ancestry, enthusiasm for knowledge and the knowable past of man, unfettering of the individual . . . indeed, the Renaissance possessed positive forces which have up to now, *in our contemporary modern civilization,* never been so powerful again. . . . [I]t was the golden age of this millennium."[19]

The implications of this thought were hardly lost on Antonio Beltramelli, a restless Italian journalist from Romagna whose admiration for Nietzsche is evinced throughout his 1908 volume *The Chants of Faunus* (*I canti di Fauno*). Four years later, in 1912, Beltramelli published *A Temple of Love* (*Un tempio d'amore*), a brief narration of Sigismondo's life and his reconstruction of the church of San Francesco in Isotta's honor. His account differed from his predecessors' chiefly in its tone, which contained a note of violent lyricism celebrating the concepts of struggle and will: "The mere presence of Sigismondo was enough to impose subjection, and in this lay the secret of his fascination over the masses." Or again: "If Sigismondo failed in his effort to kill Pope Paul II, it was hardly for lack of will."[20] In his hands the salient characteristic of Sigismondo became a ruthless, indomitable will—which also signaled the arrival of a new ethical and cultural order, turning him into an exemplary figure for the imagining of a new man who would address the pervasive sense of crisis that marked the early twentieth century and modernity itself.

Eleven years later, in 1923, Beltramelli published another book, *The New Man* (*L'uomo nuovo*). It was the first biography of Mussolini published after he took power in late October 1922. Beltramelli had always been a regionalist with ties to his native province of Romagna, where Mussolini had been born and had begun his meteoric rise through the ranks of the Socialist Party. *The New Man* portrayed him as a son of his native soil, as harsh and violent as the landscape that had nurtured him. Seeking to furnish Mussolini with a cultural genealogy, Beltramelli located his forerunners in the house of Malatesta, also from Romagna. There was the founder of the dynasty, Malatesta da Verucchio: "He knows what he wants and he places his life as a pledge for his will." And the culmination was Sigismondo Malatesta, the "warrior" who had "the heart of a poet," a figure whose "desperate energy" and "passionateness" impressed itself in his every deed.[21] Mussolini was pleased and wrote Beltramelli a congratulatory letter that was reproduced in facsimile at the volume's end. It was an appropriate gesture. Beltramelli had been a member of the Fascist Party since its inception in 1919, and in the years after 1923 his role as a party militant expanded: he served as a principal speaker at the Convention of Fascist Culture in 1925, the keystone in the regime's efforts to organize the nation's intellectual life, and he signed its chief document, the "Manifesto of Fascist Intellectuals"; later he edited newspapers for the "University Youth" movement and the "syndicate" of Fascist writers. He died in 1930, and in 1937 the anniversary of his death was commemorated with an article that reprinted all the marginalia that a young socialist named Mussolini had left in his copy of *The Chants of Faunus*.[22]

Beltramelli's portrait of Sigismondo was not, however, the antithesis of the one given by the more refined and scholarly Ricci but rather its complement. His book on Sigismondo, in fact, had originated in a lecture on the church of San Francesco that he had given some years earlier, in 1907, which he had written after consulting the text of an earlier lecture on the same subject by Ricci.[23] It is true that Ricci had kept his distance from the Fascist National Party and its activities during 1919 to 1922, and in 1923 his distinguished career—he had served as director of the Brera in Milan (1899–1903), of the Royal Galleries of Florence (1903–1906), and of antiquities and fine arts for all of Italy (1906–1919)—was culminating in a shower of honors. But now those honors were being dispensed by the new regime as part of its effort to woo the qualified personnel necessary to run a modern bureaucracy, personnel not to be found among the ill-educated and violent leaders of the squads that had brought the party to power. On 1 March 1923 Ricci was named a senator of the kingdom (*senatore del regno*); on 11 April he was appointed president of the Central Commission for Antiquities and Fine Arts; and on 6 May he was named president of the Casa di Dante, one of the nation's most prestigious cultural institutions. In March 1925 he would participate alongside Beltramelli at the Convention of Fascist Culture in Bologna, and his role in the cultural politics of the regime would continue to expand, reaching its apogee at the inaugural lectures he gave in 1933 for the Fascist National Institute of Culture. Mussolini, it was reported when Ricci died in 1934, "knew him intimately and appreciated his deep learning and indomitable energy."[24]

Pound, at one point or another, examined all the works that have been mentioned so far, and when possible he sought to meet their authors. In mid-May 1922 he first saw the church of San Francesco during holiday travels with his wife, Dorothy; before leaving he took notes from Symonds and purchased a Baedeker guidebook. While in Rimini he purchased a copy of Beltramelli's book, and he made detailed use of it a month later when he wrote his earliest drafts for the Malatesta Cantos.[25] When he returned to Paris he bought Yriarte's book, later filling its pages with 150 notes and marginalia. He also purchased Hutton's novel and Soranzo's *Pius II and Italian Politics in the Struggle Against the Malatesta, 1457–1463*. In the Bibliothèque Nationale of Paris he consulted volumes too rare to be easily purchased.[26] After five months' intense work, he left Paris in January 1923 and after a brief vacation began an extensive tour of historical archives and libraries holding books and primary documents connected with Sigismondo. His travels lasted nine weeks, from 11 February to 14 April, and covered Rome, Florence, Bologna, Modena, Cesena, Rimini, the Republic of San Marino, Pennabilli, Fano, Pesaro, Urbino, again Rimini,

Ravenna, Venice, and Milan. While in Rome he met with Ricci, who furnished information about archival sources, recent archaeological discoveries, and his defense of the view of the cipher SI.[27] In Rimini he encountered Soranzo's colleague Massèra, though it was a meeting that seems to have been rather less cordial, as we shall see. In Ravenna he sought out Santi Muratori, a colleague of Ricci who had helped renovate the church, and in Milan he attempted to contact Soranzo, whose studies of Sigismondo he had read in Paris.[28] Ultimately Pound accumulated more than seven hundred pages of notes and more than sixty-five drafts and draft fragments.

For Pound the Tempio Malatestiano became a resonant symbol that encompassed a broad range of his experiences and aspirations, both literary and extraliterary. Sigismondo, after all, had been a poet, and Yriarte's attribution of the poem by Serdini to him had only given further impetus to a conception of the church as a poem in stone, a lyrical work that expressed a realm of selfhood and desire free from, and in opposition to, the everyday world of socially given meaning. The building's mélange of styles, from the severe exterior by Alberti to the luxurious sculptural decorations by Agostino di Duccio, epitomized a polyphonic eclecticism already typical of *The Cantos*. Alberti's adaptation of motifs from antiquity coincided with Pound's recurrent interest in the renewal of classical tradition. Sigismondo had written in lyrical genres linked especially to the time when Provençal poetry had influenced Italian poetry, suggesting that he, like Pound, had harbored a genuine sympathy for the culture of Provence. And a more romantic reading of Sigismondo's biography might suggest that his devotion to Isotta was a continuation of practices sanctioned in the Provençal culture of courtly love; moreover, his fatal political mistake had been to lend his support to the house of Anjou from southern France, the land of Provence; and perhaps the ecclesiastical campaign against him resulted not from mundane political considerations but from an attempt to suppress a heretical and neopaganizing ethos of the same sort that had been stifled before in Provence.[29]

There was also the motif of patronage, plainly relevant to Pound when he was preoccupied with Bel Esprit and also crucial in his own career, from the financial support he had received from Margaret Cravens (in 1910–1912) and John Quinn (in 1915–1923) to his efforts to secure patronage for Joyce, Eliot, and Wyndham Lewis. Historians in the late nineteenth and early twentieth centuries had long portrayed the Renaissance as an age unrivaled in its patrons, neglecting the link between political power and cultural display that fostered the practice of the Renaissance courts and assimilating their activity to post-

Kantian ideals of aesthetic disinterestedness. Yet even taking these factors into account, Sigismondo could be viewed as one of the greatest of the smaller courtly patrons, one who had commissioned works from Alberti, Agostino di Duccio, Piero della Francesca, Antonio Pisanello, the poet Basinio da Parma, and many others. Finally, Sigismondo had been turned into an exemplary figure whose restless individuality and unbridled will marked a crucial moment in Western cultural history, constituting a resource for the imagining of a new man who would address the endemic crisis that was gripping liberal bourgeois culture. Sigismondo, as constructed in a complex ensemble of works and cultural practices, had become a riveting image: the source of one of the highest cultural achievements in the West and a locus for nagging questions about the cost, meaning, and purpose of that ideal moment, a figure who simultaneously heralded modernity's arrival and rebuked its failure to realize its emancipatory promise. Here were lodged all the contradictions of art and modernity, imagination and power.

Having surveyed the cultural genealogies that led to the invention of "Sigismondo" and their reception by Pound, we can reconsider the two lines that "Sigismundo" (as Pound spelled the name in *The Cantos* and in his letters) speaks at the end of Canto 10 and the beginning of Canto 11. We might begin with a word-for-word translation into English, though the result will have a slightly antique word order:

> *E gradment li antichi cavaler romanj*
> And greatly the ancient knights Roman
> > *davano fed a quisti annutii*
> > gave faith to these annunciations

The interlinear translation shows that, by triangulating cognate terms from English or French or Spanish, even a reader unfamiliar with Italian can extrapolate the passage's basic meaning. Nevertheless, it also obscures several difficulties in the original. Some are due to discrepancies between contemporary Italian and earlier Italian. The definite article *li,* for example, is an older form that has disappeared and is now written only as *gli;* but as the older form occurs frequently in Dante, it is scarcely a difficulty. More puzzling is the word *quisti* instead of the more typical *questi* (these), and *cavaler* instead of the more common *cavalieri.* Are these older forms that have vanished, or simply a mistake? And if a mistake, whose? Still more troubling are three other words: *fed, gradment,* and *annutii.* The first seems to be a variant of the Italian word *fede* (faith), which derives from the Latin *fides;* but why is the final letter *e* missing? More perplexing is *gradment,* a word that is not even recognizably Italian. One might guess that it comes from Provençal, or Catalan, or some other poorly known Romance language; but then what is it doing here? Of course no word in itself radically alters the entire passage; yet to find five words out of eleven written in a manner discrepant with practice both older and modern, and to pause and puzzle over the possible motivations behind each, is plainly an obstacle to ready understanding.

These puzzles can be resolved by examining the genesis of these lines. Their source is a fifteenth-century chronicle written by Gaspare Broglio Tartaglia da Lavello (1407–1493), a soldier of fortune and counselor who served at the court of Rimini from 1443 until Sigismondo's death in 1468, when he withdrew from active political life and resumed the composition of his memoirs, a task he had begun much earlier. Because the memoirs concern events that Broglio had witnessed, they are an important source for the life and times of Sigismondo. Giovanni Soranzo, in fact, devoted several pages in the introduction to his book to praising Broglio's account: Broglio had consistently been "au courant about the diplomatic affairs, undertakings, and economic and political conditions of his master," and his chronicle was "extremely important, because often it treats events that he claims to have witnessed himself and that are not reported in other chronicles or archival sources."[30] One such event was the battle at Nidastore of 1461, where Sigismondo led his troops to victory over superior ecclesiastical forces, an event that Broglio recounts with great vivacity.[31]

Broglio's manuscript was still unpublished in 1923, and because this passage had never been quoted or transcribed in secondary sources it could be examined only by going to Rimini, where the original manuscript is preserved. Pound visited the city between 20 and 27 March 1923, stopping there in the course of his research tour of Italian libraries and archives.[32] When Pound examined the manuscript, however, he made many mistakes in his transcription. He was unfamiliar with various conventions used by quattrocento writers to save space, particularly abbreviations and diacritical marks generally known only to specialized paleographers.[33] One such device is called fusion, by which a writer would fuse or meld together the strokes from adjacent letters with commensurate shapes, saving space and time. Thus a writer might bleed together the finishing stroke on the letter *d* with the beginning of a following *e,* as in *fede,* or he might meld together the letters *t* and *e.* Because Pound could not recognize this phenomenon, he had trouble with words such as *grandemente* (where fusion occurs between *d* and *e* and between *t* and *e*) and *fede* (again between *d* and *e*): whence his rendering of *gradment* or *fed*.

Yet Pound was deeply concerned with reproducing the texture of Broglio's manuscript, insofar as he understood it. Consider the diacritical mark that also appeared in the manuscript in the word *grandemente*. In this case, a horizontal line over the *a* was used to indicate elision of a following *n*, making the word appear as *grādemente*. Whether or not Pound understood the meaning of the mark, he took pains to register it in his final typescript and included detailed instructions to the printer on how best to reproduce it. In the first printing of the Malatesta Cantos in 1923 the mark was printed as an umlaut; in the second, in 1925, it was rendered correctly as a straight line. But the mark was omitted in the third printing, in 1930, and it has been ever since.[34]

Pound took such pains to represent the abbreviation sign over the letter *a* for several reasons. The simplest was that it attested to the historical veracity of his portrait of Sigismondo. Some two weeks after he had returned from Italy in April 1923, when asked to describe his recent work for an interview published in the *New York Herald*, he stressed the issue of accuracy: "I want my work . . . to withstand all historical criticism."[35] Historical criticism, in this context, implied a kind of captious scrutiny of details that, if they were found to be inaccurate, threatened to undermine the broader vision of cultural life embodied in his depiction of Sigismondo Malatesta and the courtly culture of Rimini. The desire that his work be able "to withstand" such examination presupposes a common knowledge of protocols and procedures, shared canons of evidence and the treatment of historical sources. Pound's acquiescence to those protocols may be given reluctantly or provisionally—but it still means, at least for the moment, agreement to play the game by "their" rules. The abbreviation sign over the letter *a,* like the footnotes incorporated into the text of the poem, like the minute corrections administered to historians who had inaccurately quoted some source or other, like the careful directions to the printer concerning how he should simulate the abbreviations representing quattrocento forms of address, all presuppose an assent, however provisional, to premises and procedures grounded in Enlightenment rationalism and the practices of advanced historiography as they had evolved up to Pound's time.[36]

Paradoxically, however, the abbreviation sign over the letter *a* also epitomized the degree to which Pound's assent to these protocols was provisory, the extent to which it was a tactical maneuver, not genuine assent. For the same sign could suggest a very different set of rules by which the game might be played. Viewed in another light, the meticulous rendering of the documentary grapheme captures the aura of the original document, records the authenticity of Pound's direct encounter with an unpublished source, and testifies to the experiential reality at the foundation of Pound's evaluation of Sigismondo and the cultural achievements associated with him. It is here, in Pound's immediate and lived engagement with such resistant materials, that his perception of Sigismondo finds its genuine sanction, not in the arid protocols of rationalist historiography. The poetic counterpart to the sign, when seen this way, is located not in the punctilious mimesis of scholarly footnotes but in the almost brutal succession of raw documents, of coarse and contradictory reports that succeed one another seemingly without logic or principle, each bristling with cryptic names and dates. It is from experience and not ideology, from life and not theory, that the author has wrested his insight into Sigismondo's significance, and it is this realm of lived experience that is presented as a substantive reality posed outside and against the merely procedural, merely formal, canons of reason.

So deep is Pound's conviction of truth as experience that it is precisely this—the experience in which his vision of Sigismondo has taken shape and from which it derives its authority—that he seeks to represent in his poem. His goal is not to offer "a historical portrait" of Sigismondo, however useful that term may be as a conventional shorthand to characterize the Malatesta Cantos, for that would imply adherence to the ethos of detachment and distance that informs the protocols of rationalist historiography. Instead, he seeks to re-create, as fully as possible, the experiential immediacy in which his own understanding of Sigismondo's career has crystallized, that dark voyage amid the murmurs of a forgotten history in which, by force of will, he has glimpsed a thread of gold amidst the gloom.

The result is that the Malatesta sequence is a text of extraordinary difficulty, one that presupposes and solicits a quasi-heroic reader, one whose labors and intuitions must be responsive to the author's own. No one has described as well as Donald Davie the resistant density, the impediment to reading posed by such a text: "Indeed, 'reading' is an unsatisfactory word for what the eye does as it resentfully labors over and among these blocks of dusty historical debris. We get lost in ever murkier chaos, an ever more tangled web of alliances, counter-alliances, betrayals, changing of sides, sieges and the raising of sieges, marches and countermarches; it is impossible to remember whose side Malatesta is on at any time or why."[37] Davie's key verbs are telling: "the eye . . . labors," and "we get lost," and "it is impossible to remember." They record a progressive clotting that finally slows to absolute blockage. The text becomes an overwhelmingly hostile reality, an assault upon consciousness. It confronts the reader with a world as confusing and chaotic as the one that was faced by his predecessor, the poet before him, which in turn is like the one faced by his predecessor, Sigismondo. Each is threatened with an engulfing darkness, with being lost "in ever murkier chaos" that epitomizes a profoundly pessimistic view of human destiny, viewed as a grim and incomprehensible setting from which an evanescent victory, a momentary order, is wrested in an act of will that is simultaneously an act of memory and of vaticination:

> *E gradment li antichi cavaler romanj*
> > *davano fed a quisti annutii*
> And greatly the ancient Roman knights
> > gave faith to such annunciations

It is here, in this paradigmatic moment, that the hero realizes his own identity, largely by invoking and assimilating that of a predecessor: as the ancient Romans have been assimilated by Sigismondo, so he is assimilated by the speaker of *The Cantos,* and so all these in turn are to be assimilated by the reader.

What is recovered at such moments is difficult to define: an experiential essence, a glimpse of pure being as it stands stripped of historical and social accretions, a laying bare of fundamental identity. Yet it is important that the object of understanding not be defined more precisely, for to do so would subject it to the rationalizing discourse to which it stands inalterably opposed. Precisely because such understanding is posed outside of and against that discourse, however, the question of verification assumes such prominence, becomes so vexed and problematic: for this form of understanding defies the rationalist criteria of evidence and proof, of logic and argument, and instead can appeal only to a hermeneutics of experience, to what must be only felt and not analyzed, shown and not clarified. Which is why *The Cantos* as a whole seems to offer a repetitive sequence of models and exempla that are endlessly adduced for the reader's edification, even though it is equally true that the very concept of a model—a definable pattern with normative claims upon the reader's attention—is rejected in favor of presenting the experiential world from which a perception of the model has been wrested. The result is to put enormous pressure on the connection between sign and referent, on the linkage between the private experience that the sign encapsulates and the public status to which the exemplary figure is assigned. Indeed, nothing can really forge the linkage between private experience and public exemplum except faith: it becomes the circuit that mediates the transition from an iconic function (such as a historical portrait) to an indexical function (an index of experience) and again to a performative function (an injunction to read thus). And that is the importance of Sigismondo's invocation of the ancient Romans. It is faith without substance, faith that need not define its contents: faith that finds its validity not in its congruity with a prior referent but in action that is located in the future. It is tested not against a historical notion of veracity but against the idea of efficacy, which is to say that its validity has been relocated in experience—this time, in the experience of the auditor/reader who is spurred to action.

These hermeneutical motifs—experience, faith, action—were fundamental to Pound's understanding of literature and its social functions, and they furnished the framework in which he assimilated his emerging interest in Fascism and Mussolini in 1925–1935. Writing notes to himself in 1930, Pound assigned himself the task of defining the "biological function of literature."[38] In response he produced a list with five potential answers:

> nutrition of impulse
> relieve mind of strain
> give feeling of being alive
> set 'em off = mobilize
> energy—start dynamo

Setting aside the second item in Pound's list, we see that his answers are of two basic sorts. One function of literature is to nurture the realm of experience: "nutrition of impulse," and "give feeling of being alive." The other is to be a spur to action: "set 'em off = mobilize," and "energy—start dynamo." The two sorts, however, overlap: for if literature nurtures "impulse," or augments experience, it is also true that impulse is typically a spur to action. Pound therefore must assume that there is a continuum between experience and action, even if the action is only that of changing one's beliefs, altering one's understanding. "The aim," writes Pound in another set of notes concerning *The Cantos,* is "to create states of mind in which certain things are comprehensible."[39]

The same cluster of notions recurs in an important unpublished essay titled "Fascism or the Direction of the Will," written by Pound in April 1933. Though intended to clarify Pound's views on Mussolini and Italian Fascism, it repeatedly attacks the notion of clarification itself, dismissing rational and coherent accounts as "dogma" and "theory." As he candidly admits, "I strongly disbelieve in any general definition." In the same vein, he castigates people who "are so full of principle that they won't ride in a train." Indeed, Italy's problem before the advent of Fascism was that it had been led by "scoundrels" who were willing to "wreck Italy for the profit or for the satisfaction of dogmas." Fascism, instead, is precisely the opposite: "Fascism by its founder's own definition is NOT a body of abstract dogma." Or again: "But then fascism hasn't any theories. It has methods."[40] Or, as he would put it in a subsequent revision of the essay: "the real point of fascism being that it simply is NOT abstract."[41] Pound, of course, is doing little more than parroting the regime's self-understanding. As Giovanni Gentile, the philosopher who took upon himself the task of articulating it in "The Philosophic Basis of Fascism," expressed it: "Fascism prefers not to waste time constructing abstract theories about itself."[42]

Instead, Pound's belief in the virtues of Fascism is asserted on the grounds of concrete experience. One form of experience is observations slowly accumulated over time: "I have seen Italy off and on since 1898. I have seen Italy for several months a year since 1920. I have lived here for the last eight years. I have seen not one town but a hundred." Here the repetitive assertion of "I have seen" urges the primary nature of experience, but inadvertently it also suggests a merely quantitative distinction between less experience and more, leading to a mathematical, hence mechanical and empty, concept of experience. The real test for experience, therefore, is located not in the past but in the future, in a criterion of efficacy: "FASCISM has meant throughout all this fifteen years that the main and necessary idea should be presented to the Italian people in such a form *that they should take action*. That is the bones and marrow of it" (emphasis added). Or again: "Fascism . . . continues to be a constructive force, *directed at results* of most possible concreteness" (emphasis added). Fascism is best understood when one perceives the outcome, the action to which it leads (the future). Between past and future, and yet inseparable from them, lies that mysterious terrain that resists definition, that can be understood only in faith: "I can declare faith in Mussolini's instinct," Pound concludes.[43] It is a puzzling comment, after all: we are asked to judge Mussolini not by his words, not by his policies, not even by his actions, but by something as remote and inaccessible as his "instinct," something to which we have access by "faith." And yet this is plainly part of a coherent set of cultural motifs. As the historian Emilio Gentile (no relation to the philosopher Giovanni Gentile) observes, Fascism's appeal to faith was indistinguishable from its cultivation of activism, activism that in turn "was inseparable from fascism's irrationalist conception of politics, which affirmed the priority of lived experience over ideology and *faith* over theory in the formation of a political culture."[44] His assessment is amply confirmed by the writings of Fascist theorists. Assaying the distinctive feature that the syndicalist writer Georges Sorel had contributed to "The Philosophic Basis of Fascism,"

Giovanni Gentile singles out "faith in a moral and ideal reality for which it was the individual's duty to sacrifice himself, and to defend which, even violence was justified."[45] Or, as Mussolini would explain, six days before the "March on Rome" in October 1922: "We have created our own myth. Myth is a faith, a passion. It is not necessary that it be a reality. It is a reality in the fact that it is a spur, a hope, a faith, a form of courage."[46] Mussolini equates myth, in the sense defined by Sorel, with faith, the term that can bridge the gap between a discarded referentialism ("It is not necessary that it be a reality") and a form of validity testing by performative criteria ("a spur" to action), between the past and the future. It is no accident that Sigismondo Malatesta's speech asks his followers to place faith in the oracle he has seen, just as the Romans once did. As the foremost scholar of Fascist culture has put it: "In a certain sense, it is correct to state that, for fascism, the essence, foundation and aim of political activity could be summed by the key word in fascist language—'faith.'"[47]

Five months after Mussolini had assumed power with the March on Rome, on 20 March 1923, Ezra Pound found himself in Rimini, where he had come to examine the manuscript of Gaspare Broglio's memoirs, along with other materials related to Sigismondo Malatesta. It was his third visit to the city. The first had been in May 1922, when he had seen the church of San Francesco for the first time. The second had taken place only a week earlier, on 12 March 1923, when he had also come to the city to examine documents held in the municipal library, the Biblioteca Gambalunga. But he had been disappointed, as he explained to his wife, Dorothy, the next morning in a letter datelined "Palace Hotel, Rimini."

> Blood And Thunder.
> Library here closed *at least* until the 20th as the damn *custode* [custodian] has flu, and the boss is too lazy—or has to teach physics elsewhere.
> Am going to San Marino by the *trenino* [little train] in a few minutes and shall try to fill in time in Pesaro, Fano, etc. till the bloody *custode* recovers. IF he recovers.[48]

Plainly annoyed with the city librarian ("the boss"), Pound spent the next week touring nearby cities that were also connected with the story of Sigismondo (San Marino, Pennabilli, Fano, Pesaro, and Urbino). He returned to Rimini in the late afternoon of 20 March, once more staying at the Palace Hotel, where he wrote another letter to Dorothy the next morning. His trip had been "laborious," he reported, and he was glad to be "back here in comfort." Already he had acquired an ally in his efforts to resolve the question of the library's closure:

"I go to library here at 10:00 o'clock this a.m. Hotel-keeper ready to sack the place and have up the mayor if it isn't open; he is a noble fascist." Concluding his letter as he headed out the door, he added: "Will now try the library."[49]

Whether Pound found it open is unclear. In any event, its resources were soon at his disposition, and he spent the next week examining documents related to Sigismondo Malatesta—among them, the manuscript of Gaspare Broglio.

Pound's "hotel-keeper" was named Averardo Marchetti (1890–1942). The son of Ferdinando and Rosa Rambelli Marchetti, he had served in the armed forces from 1915 to 1918, the entire time of Italy's participation in the war. Wounded once and repeatedly decorated, he achieved the rank of lieutenant and then captain. In early 1918 he married Antonia Vittoria Podrecca (1890–1969), with whom he had two sons, Ferdinando in 1921 and Federico in 1926. By 1921 he was listed in municipal records as a hotel-keeper (*albergatore*), and by 1923, when Pound came to Rimini, he was managing the Palace Hotel, located near the railway station and yet close to the Tempio and the center of town. Little is known about the evolution of Marchetti's political views, but his career suggests a familiar pattern. During the Great War many soldiers, especially officers from the lower ranks, felt a profound sense of camaraderie that suggested the possibility of a "new" Italy, a potential that was betrayed by corrupt politicians of the old order at the war's end. Their numbers were to swell the ranks of emergent Fascism. On 24 May 1921 Marchetti and seven other men founded the *Fascio riminese,* the local chapter of the Fascist National Party that had been created two years earlier in Milan.[50]

The fascio was soon actively participating in the so-called *squadrismo,* the harassment and beating of opponents. In September 1921 the Riminese fascio joined a march on Ravenna by three thousand Fascists under Leandro Arpinati. "Everyone had to remove his hat when the Fascist emblems and banners went by," one observer reported, "and some priests who did not react quickly enough were beaten until they bled."[51] In the summer of 1922 Arpinati stepped up the pace of attack, coordinating a systematic offensive of squads from Bologna and Ferrara against the Socialist governments in various cities of Romagna, among them the municipal administration of Rimini.[52] Victory was swift. On 6 July 1922 the Socialist administration of the city resigned en masse, citing partly the failure of local banks to extend credit but chiefly "the violence committed today against the persons of the administration." They had been beaten bloody. Six days later government of the city was formally consigned to Dr. Arcangelo Leggieri, who was to manage its affairs under an "extraordinary administration" and hold the title of royal commissary (*reggio commissario*).[53] In early February 1923 he was succeeded by Dr. Luigi Marcialis, a former subprefect of the city who liked to vaunt his title of *gran cordone mauriziano*—member of the Order of the Knights of Saint Maurice and Saint Lazarus. Marcialis ran the city from February to November 1923, doing little to conceal his sympathies. When he formally consigned care of the city to the Fascist administration that followed, he praised "the living flame of faith and duty which has burned in your hearts, whether on the fields of battle or in the recent deeds of sacred civil resistance." He looked forward to "the rebirth of our Italy under the guide of our supreme Duce and artificer, Benito Mussolini."[54] There must have been many occasions when he collaborated with Marchetti, a founder of the local fascio and one of its chief leaders. In December 1922 Mussolini had organized the Volunteer Militia for National Security, a force composed of former squadristi who reported directly to him and took no oath of allegiance to the king; Marchetti was named *comandante della piazza* in Rimini and charged with maintaining law and order in the city.

It was at this conjuncture of events that Pound arrived in Rimini for his visit of 20–27 March. After a week of work in the city's library and archives, he left early the morning of 28 March, and soon after his arrival in Ravenna that evening he wrote to Dorothy to recount his recent activities. He began with his departure from Rimini: "Triumphal exit from Rimini. Reggio Commissario descended on the librarian (who may die of the shock). Very sympatique the *Gran Cordone*."[55] Pound's report makes it difficult to say exactly what occurred, but its import is plain enough. Royal Commissary Marcialis, alerted by Marchetti to the presence of a foreign poet and scholar in town, had paid his respects to Pound and publicly reproved the library's director, Aldo Francesco Massèra—the scholar whose research more than a decade earlier had helped debunk the romantic legend of the church of San Francesco—for not having shown more solicitude in meeting his needs. Here, for Pound, was swift action replacing bureaucratic delay. He would never forget it, and almost immediately he sought to commemorate the event.

The same evening that he wrote to Dorothy, he also sent a postcard to Nancy Cox-McCormack (1885–1967), an American sculptor he had met in Paris two years earlier, in July 1921.[56] As Cox-McCormack will figure largely in the rest of this account, it will be helpful to know something of her background. Born in Nashville, Tennessee, she was the daughter of a prosperous landowner. Her mother died when she was three, her father when she was fourteen. At seventeen she was sent to W. E. Ward's Seminary for Young Ladies, where she soon showed an interest in art. Two years later, before her nineteenth birthday, she married Mark McCormack. It was an "escape marriage," she recalled later, the "only means of breaking painful ropes to freedom and the beginning of self-liberation."[57] She divorced him within three years and was soon taking private art lessons. In 1909 she moved to St. Louis to take courses at the St. Louis School of Fine Arts; the next year she moved to Chicago to study at the Art Institute. For the first time she was living not "in a world to myself" but as "one of the many Chicago women who were hearing the call of emancipation."[58] In Chicago she exhibited regularly and began to sculpt portrait busts of city socialites, and in 1912 she won a competition for a public statue that still stands outside the capitol in Nashville. She also became friends with writers associated with *Poetry* magazine, acquainting her with the works of Pound. In 1921 she moved to Paris, eager to expand her horizons still further.

After their first meeting in July, when she had spotted Pound at a restaurant and introduced herself, the two gradually became friends. In December 1921 she cast a life-mask of Pound; later the same month she modeled a small portrait bust of him.[59] Though she left Paris for Rome in January 1922, she and the Pounds continued to keep in touch. When Pound and his wife went to Italy in the spring of 1922, Cox-McCormack traveled to Siena to visit them for a week, just before they left for their first visit to Rimini. When they went to Italy again in early 1923, they met her again. By now she was settled in Rome and could make all the arrangements for housing the Pounds when they stayed in the city from 16 February to 1 March, a few weeks prior to Pound's encounters with Marchetti in Rimini.[60] All but inevitably, one subject of their conversation was the new regime that had seized power only months before. Cox-McCormack, in fact, had seen the March on Rome at first hand. She later recalled the "armored wagons . . . rushing with soldiers to all critical points," and the day after Mussolini assumed power she stood "under a threatening sky" and "watched the Duce, Balbo and others heading this blackshirted procession" from the Piazza del Popolo to the Altar of the Nation. Much later, in the unpublished memoirs she wrote in 1939, she remembered: "The creative impetus back of it all swept most of my Italian friends into a world of bright expectations. Their eyes blazed with the blinding light of Fascist 'glory.'"[61] In reality she was describing not just her friends but herself.

When Cox-McCormack moved to Rome in early 1922, she soon developed two circles of acquaintances. The first centered on Lilliana de Bosis, whom she met in the summer of 1922; she was the wife of Adolfo de Bosis, a poet formerly associated with Gabriele D'Annunzio and now a frequent guest of the royal

22. Nancy Cox-McCormack and Ezra Pound, Paris, 1922, in the
garden before Ezra Pound's studio apartment. An inscription in
Cox-McCormack's hand reads, "N. C. McC. & E.P. / 70 bis rue
Notre Dame des Champs / 1922." Courtesy of the Poetry/Rare
Books Collection, State University of New York at Buffalo.

family. Adolfo de Bosis called Mussolini "the King's expedient for avoiding
worse conditions," Cox-McCormack recounted, and she went on to say, "Every
artist I knew . . . was enthusiastic about the 'stellone' (great star) who had
appeared in the sky 'to save Italy from utter ruin.'"[62] The Bosis family soon
introduced her to Giacomo Boni, a famous archaeologist who would be appointed senator by Mussolini in March 1923. He would cast the decisive vote
against the first motion of no confidence presented a month later and would go
on to design the official insignia of the party, an archaeological reconstruction
of the fasces that had been carried by the magistrates of ancient Rome.[63]

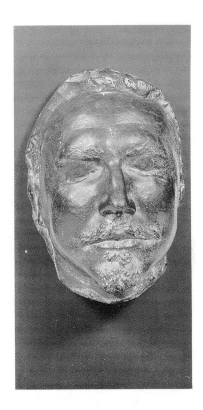

23. Life-mask of Ezra Pound, by Nancy
Cox-McCormack, Paris, December 1921.
Bronze, 60 × 20.5 × 26.7 cm. Courtesy
of the Yale Collection of American
Literature, Beinecke Rare Book and
Manuscript Library, Yale University.

The Bosis family also introduced her to Ansel Edgar Mowrer, a correspondent
for the *Chicago Daily News,* who in turn introduced her to Vittorio de Santa, a
journalist working for the *Chicago Tribune.* On 3 January 1923, Santa wrote a
letter to Mussolini urging that he accept a proposal by Cox-McCormack to
sculpt a portrait of him.[64]

More than a fortuitous chain of circumstances had led Cox-McCormack to
Mussolini. She was cultivating friends with just that goal in mind, and her
second circle of acquaintances pointed in the same direction. In the autumn of
1922 she met Thomas Judson, an American expatriate who had come to Rome
in 1914 to study archaeology and had remained as a consultant to dealers in arts
and antiquities. Judson, in turn, had introduced her to Lidia Rismondo, a
young and attractive demimondaine who had cultivated contacts with the
fringes of the Fascist leadership in Milan and now was hosting a political salon
conveniently located near Mussolini's residence. Cox-McCormack soon made a
portrait bust of Rismondo and began to frequent her political salon. In an
apartment "crowded with treasures" Rismondo entertained "groups of officers
and their wives," for whom she would "sing a few arias" while "accompanying

24. Portrait of Ezra Pound, by Nancy Cox-McCormack, Paris, December 1921.
Painted plaster, 23 × 24.3 × 11 cm. Inscription: "Ezra Poeta." Courtesy of the
Poetry/Rare Books Collection, State University of New York at Buffalo.

herself on the piano." On 18 March 1923 she took Cox-McCormack to watch
Mussolini open a meeting of the International Chamber of Commerce. Five
weeks later, Cox-McCormack was introduced to Mussolini himself. In early
May they had a second meeting in Mussolini's apartment in Palazzo Trittoni.
After a brief discussion, Mussolini agreed to let her sculpt his portrait.[65] The
work required ten sittings that took place in May and June; when finished, it
was the first bust to be made of the new ruler. The sculptor was utterly
captivated by Mussolini. In October 1923 she published an essay that praised
him for being "wholly concerned with welding Italy into a prosperous and
happy entity." He was "a creative force evolving and directing the beginnings of
a renaissance." He was "much an artist," and his eyes, which were "the kindliest
I have ever looked into," revealed "a man guided by tremendous and admirable
qualities of heart."[66] Two years later she wrote a preface to the English translation of Mussolini's *My Diary,* hailing him as "the inspiration of the new epoch
in Europe."[67] (Cox-McCormack later lost faith in the regime, however, in the

early 1930s, after a member of the Bosis family incurred the government's wrath by dropping anti-Fascist leaflets from an airplane over Rome; the programmatic harassment of the entire family finally disillusioned her.)

When Pound visited her in Rome in February 1923, she introduced him to Giacomo Boni, who in turn introduced him to Corrado Ricci, the art historian and cultural administrator who was completing his monumental study of the Tempio Malatestiano.[68] Evidently she also informed Pound about her contacts with Lidia Rismondo, her favorable views of the new regime, and her efforts to meet Mussolini. For Pound was plainly aware that she was moving among influential circles close to the center of power when he wrote her a postcard from Ravenna on 28 March 1923, the day after he left Rimini: "If you have *any*

25. Portrait bust of Lidia Rismondo, by Nancy Cox-McCormack, Rome, 1922. Terra cotta, 47.7 × 40.7 × 24 cm. Courtesy of the Herbert F. Johnson Museum of Art, Cornell University.

26. Nancy Cox-McCormack, with Benito Mussolini, modeling a portrait bust of Mussolini, Rome, May–June 1923. Courtesy of the Sophia Smith Collection, Smith College Library.

real political power, please see that the Gran Cordone Mauriziano Dr. Luigi *Marcialis, Reggio Commissario pel Comune di Rimini* [royal commissary for the City of Rimini] and also Signor *Marchetti,* Direttore del Fascio [of] Rimini, both receive *all* possible honors and advancements. They deserve well of Italia."[69] Alas, in March 1923 Cox-McCormack was still some two months away from her goal of meeting Mussolini; she could do nothing for Marchetti or Marcialis. Pound, meanwhile, continued to commemorate the events that had taken place in Rimini. When he returned to Paris he sent Marchetti a copy of his recent volume *Lustra* with an inscription reading: "Al amico Marchetti, dono del autore suo amico. Ezra Pound 1923."[70] But that was only the beginning.

Pound's postcard to Cox-McCormack was more than just a hasty gesture. His experience writing the Malatesta Cantos was important to him, as scholars have long known. After completing them in April 1923, Pound finally realized what form he had been seeking for his long poem; he swiftly revised all the previous cantos, added five more, and completed the first sixteen cantos in their modern form, leading to the publication of *A Draft of XVI. Cantos* in January

27. Portrait bust of Benito Mussolini, by Nancy
Cox-McCormack, Rome, July 1923. Bronze, 48.2 ×
20.5 × 21.5 cm. Courtesy of the Herbert F. Johnson
Museum of Art, Cornell University.

1925.[71] For Pound, Marchetti's aid had been invaluable. In June 1925 he returned to Rimini for a fourth visit, this time to commemorate Marchetti's
actions by presenting him a proof copy of *A Draft of XVI. Cantos,* an event that
was celebrated in the newspaper of the local fascio, the *Bridgehead* (*La Testa di
Ponte*), in its issue of 6 June 1925.[72] A copy of *The Cantos,* as Pound recalled a
few weeks later, "was carried through the village, not on a triumphal ox-cart
draped with scarlet, but at any rate with due order by il Comandante. . . .
Marchetti stated that he had shown my poem 'anche a Domini Deo' [even to
the Lord God]." Pound even asked his publisher for a special set of page proofs
containing only the Malatesta Cantos; he wanted them for a gift, as he would be
"sending them to il Comandante" in Rimini.[73]

Nor was this the last time that he commemorated Marchetti. Eight years later he recalled him again in *Jefferson and/or Mussolini:*

> "NOI CI FACCIAMO SCANNAR PER MUSSOLINI" [We're willing to cut our throats for Mussolini], said my hotel-keeper in Rimini years ago, thinking I knew nothing about the revolution and wanting to get it in my head. Nothing happens without efficient cause. My hotel-keeper was also Comandante della Piazza, we had got better acquainted by reason of his sense of responsibility, or his interest in what I was doing. The local librarian had shut up the library, and the Comandante della Piazza had damn well decided that if I had taken the trouble to come to Romagna to look at a manuscript, the library would cut the red tape.
>
> "Scannar" is a very colloquial word meaning to get scragged. It has none of the oratorical quality of "we will die for," but that's what it means. And my friend M. was expressing a simple fact.
>
> This kind of devotion does not come from merely starting a boy-scout movement.[74]

Pound's recollection of "il Comandante della Piazza" is cited as a landmark in his understanding of Fascism; Marchetti's devotion, even his style of expression, are indices of Fascism's virtue: what inspires "this kind of devotion" must be something of genuine power. Again the critical term is faith, "devotion," and again it is inseparable from action, Marchetti's resolve that "the library would cut the red tape."

Taken together, Pound commemorated his encounter with Marchetti six times between 1923 and 1933: in the letter to his wife, in the postcard to Nancy Cox-McCormack, in the dedication copy of *Lustra* that he gave him, in his visit to Rimini to present *il comandante* with *A Draft of XVI. Cantos,* in a later gift of page proofs for the Malatesta Cantos, and in published recollections in *Jefferson and/or Mussolini.* For Pound their encounter marked a turning point: only thus had he been able to secure access to the world of experience epitomized by the abbreviation sign over the letter *a* in Broglio's manuscript.

Pound's experiences with Cox-McCormack and Marchetti in February–March 1923 were not his earliest encounters with Fascism. His first had already taken place in Paris during the latter half of 1922. In August, while his wife was away in London, he wrote her that he had recently "dined several times" with the Marchesa Luisa Casati, a former mistress of D'Annunzio who frequented the Paris salon of Natalie Barney and Romaine Brooks, the latter having once painted her portrait. A few days later Pound reported that Casati had left Paris; "her fascisti have taken her back to Italy." (It is his first use of the term "fascist" in all his correspondence.) When Dorothy replied with salacious anecdotes about Casati and the portraitist Augustus John, Pound took it in stride: the tales "sound likely," he answered, as she had the carefree qualities "of the Rimini figures," the sculptures in the church of San Francesco.[75]

A month later, in September 1922, Pound was introduced to the American journalist Lincoln Steffens, and on 30 October he went to hear him lecture on the Russian Revolution and his firsthand impressions of Lenin. When Steffens came back to Paris a month later, returning from the Lausanne peace conference at which Mussolini had made his debut before the international press, he gave another lecture on modern revolutions, synthesizing his earlier experiences in Mexico and Russia with his recent observations of Mussolini. Steffens had found Mussolini as impressive as Lenin, and he especially admired *il Duce*'s disdain for parliamentarian politics: "He despises the old game of politics and diplomacy, democracy as we pretend it is. . . . He has risen into an empty throne by dint of his contempt for the present type of government." Mussolini, as Steffens put it in his contemporary *Autobiography*, was "as bold as Einstein." He and Lenin were the only contemporaries who knew how to "read history, and not as scholars do, for love of a growing body of knowledge, not even as scientists seeking the laws that govern events, but as men of action, reading a record of human experimentation to find out what can be done and how." Steffens had left his first interview with Mussolini "sure that here was a man and that that man knew something and meant something and had the will to and the way to do something. I would go and live in Italy," he concluded, "to see . . . this dictator work."[76] Pound attended Steffens's talk, and he "dragged" along the Irish critic Mary Colum. To her the evening was one of "appalling dreariness," but Pound listened with "rapt attention, his eyes glued to the speaker's face, the very type of a young man in search of an ideology, except that he was not so young."[77] Steffens had sketched an answer to the question of history that had acquired such urgency in the aftermath of the Great War. He might almost have been outlining the project of *The Cantos:* to "read history . . . as men of action [do], reading a record of human experimentation to find out what can be done and how."

Although Pound's experiences with Marchetti were anticipated by preliminary encounters with Fascism in Paris, they were also followed by others that took place when he returned there. Once more it was Cox-McCormack who provided the occasion. After completing her portrait of Mussolini on 1 July 1923, she returned to Paris for several months. To Pound she avidly recounted her experiences with Mussolini, her impressions of his abilities, and her belief in the sincerity of his interest in the arts. After one such conversation, Pound wrote her at length, on 15 August (a month after publication of the Malatesta Cantos):

> To clear up what I said the other day, it would be quite easy to make Italy the intellectual centre of Europe; and that by gathering ten or fifteen of the best writers and artists. . . .
>
> The experiment would not be expensive; the whole thing depends on the selection, and on the manner of the invitation. I shouldn't trust any one's selection save my own. There is no use going into details until one knows if there is or could be any serious interest in the idea; that is to say, if the dictator *wants* a *corte letteraria;* if he is interested in the procedure of Sigismundo Malatesta in getting the best artists of his time into Rimini, a small city with no great resources. I know, in a general way, the fascio includes literature and the arts in its programme; that is very different from being ready to take specific action.
>
> You have to avoid official personages, the deadwood of academies, purely pedagogical figures. The life of the arts is always concentrated in a very few individuals; they invent, and the rest follow, or adapt, or exploit.
>
> Italy has an opportunity *now,* an opportunity she would not have had thirty years ago, or even ten years ago. Germany is busted, England is too stupid, France is too tired to offer serious opposition; America is too far from civilization and won't for a hundred years distinguish between the first rate and the second rate; she will always stay content with copies.[78]

The terms of Pound's proposal are remarkably revealing. When he defines a "serious interest in the idea" as desire to have "a *corte letteraria,*" he is quoting from the title of a book that had surveyed the humanists who worked at the court of Sigismondo, a parallel made fully explicit when he urges Mussolini to follow "the procedure of Sigismundo Malatesta in getting the best artists."[79]

Cox-McCormack evidently decided not to act on Pound's proposal until she was back in Italy and could make use of her personal contact with Lidia Rismondo. But her return had the unintended effect of multiplying Pound's requests for contact with Mussolini. In early January 1924 he wrote her anew, this time asking that she use her influence with Mussolini to get him to write an essay for the *Transatlantic Review,* Ford Madox Ford's new literary journal:

> CAN you get a few choice words from Muss. exclusively for the Transatlantic, one or two pages, or as much more as he likes on his scheme for restoration of ROME; tell Judson that the Trans. is THE intellectual organ. (Jud. can have a try writing for it himself re Etruscan research.)
>
> Get Muss. to write a line on new building in Rome, new paving, etc. (possibly as link in revival of Italian intellectual life—that leads on to our other affair).

Ford wants this message at once; i.e., as soon as possible. ANY how in time for second number.

The Transatlantic is a free international avenue of communication. Muss. wd. reach the PENSEURS partout; and they "make the opinion of next week." [80]

Cox-McCormack evidently declined this request, but it was hardly long before Pound returned to "our other affair," his proposal for Mussolini to pursue a program of cultural patronage that would turn Italy into an international cultural center. On 13 January 1924 Pound wrote that "I would come [to Rome] if the moment were opportune" to discuss his earlier proposal for cultural patronage.[81] On 28 January he raised the subject again, this time at length. He dismissed as "slither and blah" the notion that his proposals be forwarded to Mussolini in a letter; he wanted something quite different: "The matter will be settled man to man between M[ussolini]. and me, or else it will be merely bitched, botched, and bungled, bureaucratized, bastardized, boozled, boggled, and altogether *zum wasser*." As if momentarily sensing difficulties posed by his truculent demand to meet a head of state, he also proposed another scheme:

> It [the topic] can be *opened* by *your* asking M[ussolini]. one simple question—or even getting R[ismondo]. to ask it—so long as you get a direct definitive answer. And the question is . . . Does he want Italy to be *veramente IL centro, non UN centro, della vita europea (centro dell'intelletto e della coltura della Europa)* [truly THE center, not A center, of European life (the intellectual and cultural center of Europe)].
>
> *COME ERA nel quattrocento e nel cinquecento* [As it was in the fifteenth and sixteenth centuries].
>
> If so he can have *il mio sostegno* [my support] and I will come to discuss or tabulate QUALCHE MISURA SEMPLICE che si può prendere con piccolissimo spese e ANCHE SENZA SPESE ALCUNO [some simple measure that can be adopted with little or no expense at all].
>
> That is about as briefly as I can put it.[82]

What became of these discussions is not clear. Most likely Mussolini's confidants informed Cox-McCormack that he had no time for such matters with the approaching elections. Shortly afterward she left Rome for good, ending the opportunity. To be sure, the affair is not without touches of the comic—as when Pound offers "my support," on the egocentric assumption that it might really matter to Mussolini that he have it—or even the absurd, as we are left to contemplate an issue of the *Transatlantic Review* that might have contained the first sections of what became *Finnegans Wake* alongside writings by Pound, Ernest Hemingway, Gertrude Stein, and Benito Mussolini! Yet beyond that, there is also a thread of connection that winds its way among all these events:

from Pound's admiration for the Marchesa Casati with the carefree qualities "of the Rimini figures" (August 1922); to his encounters with Boni and Ricci in Rome (February 1923) or with Marchetti in Rimini (March 1923); to his proposal that Mussolini adopt "the procedure of Sigismundo Malatesta in getting the best artists" (August 1923); even to his hope that Mussolini will want to make Italy "as it was in the fifteenth century" (January 1924). That thread is the intricate complex of motifs invested in the cultural invention of Sigismondo, the ideal patron, a complex by which Pound is able to address and assimilate the emerging culture of Fascism.

Critics have often claimed that Pound turned to Fascism in response to the global economic crisis that followed the Great Crash of 1929. His interest in Mussolini, in these accounts, was the result of goodwill marred by naïveté, a noble urge to better the world mistakenly diverted into hero worship. More recently this argument has been reproposed, with some important modifications. Pound's "conversion to fascism" is assigned to 1931, the year he began dating most of his letters by the Fascist calendar; and it is urged that Pound's "growing sympathy for Italian fascism was always based in part upon Mussolini's socialist roots." His "was a left-wing fascism," one that "emphasized its socialist roots" and correctly perceived that "many of [Fascism's] programs" originated "in Mussolini's early advocacy of Syndicalism and Socialism." Evidence for this view is found in a letter written to Oswald Mosley in July 1934, advising him that "the only fascism that CAN work in Engl' or France or America is fascismo di sinistra [left-wing fascism]."[83]

Several points in this view are dubious. None of Fascism's programs had roots in Mussolini's early adherence to syndicalism. What Mussolini knew of syndicalism was Georges Sorel's *Reflections on Violence* with its theory of myth, the notion that the revolution would come into being only if workers believed in a myth, a transfixing image of cataclysmic change and social transformation that would seize the imagination, not appeal to reason or logic. Mussolini reviewed the book at some length in 1909, and from it he learned much about a politics of the imagination that he would use both as radical socialist and as Fascist.[84] But that is a far cry from the kind of governmental legislative initiative usually encompassed by the term *program*. Indeed, syndicalism had no program to offer. It urged revolutionary violence, not reformist "programs."

It is still less tenable to urge that Pound's interest in Fascism stemmed from a systematic comparison of the guild syndicalism he had observed in London in the 1910s with the economic policies of the regime. Such arguments confuse rationalizations with reasons. When Pound mentioned Mussolini's socialist background, he was not analyzing the grounds of his sympathy for Fascism but parroting a commonplace of Fascist propaganda, which consistently called attention to Mussolini's early socialism in order to imply that he would bear in mind the interests of workers. Likewise, in his letter to Mosley, he was dispensing advice about tactics for success in England, not affirming principles that had guided his intellectual development. It is true that he came to believe that Mussolini would eventually adopt economic policies of the sort that attracted Pound after 1935. But those were later developments: they were the elaborate self-deceptions with which he rationalized his ongoing support of a regime whose moral bankruptcy was already patent to most observers. They were not the reasons that had sparked or sustained his initial interest. Those more genuine reasons were already fully formed by late 1923 and early 1924, as Pound himself acknowledged. As he put it in early 1933, echoing Lincoln Steffens's view: "I bet on Italian fascism years ago and came here to live in the middle of it."[85] Pound, we recall, had left Paris for Italy in late 1924.

When drafting his original notes for Canto 41, which offers its famous portrait of Mussolini, Pound included a sketch of Mussolini's military service in World War I that says much about the origins of his attraction to Mussolini.

> "would have called that a portent"
> saw then the white thorn hedges, albassina,
> stiff silvered [with] frost, by San Casciano
> twenty metres between their trenches.
> "identified as the hospital where Mussolini . . . ["]
> from cliche in the Corriere and therefore bombed
> by the austrians, that was his worst day in the war.[86]

Pound's sketch follows a commonplace of Fascist propaganda, which urged that the Austrians during World War I had bombed the hospital that housed Mussolini in order to kill him. More important, however, is the opening line, "would have called that a portent," for it is Pound's recollection of Sigismondo's speech to his troops at the end of Canto 10:

> And they came at us with their ecclesiastical legates
> Until the eagle lit on his tent pole.
> And he said: The Romans would have called that an augury
> *E gradment li antichi cavaler romanj*
>   *davano fed a quisti annutii,*
> All I want you to do is to follow the orders

Pound's evocation of the earlier passage suggests how fully his understanding of Mussolini was shaped in, and by, the experience of writing the Malatesta Cantos in 1922 and 1923. The echo becomes a cipher in which the mystery of the protagonist's identity is finally resolved: Mussolini is a reincarnation of Sigismondo Malatesta, and it is faith, rooted in experience, that will enable us to perceive his identity amid the apparent confusion of contemporary history.

The question of identity, after all, is one of the major motifs of *The Cantos,* one already thematized in the work's opening lines: "And then went down to the ship, / Set keel to breakers, forth on the godly sea." Who performs these actions? The subject's identity is conspicuously absent, and it is not until the next line that the reader learns: "We set up mast and sail on that swart ship." But in that momentary yet crucial gap in the poem's first two lines, in that suspended space where actions occur without an agent to perform them, the text lays out its great theme of a subject internally split and dispersed through time, defining its heroic task as the reconstitution of that lost identity, an effort that will consist in closing the gap between narrator and hero, author and reader—so forming "we." That is also what is at stake in the closing lines of Canto 10, when Sigismondo assumes the vatic function of the augur who interprets the eagle's landing on his tent. For a moment the figure of Sigismondo becomes blurred, his identity attenuated amid the multiple embedding of quotations: the speaker of the poem quotes Gaspare Broglio, who quotes Sigismondo (here cited only by the pronoun "he"), who in turn quotes the ancient Romans, who in turn . . . : "And he said: The Romans would have called. . . ." Identity is fragmented and dispersed, then reconstituted in an experience that demands faith. Which leads to action: "All I want you to do is to follow the orders." Heroic individualism, the discursive sweep of this passage tells us, is the other side of corporate conformity, and the question of the subject is resolved in the affirmation of subjection. The identity of the speaker is reestablished in the restoration of clear distinctions between "I" and "you," between the subject and the object, between active volition ("I want") and passive obedience ("follow the orders"). That is also the distinction that was at stake in the strained relations between Pound ("I want") and the librarian Massèra of Rimini ("follow orders"), the sedate scholar who was so underpaid that to make ends meet he had to teach physics at a local naval academy and who felt reluctant to assume as well the functions of a custodian for an American tourist, living in Paris, who vaunted his erudition about a historical subject that Massèra, in many ways, understood in greater depth.

More than Massèra's personal difficulties, however, were at stake in his encounter with Pound. For Pound, Massèra epitomized the cultural bureaucracy with its adherence to anonymous norms and impersonal criteria of assessment, its incapacity to perceive the needs of the artist. Abetted by the Fascist Marchetti, his momentary patron in Rimini, Pound staged a symbolic victory over a figure in whom resided all the forces of modern expert and professional systems. Doing so, he gained access to the passage from Broglio, and through that passage, as used in the Malatesta Cantos, he restaged a second victory in which the anonymous soldiers of Sigismondo, allegorical figures for the masses of modernity, give their consent and pledge their faith to the grand figure of the exemplary patron—at his behest.

They consent to take orders, of course, although they do not reach consensus. The basis of their consent, within the terms of the poem, is "faith." But if the case of Massèra can tell us anything, it may be possible to specify those grounds a bit further. When Massèra saw Pound and Marchetti huddled together with Marcialis, who now wielded absolute power over the city government, he knew what it could portend—perhaps the loss of his job, and perhaps much worse. For Massèra knew well what a visit from Marchetti could mean: he had heard the reports of those priests bloodied in nearby Ravenna; he had seen the spectacle of the city officials of Rimini (his former employers!) being beaten in the streets. They were not matters to be weighed lightly. The "faith" and "devotion" of Marchetti were not unknown to him, though his assessment of their merits probably differed from Pound's. And so, on that last day of Pound's visit in Rimini, he swallowed his pride and accepted the humiliation of public rebuke by Marcialis. No wonder, as Pound put it, he seemed ready to "die of the shock."

And yet, in Pound's words, it was Massèra's public humiliation that defined his "triumphal exit from Rimini," just as that triumphal exit signaled the beginning of his inexorable entry into the ranks of militant Fascism. We err, I suspect, in urging that that adherence had its basis in a reasoned examination of competing economic theories or a sustained comparison of Mussolini's programs with those of guild socialism or revolutionary syndicalism. No one, that day in Rimini, brought up those subjects to Aldo Francesco Massèra. Yet I suspect he understood all too well the genuine basis of Fascism. The solemn rhetoric of "faith" and "action" scarcely concealed the taut fist of terror.

Chapter 5 Patronage and the Poetics of the Coterie: H.D. in the Modernist Canon

the elixir of life, the philosopher's stone
is yours if you surrender
sterile logic, trivial reason
H.D., *Trilogy*

I did not conceal from you that I think you overrate H.D.'s poetry. I do find it fatiguingly monotonous and lacking in the element of surprise. I mean that this last book *Hymen* is inferior to her earlier work; that many words should be expunged and many phrases amended; that the Hellenism lacks vitality; and also morally, I find a neurotic carnality which I dislike.
T. S. Eliot to Richard Aldington, 17 November 1921

When historians of the future seek to characterize the past decade of cultural life in the United States, they may just decide to name it "the decade of the canon debate." Its key moments are well known. Leslie Fiedler and Houston Baker inaugurated the discussion with *Opening Up the Canon;* this was followed by a special issue of the influential journal *Critical Inquiry,* which lent the topic theoretical respectability.

A few years later Allan Bloom issued *The Closing of the American Mind,* a work that became a national best-seller and briefly turned Bloom into a media celebrity, and E. D. Hirsch published his prescriptions for "cultural literacy," a list of books and informational nuggets supposedly indispensable to participation in literate culture, a list that critics promptly damned as "Eurocentric."[1] When Stanford University announced in 1988 that it was altering its required introductory course in the humanities to reflect more adequately the ethnic heterogeneity of its students, it sparked still more debate. "The canon" was now a topic for the front page of national newspapers. Inside the university, interest in the canon accompanied a broader shift in critical focus, a turn away from the systemic and purely linguistic paradigms of the recent past and toward concern with questions of sociohistorical context of a sort that fueled the interest in New Historicism. But that development may have been only part of a wider change: in American society at large there has been a perceptible politicization of discussion about art and culture, a trend confirmed by bitter confrontations that have exploded everywhere in recent years, from the controversy over the Robert Mapplethorpe exhibition to the ongoing struggle over proposed cuts in funding for the National Endowment for the Arts, from theatrical confrontations over "political correctness" to endless discussions of "multiculturalism" in the humanities. Not only have cultural questions become sharply politicized, their politicization has been increasingly shaped by a climate of heightened awareness about ethnicity, race, gender, and sexual preferences—a kind of awareness that seems at odds with basic ideas about the relative autonomy of artistic judgment, or about the relative independence of artistic quality, that have been central to evaluative criticism as traditionally practiced.

Such issues attract media attention only when accompanied by sensational events or immediate political repercussions. But for most scholars their effects are felt at the local level of debate about canons in specific periods or generic traditions. In literary modernism the debate has been as fierce as anywhere, and perhaps more so because the canon of major poets—Yeats, Eliot, Pound, Wallace Stevens—seemed the outcome of a substantial consensus that was relatively stable and difficult to dislodge.[2] That too has changed. The discourse of postmodernism has been fashioned partly through an increasingly reductive view of the modernist moment and its achievements, often treated as little more than the sum of the most reactionary political or ideological positions that the modernists assumed at various points in the 1920s or 1930s. As many of those views have become unacceptable or repugnant to more recent consensus about ethics, politics, or religion—and many were already sharply contested in the modernists' time—scholars have turned to neglected figures who better conform to ideological paradigms that facilitate a revisionary account of the modernist achievement. And for a growing number of critics, H.D., the name under which Hilda Doolittle wrote from the time she published her first poem in 1912, has become the writer who marked a difference. Virtually forgotten at the time of her death in 1961, her work, says one writer, "can finally assume its rightful place in the canon of the great modernist writers."[3] It has acquired, says another, "a central place in the history of twentieth century poetry."[4] Her long poem *Trilogy*, writes yet another, "must be ranked with *Four Quartets* and *The Pisan Cantos* as the major poems in English to come out of the war."[5] H.D., in fact, should be considered "one of the most original poets . . . in our language."[6] Such claims, moreover, have often been explicitly advanced against the background of the new awareness of ethnicity, race, gender, and sexual preferences. H.D. was a lesbian; she had an important relationship with a black artist, Paul Robeson; she was ostensibly responsive to the plight of Jews in the 1930s; and as a consequence, it is claimed, she developed a "particular modernism" that differed from that of her contemporaries, "a modernism of the margins rather than the reactionary center."[7] H.D., it would seem, might almost have been made to meet all the criteria that potential critics could raise for entrance into the canon of the 1990s. She was a victim of ugly social prejudice, and her status as a victim led her to identify with history's other victims. What still remains to be established, though, is whether she was a great poet.

To address that question, we need to assess her control of poetry's basic formal resources (rhythm, syntax, diction), her use of specific genres and generic conventions, and, just as important, the relations that her literary practices presuppose between her works and her audience—their social setting. All these dimensions of her writing, of course, were profoundly affected by the circumstances in which she worked, circumstances that were a consequence of a single event that irrevocably changed her life forever: in late 1918 she met Winifred Ellerman, more commonly known by her pen name Bryher, who was the only child and heir of a shipping magnate considered the wealthiest man in England. In Bryher, H.D. found first a lover, then a friend. More important, she also found a lifelong patron of endless bounty. Paradoxically, such bounty may have had its price. For its effect was ultimately to cast H.D. in the role of a coterie poet, one whose writings circulated, like bonbons at a dinner party, among a cénacle of friends and hangers-on in wealthy bohemia. Bereft of a genuine public, deprived of critical give-and-take, she wrote against the backdrop of travel between her psychoanalyst in Vienna, Sigmund Freud, and the

28. H.D., circa 1930. Courtesy of the Yale Collection of
American Literature, Beinecke Rare Book and Manuscript
Library, Yale University.

beaches at Capri and Greece, between the villa overlooking Lake Geneva and
the furnished apartment that awaited her in London. Eager to please Bryher
and the clique that gathered around her limitless wealth, H.D. may have
become a victim not of social prejudice but of something seemingly more
benign—patronage. Which is why her career serves as such a distinctly modernist fable.

To assess the achievement of H.D. is not an easy task. In part it is complicated
by the genuine difficulties that attend all evaluation—ineradicable tensions
between cultural and aesthetic assessments, between historical and supra-
historical values and evaluations. But in part it is complicated by the fact that

29. Bryher (Winifred Ellerman), circa 1935. Courtesy of the
Yale Collection of American Literature, Beinecke Rare Book
and Manuscript Library, Yale University.

the apparently simple pronoun "she," as well as its antecedent, "H.D.," can
refer to a number of entities that are quite distinct and perhaps even incompatible. One H.D., for example, might be the poet who lived and wrote primarily
between 1915 and 1960, who, exercising certain legal and proprietary rights,
engaged in various arrangements for publishing the works that are ostensibly
the subject of the current debate. Another H.D., however, might comprise a
much looser and more ill-defined entity: this H.D., created largely in the 1980s,
has been instituted without the active participation of the earlier H.D., constructed through different legal, textual, and ideological conventions, fashioned through an accessible canon of works unlike any that prevailed in her

lifetime, and forged with the assistance of support literature issued by biographers and scholars offering new evaluations of her work. The identity of this H.D., in short, has been textually and culturally constituted by a far more recent array of agents, among them literary scholars, acting at a conjuncture of cultural, ideological, and institutional interests. And one may legitimately wonder to what degree this complex individuality articulated within specific worlds of signification, worlds that are inevitably textual and even editorial in character, coincides with that of the earlier H.D.

In a 1960 review of the last novel that H.D. published in her lifetime, *Bid Me to Live,* William Hogan, then book critic for the *San Francisco Chronicle,* confessed to his mistaken belief that H.D. had already died "years ago."[8] Hogan's remark, however cruel it seems in retrospect, suggests the extent to which H.D. had been forgotten by critics and literary historians. When H.D. actually died a year later in 1961, the accessible canon of her work was exiguous.[9] Only four volumes were in print: the novel *Bid Me to Live,* a truncated version of her memoir *Tribute to Freud* (published in 1956), her long poem *Helen in Egypt* (published in 1961, only a few days before her death), and a volume of *Selected Poems* (published in 1957). They represented but a fraction of her work in the three genres that she had favored, poetry, prose fiction, and autobiographical writing. The *Selected Poems,* for example, contained forty-two poems and four excerpts from longer works; her *Collected Poems,* first published in 1925 and reissued in 1940, had contained twice as many poems, and in the years since 1925 many more had accumulated.[10] Readers could consult only a tiny portion of a canon far more extensive than most anyone dreamed.

Thirty years later, one is struck by the profound changes that have reshaped the accessible canon of H.D. More of her works are available today than was the case at any point in her lifetime, creating a wholesale transformation in the bibliographical context for the study of her career. Consider briefly the poetry. In 1983 Louis Martz issued *The Collected Poems of H.D., 1912–1944,* a volume that contained almost two hundred pages of previously uncollected or unpublished material.[11] Aside from the long poem *Trilogy,* the volume contained 160 poems, almost double the number (84) of the earlier *Collected Poems* of 1925/1940. In addition, the other long poems, *Helen in Egypt* and *Hermetic Definition,* have been kept in print for almost twenty years running.

H.D.'s fiction and autobiographical prose have also proliferated. Between 1980 and 1990, thirteen books have been issued by the new H.D., of which nine were fiction or autobiographical writings. Six, it should be noted, had been out of print for more than half a century—no small amount of time during a period when a decade seems an eon—and the other three had never been published before. Since 1990 two more volumes of fiction and one of correspondence have appeared.[12] Still, even these do not exhaust the extent of the H.D. phenomenon, for the outpouring of "new" materials by H.D. has also been accompanied by an apparatus of support literature, such as popular biographies (by Janice S. Robinson in 1982 and Barbara Guest in 1984), critical monographs (by Susan Stanford Friedman in 1981, Rachel Blau Duplessis in 1986, and Friedman again in 1990), new journals (the *H.D. Newsletter* and *Sagetrieb*), and numerous academic articles. The intertwining of these phenomena should not be underemphasized: the critical monographs repeatedly stressed that the unpublished works of H.D. were "deserving of publication" and suggested that H.D. had "suppresse[d] these books out of a pragmatic fear" of a climate hostile to their sexual or other concerns.[13] The unpublished works, it was hinted, had been suppressed by a regime based on gender, and critics were urging "full disclosure." But to a large degree the rhetoric of moralism merely obscured the institutional relations that were bringing pressures to bear: the formal curriculum of the university is not only a canon but also the gateway to a market, for more than anything the canon shapes what is now the principal source of demand for works of poetry and literature: college class sales. Scholars, in effect, were assuming the task of market preparation and advance advertising for the commercial editions to follow. Behind the rhetoric of "the Other," in other words, scholars were working comfortably within the institution of mainstream publishing. What ensued was the massive transmission of H.D.'s writings to a large new public commanded by the professoriate and the agency of university curricula—a readership quite alien to the limited circle of friends and hangers-on who formed the coterie audience for H.D.'s works during much of her lifetime.

The smallness of the accessible canon of H.D.'s works at the time of her death was not entirely because of critical neglect—it was due partly to personal anxieties about publication on the part of H.D. herself and partly to the social setting that helped to generate those anxieties, her status as a coterie writer. H.D. herself published only one of her autobiographical writings, *Tribute to Freud,* during her lifetime. With regard to her novels, her output was equally restrained, if not always by her own choice. Though she had written eleven novels and part of a twelfth, only one (*Bid Me to Live*) was in print at the time of her death, and only two others were published during her lifetime: *Hedylus,* originally issued in 1928, and "Tatter," a section of an uncompleted novel, published in an anthology of 1931. Nor does it appear that H.D. was always prohibited from publishing the others by malevolent forces. On the cover page of her novel *Asphodel,* for instance, she voiced her own injunction regarding its fate in no uncertain terms: "Destroy." When this was written cannot be ascertained; but it says much about her own opinion of her work—which may have been prompted by shrewd self-assessment—and it raises important questions about possible editorial approaches to her canon. In 1934 H.D. submitted another novel, *Pilate's Wife,* to a mainstream publishing firm, which after due consideration decided that it lacked both quality and commercial promise. Another novel, *White Rose and the Red,* was also "probably rejected" in 1948.[14]

Her shorter fiction had endured much the same fate as her novels. *Palimpsest,* a collection of three novellas first published in 1926 by Contact Editions in Paris and Houghton Mifflin in the United States, had never been reprinted. Three other collections of fiction (*Kora and Ka, The Usual Star,* and *Nights*) had been privately published in 1934–1935, issued in limited editions of one hundred copies that were addressed, in the words of the title page, to "the author's friends." A fourth book, the delightful child's tale *The Hedgehog,* had been issued in London in 1936 by the Brendin Press, an operation owned by H.D.'s companion Bryher that was effectively "their own privately subsidized firm."[15] It was a deluxe edition, ornamented with illustrations by the fashionable artist George Plank, limited to three hundred copies. None of the four works had been submitted to a commercial press, and at the time of her death all had been out of print for a quarter century or more.

It is worth pausing over the four volumes of fiction issued between 1934 and 1936, for they epitomize key motifs in the evolution of H.D.'s career between roughly 1920 and 1940. Fine editions and small presses were, of course, typical venues of publication in the formation of modernism, playing a crucial role in its emergence and development. One need only recall a few names and dates of an extensively documented phenomenon: the Dun Emer Press (later the Cuala Press), which Yeats dominated from its foundation in 1902 and through which, from that time on, he issued nearly all of his works in limited editions; the fine editions issued by Elkin Mathews from his famous shop in Vigo Street, which published Yeats, Joyce, Pound, and William Carlos Williams; the Ovid Press of John Rodker, who issued deluxe editions of Eliot's *Ara Vos Prec* and Pound's *Hugh Selwyn Mauberley* in 1920; the lavish edition of *Ulysses* issued in 1922 by Sylvia Beach; the fine press edition of *The Waste Land* that Eliot originally planned with Maurice Firuski in February 1922, before he finalized his arrangements with Horace Liveright; or the deluxe editions of *The Cantos* that appeared in 1925, 1928, and 1930.[16] While the deluxe and limited editions responded to several conflicting imperatives, one important motive was economic. Authors, by restricting supply, could exploit the limited demand for modernist literature, turning each book into an objet d'art that acquired potential investment value for collectors. After 1930, however, this strategy no longer made sense: the onset of the Great Depression destroyed the economic climate that had sustained the market for fine editions, and in subsequent years the practice declined in importance.[17]

The works published by H.D. between 1934 and 1936 were therefore unusual in adopting a form of publication that was conspicuously outmoded. The 1936 publication of *The Hedgehog*, with its illustrations by Plank, was realized only because H.D.'s companion Bryher owned the publishing firm and was willing to underwrite the book's costs. The three other volumes were somewhat different. They were not, properly speaking, fine editions that appealed to a restricted market but private editions that addressed a minute coterie, an audience that was explicitly described in their colophons, such as this one from *Kora and Ka:* "This edition of one hundred copies has been privately printed for the author's friends." Or this one from *Nights:* "This edition, of 100 copies, has been printed by friends of the author for private circulation." Many of H.D.'s works thus actively avoided contact with a wider public, not because H.D. was fearful of public reaction but because she assumed that the public was unworthy of being addressed. Her works, instead, circulated within a comfortable and "private" circle of well-to-do "friends." Significantly, all three volumes were printed at Bryher's expense by the same firm, Darantiere, that had issued *Ulysses* in 1922. Then, recourse to Darantiere had been prompted by a legal obstruction of cultural circulation and debate; now it was merely a mechanism to avoid the public sphere altogether. H.D.'s works of these years represent a new privatization of culture, a regression to the world of Pamela Tennant, Lady Glenconner, in whose private gallery Ezra Pound had given his lectures long ago in 1912, the kind of setting that modernism had long since abandoned.

Much the same was true of the periodical publication of her poetry: of thirty-one new poems published between 1931 and 1950, twenty-three appeared in *Life and Letters Today,* a journal that Bryher purchased from Desmond McCarthy in 1931. Such publishing practices were an outcome of H.D.'s personal and financial situation after 1919, when the combination of income from her modest inheritance and the massive patronage of Bryher ensured that she would live like the Victorian sages whom Robert Lowell once described as "breezing on their trust funds through the world."

The effects of this situation were not entirely happy. H.D.'s financial dependency on Bryher created an absorbing isolation that shaped much of her work. In the generic configuration of her canon, its effects are perceptible in the tiny quantity of her nonfiction or critical prose: from 1916 until her death in 1961, H.D. published only forty-three articles—less than one per year.[18] Compare this with the canon of other modernists: T. S. Eliot, in a career that spanned exactly the same period, published well over five hundred essays and reviews; Marianne Moore, more than four hundred; Ezra Pound, more than fifteen hundred; and W. B. Yeats, at least four hundred. An explanation for this is obvious enough: the income and hospitality furnished by Bryher meant that H.D. felt little pressure to engage in literary journalism. Yet the lack of critical prose is itself only symptomatic of another, more ambiguous result of Bryher's munificence. It is a commonplace that literary modernism is distinguished by an unprecedented production of critical and theoretical writings that articulated the historical, formal, or ideological grounds for the modernist experiment, that sought to create or shape an audience receptive to modernist artworks. And yet one will search in vain for such writings within the minuscule corpus of nonfiction produced by H.D., for she felt little impetus to engage in an active or genuine dialogue with her contemporaries. For many years she could simply ignore them altogether: from 1918 through 1924, from 1930 through 1936, and from 1947 through 1960, H.D. published no critical prose at all—all together, twenty-eight years of silence, over half her career. And there is little doubt about why H.D.'s silence began precisely in 1918. As Bryher offered at the start of their relationship: "I was glad of your letter and I hope if there is anything I can do for you, if another few pounds would be useful to you in a month or so, you will not hesitate to ask it."[19] Lonely and often depressed, H.D. divided her middle years between Bryher's palatial residence, the modernist Villa Kenwin overlooking Lake Geneva, and the furnished flats she leased for her in London. Her journeys back and forth were assisted by a retinue of bustling chauffeurs; her changes of trains called forth an army of "porters at every stop."[20] As her daughter recalls, H.D. was "isolated from the world" in Kenwin, "well-buffered" by "a staff" of servants that was "almost a bodyguard."[21] Her world was a cocoon, and she neither needed nor pursued the give-and-take of exchange with others. Nor did she need or seek an audience, be it small or large; her audience had already been acquired for her by the wealth of Bryher: "one hundred copies . . . for the author's friends," or "for private circulation." In extreme cases, even they might be dispensed with. In 1919, when H.D. published *Hymen* in a small edition of three hundred with Harriet Shaw Weaver's Egoist Press, Bryher bought all three hundred copies of the book, then left them with Weaver to sell again, ensuring that she would make a profit. Bryher, in effect, had become the book's only reader. It was a modernist dream—or perhaps nightmare—come true.[22]

H.D. had little interest, and no reason to have an interest, in addressing anyone who stood outside the coterie that surrounded her and Bryher. Significantly, fourteen of her forty-three book essays and reviews are unsigned, and another four are pseudonymous, so that in some 42 percent of her nonfiction prose H.D. avoided a declaration of her own authorship. To be more chary of public engagement would be difficult indeed. Likewise, ten of the reviews treat scholarly works on ancient Greek sculpture and art, topics that reflect her private interests, but scarcely any treat contemporary works issued by other poets or novelists, the kind of materials indicating a public dialogue with peers. After 1942 virtually all her nonfiction prose consists of her reminiscences about Freud, a kind of writing that suggests the solipsistic reverie that became her habitual state under Bryher's benevolent but narcotic and claustral care.

H.D.'s isolation after 1920 shaped not only the genres in which she worked but the way in which she approached them. Typical is her practice in the novel, which she characteristically approaches via the roman à clef, a subgenre that originated among aristocratic circles of the seventeenth-century French salon

30. Kenwin, Bryher's villa near Burier, Switzerland, above Lake Geneva; designed by Hans Henselman, 1930–1931. Courtesy of the Yale Collection of American Literature, Beinecke Rare Book and Manuscript Library, Yale University.

and has been occasionally revived in French and English novels.[23] Whatever its permutations in the course of time, the roman à clef has always been marked by its restricted appeal to social formations that resemble or imitate an aristocracy, not least among them the aristocracy of sensibility that made up the wealthy bohemia surrounding H.D. and Bryher, an elite whose circulation among the "right" circles was itself the clef to a code of personal and autobiographical references. Which is why, no doubt, H.D. published only three of her twelve novels in the course of her lifetime: to anyone outside the inner circle, they were hardly of interest. Her prose fiction, as she herself may have realized, testified to "the peculiarly modern mix of the egotism of artistic ambition and the vanity of upper-class leisure."[24]

Recent critics, it is true, have tended to view H.D.'s use of the roman à clef differently. According to Susan Stanford Friedman, H.D. turned to the roman à clef because it was a "marginal prose genre."[25] It is accurate, of course, to characterize the roman à clef as "marginal," insofar as its insistent topicality seems to violate universalist norms of aesthetic value; yet, however inadvertently, her usage also suggests that we view H.D.'s employment of this genre within the context of Friedman's larger thesis that H.D. developed a "modernism of the margins," which she defines as "a modernism based on an identification with those left out of the cultural mainstream."[26] More broadly, Friedman argues that H.D.'s work "expressed a progressive politics originating in an exploration of the power structures underlying the personal," a politics that evolved in the course of her response to two kinds of cultural experience. "In the black experience . . . epitomized by Robeson, she found an eloquent mirror for her own marginality, her sense of spiritual exile and alienation." Further, "her involvement with psychoanalysis carried with it a profound identification with Jews." H.D. consistently displayed "sensitivity" and developed an "identification with Otherness." Thus, we are left to assume, her choice of a "marginal prose genre" such as the roman à clef was only another aspect of her "identification with all the others who have been 'dispersed and scattered' by the forces of history: Blacks, Jews, Indians, homosexuals and lesbians, women, even artists."[27] Such an implication, while appealing to current moral concerns, is achieved largely through an abuse of literary terminology and history, an abuse that conflates a quintessentially aristocratic genre with the politics of egalitarianism implied by the rhetoric of "marginality." It is a maneuver accomplished by an intellectual sleight of hand and a distortion of literary history. The roman à clef can be called a "marginal" genre only in a form of perverse logic that would enable us to describe the palace of Versailles as "marginal housing."

The effort to revaluate the work of H.D. by assimilating it to current interest in "the marginal" and "the other" has transformed not only the accessible canon of her own works but how specific poems within that canon interact with others in the shaping of various larger canons, such as those of modern poetry or American literature. Textbooks and anthologies, the mundane forms of any canon, are the principal agents and registrars of these changes, and doubtless the weather vane of the anthology is *The Norton Anthology of American Literature*. Although not one poem by H.D. had been included in editions prior to 1985, more recently her work has been given relatively extensive representation, comprising six poems (seven in the third edition of 1989) and sixteen selections from *The Walls Do Not Fall*. The excerpts from a long poem are the editorial manifestation of recent claims that H.D.'s best work is found in the later "epics," even as the selection of earlier poems follows the touchstones established by recent revisionists. Notable, for example, is the inclusion of the poem "Leda," a work omitted from the 1957 *Selected Poems,* the works in which may have been chosen by H.D. herself, as well as the 1983 *Collected Poems,* which were selected by Louis Martz. Yet the poem has been highly praised more recently for its "critique of classical tradition from a woman's perspective," and accordingly it is now included.[28] Accompanying the poems are introductory comments that furnish students with explicit instructions to read largely for content: the "essential dilemma" explored in H.D.'s work is "how to be a woman poet speaking in a world where women were spoken for and about by men." Biographical information is presented in a similar vein: H.D.'s relationship with Bryher, we learn, "developed first as a love affair and then into a lifelong friendship," and "with Bryher's financial help she raised her daughter and cared for her ailing mother." What emerges is a sentimental portrait of solidarity based on gender, solidarity disturbed only by the occasional intrusions of men: "Freud and H.D.," the editor notes, "had many arguments, especially over the destiny of women, for H.D. by this time had become a feminist." Bibliographical information, in contrast, is dispensed very sparingly. "During the thirties," we are informed, "H.D. worked mostly in prose forms and composed several autobiographical pieces (some of which remain unpublished)"; nothing is said about the private editions, the subsidized printing, or the publication of poems in journals owned and edited by Bryher.[29]

In such remarks, the introductory comments replicate a certain one-sidedness perceptible in the recent surge of critical writing about H.D., a tendency to assess her poetry wholly in terms of its subject matter and content and to exclude questions of aesthetic value plainly relevant to a discussion of poetry.

Typical in this regard is Friedman's landmark essay "Who Buried H.D.? A Poet, Her Critics, and Her Place in 'The Literary Tradition,'" which issued the earliest and most significant call for a revisionary view of H.D.'s achievement. Friedman's goal is to advance new evaluative claims about the quality of H.D.'s poetry: she urges that "her poetry is magnificent," adding that "her poems captivate, enchant, and enlighten me." In explaining this evaluation, Friedman says only that her view is "single" and "necessarily subjective," pointedly resisting pressures for a more critical account of her captivation, enchantment, and enlightenment, and tartly dismissing "the thorny question of what makes literature 'great,' who determines the standards for greatness, or even whether the literary reputation of an author has much of anything to do with genuine genius." And when she adduces specific works to substantiate her evaluation, she praises them wholly in terms of their content: a passage from *Winter Love* is important because it portrays a "woman's anguish"; the long poems *Helen in Egypt* and *Hermetic Definition* are notable because they offer "poetic arguments for a belief . . . [that] the dominance of masculine values has brought destruction and suffering, like the catastrophe of the two world wars."[30] And in a more recent discussion of H.D.'s earlier poems, Friedman pursues the same style of evaluation. The early poems are "brilliant" because they "reveal central conflicts in her identity as a woman poet"—note the same claim that appears in the *Norton Anthology*—and on this basis we can assess the individual works. The poem "Eurydice" deserves recognition because it "present[s] a defiant Eurydice who angrily condemns her husband"; the poem "Helen" is noteworthy because it is "*about* the paralyzing misogyny at the heart of male worship of woman's beauty"; the poem "Cassandra" is praiseworthy for being "*about* gynophobia"; and the poem "Demeter" merits our attention because it "carries lesbian overtones" (emphases added). The poet's crowning achievement is "Leda," published in 1919, for it "reverses centuries of literary and artistic tradition," insofar as "there is no rape or violence in H.D.'s poem, in which the red swan and the gold lily commingle in the gold-red sunset, 'Where tide and river meet.'"[31]

Still, one may wonder whether such judgments do not privilege a constricted range of poetic and intellectual possibility. If H.D.'s "Leda" lacks the power of a poem such as Yeats's "Leda and the Swan," perhaps it is because the latter is so forthright in confronting the sheer otherness of violence, responding to a richer, more contradictory range of experience and thereby creating a more dialogical understanding of alterity. Consider, for example, the disparate tonalities articulated in the syntactic range of Yeats's poem: the omission of any verb in the famous opening phrase ("A sudden blow") evokes an event with no discernible agent and places the reader in a dilemma analogous to that of Leda, who must decipher the source and meaning of an alien, overwhelming experience; subsequently a magisterial sequence of verb tenses and temporal adverbs is unfolded to make the transient event reverberate in tragedy and beauty of immense proportions.[32] A similar dissonance is encompassed by the poem's linguistic texture: no sooner does Yeats invoke the diction of conventional eroticism, with the phrase "her thighs caressed," than he transmutes it into an experience of alien ecstasy: "by the dark webs." His word choice emphasizes the encounter of the pathetically human ("her thighs") and the indifferent other ("the dark webs"), probing discordant extremes of experience. H.D.'s poem, in contrast, explores a terrain of sensibility that seems more restricted: its verbs are all in the present or present perfect tense, emphasizing a flow of erotic pleasure that lingers into the poem's discursive present (the time of the reader's reading); and in her poem the verb "caress" serves only to reinforce this motif of prolonged languor, evoking little more than conventional tenderness: "the level ray of sun-beam / has caressed / the lily." And whereas Yeats depicts the swan in terms that signal its radical otherness, emphasizing the "bill" and "dark webs," H.D. uses a vocabulary that humanizes and softens its alterity, as in "the red swan . . . uncurls his coral feet." H.D.'s preference for a phrase such as "coral feet," rather than "dark webs," assimilates the alien beast to human prettiness, a tendency only accentuated by the adjective "coral," which decoratively echoes the unvoiced guttural (or hard *c*) of "uncurled" and drapes the bestial with a gauze of tintinnabulation. And Yeats portrays "the great wings beating still / above the staggering girl," as if to underscore the incongruity of divine power and human pathos; H.D. avoids such potential discordance by turning the woman into a "day-lily" that "rests / beneath soft fluttering of red swan wings." The emphasis on "soft fluttering," like the earlier "caressing" of the "sun-beam," reinforces a single note of tender eroticism, the pleasures of which are extended into a discursive present of infinite leisure—as if to incorporate the reader into the economy of patronage itself, at least as H.D. experienced it. Here is a monological texture that differs from the pluralism embraced by Yeats's poem, which encompasses disparate and often powerfully opposed tonalities.

H.D.'s "Leda" has been praised because it lacks "rape or violence," a deliberate omission that "reverses centuries of literary and artistic tradition, which usually features Zeus in the shape of a swan raping Leda."[33] Such accounts rehearse an increasingly familiar pattern of narrative in professional literary studies: "centuries of literary and artistic tradition" coalesce into a uniform history of cultural oppression that is "reversed" at the stroke of a pen. But the cultural tradition may be more complex than such accounts allow, and in crucial respects it may suggest a narrative that is significantly different. As has long been known, the iconology depicting the story of Leda and the swan was produced in fairly distinct periods with corresponding styles of treatment. From late antiquity there are bas-reliefs, gems, terra-cottas, lamps, and scarabs that show Leda standing as she gently presses the swan in her thighs or caresses its neck, and some show her reclining and clothed, pressing the swan to her bosom. It is the latter image that was recovered and reformulated during the Renaissance in a series of well-known paintings by Leonardo, Michelangelo, Correggio, Tintoretto, and Veronese. The setting is often a *locus amoenus;* the rape is aestheticized into seduction or, in Correggio's case, turned into a bathing party; Leda is elaborately coiffured and caresses the swan in graceful and stylized gestures. Little indeed suggests "rape and violence" in these works from the mainstream of the Western pictorial tradition, and even that little vanishes in still later works, such as the elegant sculpture of Jean Thierry or the graceful erotic bronze of Raymond Sabourand. In the mid–nineteenth century when new interest in the Leda story arose, fear of its sexuality and bestiality once more ensured that visual and plastic representations of the tale firmly adhered to decorative conventions. When the symbolist painter Gustave Moreau depicted the incident, in a work that Yeats probably knew well, he presented not a bestial rape but a sacred marriage, not violence but hieratic arabesque, not conflict but evasion. In short, as Ian Fletcher concludes his comprehensive survey of the iconological tradition surrounding the story: "Rape is found in the remoter myths and in Post-Yeatsian art, but not in the sources that were probably available to the poet."[34] It is Yeats, in other words, who "reverses centuries of literary and artistic tradition." It is H.D., instead, who continues and prolongs the decorative aestheticization of the story that has dominated both the pictorial and the literary heritage.

When critics praise H.D.'s "Leda" so highly for shunning "rape or violence" in its presentation, doubtless they intend to commend the poem for expressing attitudes that are socially or didactically useful, *utile* in the most traditional formulation. Their aims derive from a venerable tradition of criticism emphasizing the moral dimensions of literary study and the ethical effects of specific works. Yet in pursuing this emphasis with provincial excess, one may lose sight of other truths no less important: that the aesthetic character of a literary work is not extraneous but essential to questions of its social or ethical effects; that the morality of poetry is not exhausted in subject matter ("about gynophobia") or content but also resides in details of syntax, rhythm, diction, rhyme, and musicality, where an intangible yet perceptible integrity is also nurtured and sustained; and that much of the ethical character even of "content" consists not in how this accords with political positions selected a priori but in complex relations binding content and style to audiences and occasions, to interpretive communities in contingent circumstances—settings registered precisely in the sociomaterial instance of the work.

If recent assessments of H.D. diminish the possibilities of poetic experience and constrict the range of values that poetry can accommodate, they may be only echoing a habit of H.D. herself. For in the poem "Leda," when the speaker longs for "no more regret / nor old deep memories / to mar the bliss," many readers will sense not only a certain vacuity—no doubt exacerbated by the rhyme of "bliss" with "kiss"—that recurs in H.D.'s poems early and late, they will also detect the deeper intellectual limitations exposed by the wish itself.[35] Those limitations, in turn, are inseparable from a more fundamental weakness that bears directly on the problems of audience and evaluation of her work: for H.D.'s is poetry that flatters its audience, that gratifies its readers' wish to believe that knowledge comes without pain, and transcendence without suffering—that encounters with divinity can be as pleasant as "a kiss," and yet bring "no regret . . . to mar the bliss." This impulse to indulge her audience, to oblige it with comforting truths, is what lies at the heart of her early triumph as the most popular of all the Imagists and her subsequent success as a coterie writer, the kind of writer who thrives by gratifying an inner circle. And it is especially evident, I think, throughout the long poem *Trilogy*, in H.D.'s ambivalent use of the pronoun "we," a usage that accommodates any potential reader or embraces only the initiates who already share the poet's belief in a heady brew of astrology, Tarot cards, and séances. When she defines the status and function of writers in the crisis of the modern world, articulating the task of her own poem, she writes:

> we [are the] authentic relic,
> bearers of the secret wisdom,
> living remnant
> of the inner band
> of the sanctuaries' initiate

Readers are encouraged to choose the most obliging interpretation, and to regard H.D. as the mystagogue who leads "us" to secret yet comfortable wisdom, insight that demands nothing and threatens no one; few readers, after all, will want to disagree that "we" are the "authentic relic" or "the living remnant / of the inner band." Yet as one critic has written: "Only poor poets flatter their audience interminably; only negligible ones play always to the reader's prejudices."[36]

Ultimately, H.D.'s confidence betrays the complacency of the coterie in its assurance that "we" can rest secure in the sense of our difference from "you others."

> So, in our secretive, sly way,
> we are proud and chary
>
> of companionship with you others

This way of using pronouns stems, no doubt, from H.D.'s twenty years' participation in the coterie that surrounded her and Bryher. And its assurance is only echoed in the ease with which H.D. claims privileged access to unequivocal truth:

> so let us search the old highways
>
> for the true-rune, the right-spell,
> recover old values;

Or again:

> let us entreat
> that he, by his tau-cross,
>
> invoke the true-magic,
> lead us back to the one-truth

H.D. never really doubts that "we" can find "the true-rune" or "the true-magic," or even "the one-truth," a realm of absolute verity signaled by the definite article. It is, again, the confidence of the coterie, assured that its privileged vision—at once portentous and yet accommodatingly vague—is also a vision of totality, "*the* one-truth."

Oddly, in spite of extensive evidence of this totalizing, if not totalitarian, vision, recent criticism of *Trilogy* has deftly converted the poem into a hymn to "a poetics, and a politics, of openness."[37] For Alicia Ostriker, this openness is articulated in H.D.'s description of a May-tree, in *Tribute to the Angels:*

> yet no trick of the pen or the brush
>
> could capture that impression;
> music could do nothing with it,

nothing whatever; what I mean is—
but you have seen for yourself

In Ostriker's view, the apostrophe to the reader ("but you have seen for your-self") constitutes a break "in the history of meditative poetry," for "no poet before H.D. invites us to trust not a still point outside of ourselves, transcend-ing this world, but our own interiority."[38] Another critic, citing the same passage, concludes that H.D. shapes "a new community" that "sweeps away" the "old hierarchies, linearities, and teleologies of male interpretation of experi-ence," creating a brave new world in which "Divinity . . . is immanent in the experience of us all," one that differs radically from the "God [who] is outside or inaccessible to Eliot [in *Four Quartets*]."[39] Reading such claims, one cannot but recall the mystical poetry of the German baroque tradition, the great lyrics of the early Goethe, Wordsworth's "Intimations of Immortality" or *The Pre-lude,* as well as the collected poems of Emerson—surely works that "invite us to trust . . . our own interiority" and ponder the "Divinity . . . immanent in the experience of us all." Even so, one must concede that these claims do indeed describe an essential element of H.D.'s thought, merely endowing it with pseudohistorical uniqueness. For H.D. really does believe in the nebulous and benevolent divinity of the self described by her admirers; she really does believe, as one critic says, that the grace of vision is "free and joyous, and acceptance of the miracle certain, unavoidable."[40] She really does believe in a mix of bland notions from popular occultism and generalizations that denounce contempo-rary humanity in the abstract and yet promise everyone that he or she is assured of becoming a god. Yet are these ideas, even viewed only as "content" apart from questions of aesthetic value, truly the best that have been thought and said in the poetry of this century? Many, I suspect, will find room for doubt. And yet if we assume that values are not intrinsic but are constituted in relation to specific interpretive communities in limiting historical circumstances, then the ques-tion of how these ideas have come to be so highly regarded becomes urgent.

At the level of critical theory, evaluation of the new H.D. has pursued its aims through contradictory assumptions about the possibility of objectivity in political and aesthetic judgment. Friedman's defense of her view of H.D.'s poems is telling in this regard. For it might be objected that her readings are exactly that—readings, interpretations, perhaps partial or limited construc-tions rather than full or objective representations of the issue in question. Friedman, however, insists on their correctness. She castigates those who have failed to perceive that H.D.'s later works articulate a belief that "the dominance of masculine values has brought destruction and suffering," and she urges: "Let no one argue at this point that as long as all reading is subjective one person's theories are as valid as another's." The remark implies a curious double standard: apparently when we discuss a work's political values or content, it is illegitimate to defend our claims by appeals to subjectivity; yet when we discuss poetic or aesthetic value, as in Friedman's view that H.D.'s "poetry is magnificent," it suffices to invoke "my single, necessarily subjective perspective." Friedman never offers an argument in support of this curious assumption. She does, however, offer reasons why appeals to subjectivity are inadmissible when we consider questions of content: in such cases, appeals to subjectivity can veil "prejudiced political and cultural categories," such as "a misogynist set of psychoanalytic presuppositions," and lead to "distortions of a literary work" that "have real consequences for the reputations of many writers—those of different races, nationalities, classes, and . . . sex."[41]

Paradoxically, this claim assumes that we really can achieve undistorted or objective truths at the level of "political and cultural categories," whereas when we assess the aesthetic properties of cultural works, it seems, we can only record "single, necessarily subjective" impressions. The discrepancy, however, is more apparent than real; it is part of a rhetorical stratagem in which the motifs of subjective impression and objective argument are separated only in order to reinforce each other, the more effectively for their apparent logical contradiction. The local blindness of aesthetic subjectivity is strategically placed only to guarantee its obverse—universal and undistorted understanding of "the political or cultural categories" that inform a work and its interpretation. And yet it is self-evident that the insights Friedman ultimately achieves are little more than commonplaces in current academic literary studies, claims that are historically limited, recent in origin, and hardly the subject of universal agreement. It is, in other words, largely through the mystification of aesthetic value, through its removal to a realm of subjectivity beyond discussion or debate, that such criticism erases the historical and contingent nature of its own assessments.

At the level of critical practice, the new H.D. has become a canonical figure for the kinds of values that have earned the opprobrious label of "political correctness" largely by purifying her work of the material complexity in which it was formed, a task concretely accomplished through the neglect of bibliographical, textual, and editorial considerations in assessing her work's genesis and development. To date there is not a single critical edition of a work by H.D.; little awareness that the texts currently in circulation may differ in important ways from those that prevailed in her lifetime; and scarcely any discussion of the bibliographical codes embodied in the transmissive history of her work. Omitting such matters, criticism of the new H.D. erases from view the dynamics of coterie publishing that prevailed in the original setting of her work's production, dynamics that pose resistances to the aims and ambitions of recent criticism and exert constraints on the ease with which H.D. can be assimilated to the egalitarian tenor of the present. Recent criticism of H.D., in constituting the authority of its own interpreting self, must also construct a cultural other of textual and more genuinely social criticism. Only then is such criticism free to construct its accounts without hindrance, to bypass the socio-material instance of the work and the heterogeneous histories it encodes, to overlook the communicative conditions informing the work's production and transmission. Only thus can a poet of the coterie be turned into the victim of malevolent neglect, the roman à clef be transformed into a "marginal" genre, a tradition of decorative aestheticization become "centuries" of "rape and violence," a commonplace of late and derivative romanticism be called a novelty "in the history of meditative poetry." Subtly and yet surely, the rhetorical economy of such criticism insinuates its own form of flattery: only "we," it assures us, have the acumen and understanding to appreciate truly the work of H.D.; only "we" are the "authentic relic" and "the living remnant of the inner band," a notion that gratifies our own pretensions to new insight even as it transforms us into members of the discursive coterie constructed around the new H.D. But only poor critics flatter their audience interminably.

It is not, of course, to be deplored that the works of H.D. have recently been transmitted in ways inconsistent or incommensurable with the logic of their original production. All works, in the course of time, must move from some specific sociohistorical matrix into others that are structured by different sets of values and concepts, different backgrounds of practice and knowledge in which those are integrated. Yet if our exchange with works from the past is not to be unduly curtailed by the intellectual preoccupations and modes of the present, we must employ a wide range of critical stratagems to keep us aware of the historical discontinuities that are not impediments to but the preconditions of our engagement with the past. Women's studies, in the course of the past three decades, has recognized just that and patiently reconstructed the material and discursive conditions that shaped—maimed, one might say—feminine experiences in different class and social settings. But revisionist critics of H.D. may betray that heritage when they offer an oversimplified historical account in which gender has been unilaterally reified, dissevered from the material conditions and social relations in which it acquires its significance.

When the *Norton Anthology* advises readers that H.D. quarreled with Freud because "by this time [she] had become a feminist," it encourages us to conflate our sympathies for contemporary feminism with the assessment of H.D.'s literary achievement—to transform the question of H.D.'s work into a referendum on current feminism. But they are not the same. To reject the claims that revisionist critics have advanced for H.D.'s work does not entail that one reject or undervalue feminism, past or present. Further, as a matter of historical accuracy, it is by no means clear that H.D. "had become a feminist" by 1933. In the course of a long life, H.D. chose not to participate in any of the numerous organizations, British, American, or international, devoted to advancing women's issues, nor did she choose to take up those issues in her nonfiction prose. Similarly, despite receiving massive gifts of eight thousand pounds (in 1933) and more than twenty thousand pounds (in 1945) from Bryher, H.D. also chose not to make a single donation in support of feminist groups or causes.[42] True, she did indulge in mystical speculations about the maternal; but whether those constituted a contribution to feminism is very much an open question.

Likewise, it is also not clear that H.D. was especially responsive to the plight of Jews under the encroaching menace of Nazism. Though she evinced concern over Freud, her own analyst, there is little to suggest that her concern became more generalized. Bryher, it is quite true, developed a genuine appreciation of the Jewish intellectual heritage in German-speaking culture, an outgrowth of her interest in psychoanalysis; she actively helped Walter Benjamin leave Berlin in 1933, and she used her money and influence on his behalf during the difficult period from September 1939 to June 1940. But in the extant correspondence among Bryher, Benjamin, Sylvia Beach, and Adrienne Monnier—Beach and Monnier acted as agents for Bryher's gifts to Benjamin, whose plight they had brought to her attention—the name of H.D. is not mentioned.[43] The moral credit for these actions, which is real, must go to Bryher, not H.D.

Finally, there is the claim that H.D.'s sexual orientation enabled her to achieve probing insight into the experience of subordinate cultures, insight that enhances the aesthetic richness of her oeuvre and endows it with emancipatory significance. But H.D.'s identity, like anyone's, was a composite and complex affair, and such claims overemphasize one aspect of her identity at the expense of others that were equally or more important, in particular her role as the recipient of lavish and virtually limitless patronage. Further, despite the appeal that such claims make to left-inclined sentiment, they may harbor much that is ethically and politically regressive. For if it is true that the emergence of the public sphere is characterized by norms of reasoned discourse in which arguments, not the status or identity of participants, are to be decisive, then such straightforward appeals to sexual identity may signal a worrisome withdrawal from procedural protocols that are a precondition for genuine cultural dialogue. Aesthetic rationality is still a matter of basing judgment on reasons, not identity.

No one, of course, can predict how critics of the future will regard the new H.D. or the evaluations of her work that have been offered in recent years. I suspect that they will come to recognize that the circumstances in which H.D. worked ensured that many of her works were poorly known and consequently undervalued by critics of the 1960s and 1970s; that the massive publication of her works in the 1980s made it possible for critics to assess a range and variety of writings far richer than previously supposed, among them some gems such as the *The Hedgehog* and her reminiscences of Freud; but that the new publications also made clear that previous evaluations of H.D.'s poetry were largely accurate in finding that she had written a few short poems with astringent charms in her early years, and that later she had written longer works whose limited insights and impoverished command of diction, rhythm, and syntax left them irreparably flawed. She was the author of a few minor classics in prose and verse, and she was a figure of interest for the life of her times as experienced by privileged bohemia. But the genuine limitations discernible in her work as a whole tell us much about the risks inherent in the modernist culture of patronage, the culture that sustained but may also have ruined her career, encouraging her to indulge in the evasive complacency of coterie poetics and to shun a more genuine, more probing engagement with her contemporaries.

Epilogue

H.D., ultimately, became the kind of poet that Pound might have become had he chosen to pursue the course of ingratiating himself with Pamela Tennant, Lady Glenconner. But that was not to be—for a while, at least. Prodded by the exploits of Marinetti, consumed by his desire for public attention, and impelled by his passionate conviction that the arts are a serious social concern, Pound pursued a very different career. Out of its discrepancies and contradictions he was able, for a brief period, to fashion a public persona and a jagged style of poetry and critical prose that distilled his restless aspirations, and those of a significant part of his age. Equally important, he came to play a key role in shaping a fragile institutional structure in which those aspirations could find voice, a social and discursive space that was half withdrawn from, yet also half nestled within, the larger culture of which it was a part. Patronage was a crucial institution within that structure, and in the end Pound succumbed to its illusory allure, caught by the glimmer refracted from the grand myth that the Renaissance was the achievement of a small group of elite spirits, the patrons and artists mysteriously charged with the task of giving birth to a new culture, a myth that Pound would elaborate and project upon the phantasmic screen of Mussolini and Italian Fascism. Paradoxically, as his allegiance to Fascism and his desire for social transformation deepened, his assimilation of these to an obsessive anti-Semitism resulted in his own isolation, effectively cutting him off from genuine dialogue with his contemporaries. Pound's poetic and critical voice sank into a hoarse monologue, leading to the unremitting tedium of the poetry and prose written between roughly 1930 and 1945. The notorious radio broadcasts of 1941–1942 hark back to Pound's aspirations and experiences with the emerging mass media in 1912–1915, but they do so in the form of macabre parody: his words echo in a shrill emptiness that bears witness only to an utter lack of community and mutual exchange.

In different but complementary ways, the careers of Pound and H.D. attest to the risks that attended the modernist creation of a counter-realm to the public sphere. In H.D.'s case, it led to a withdrawal from genuine social exchange, a retreat into the complacency of the coterie and solipsistic reverie; in Pound's case, to an attempt to bypass social dialogue through a direct but wholly imaginary rapport with the charismatic figure of the ideal patron, a figure whose person is transformed into a spurious substitute for the body politic. They are exemplary fables of modernism's fate.

Patronage could nurture literary modernism only to the threshold of its confrontation with a wider public; beyond that point, it would require critical approbation and some measure of commercial viability to ratify its status as a significant idiom. The modernists understood that. They were shrewd in turning the early mass media to account, adept at melding together workable niches into a sustainable submarket, skillful in shaping an institutional structure that, though extraordinarily fragile, enabled them to pursue their aims. They entertained no illusions about the increasingly pervasive effects of the commodification of culture, though if Joyce is any example, they could discern the traces of human dignity to be found even in cultural detritus. But they also entertained no illusions about utopian alternatives; to live completely outside market relations was no more possible than breathing without air. One could temporize, hold them at bay, gain time—but no more. When the moment of reckoning came, as inevitably it must in a capitalist order, modernism found pragmatic means to marshal those relations in its own behalf, and it invoked the operations of the market as confirmation, or justification, of its claims to aesthetic dignity—eroding, however unintentionally, the status of that dignity itself.

Modernism is commonly depicted as an intransigent defense of the aesthetic, a conceptual category that, in turn, is routinely dismissed as a form of "bourgeois ideology" that was jettisoned by the historical avant-garde and today can evoke no more than a sardonic smile from their postmodernist successors. But that account omits too much. It slights the probing engagement with popular culture apparent in the work of figures as diverse as Joyce, Marinetti, Eliot, and even to some extent Pound. It loses sight of the uneasiness and ambiguity always embedded in the notion of the aesthetic, that equivocal synthesis of the timeless and the contingent, universal and particular, sensual and contemplative.[1] It fails to perceive that the aesthetic, already in the early years of this century, had become a category that was tenuous, eroded by the increasing penetration of market relations in every aspect of life, penetration that creates a tacit but pervasive consensus that the market is the sole arbiter and guarantor of value, and chafed by the theoretical assaults of the avant-garde in the wake of Marinetti and the Futurists. And it fails to acknowledge the extent to which modernist institutional structures themselves embodied divided allegiances. The owners of the Sunwise Turn could never agree on whether to turn a profit or proceed with the support of patronage, just as no one, including its owners, could decide whether the *Dial* was "a business house" or "a patron of literature." Even patronage, with its seemingly ideal realization of a noncommodified mode of cultural production, was so uncertain of its aims and status that it had to disguise its activity as investment, conceal its largesse under the pretext of royalties for books that never earned any, or pretend to make payments for manuscripts, editorial services, and artistic consultation. Only rarely, when justified by special circumstances or occasions, did it assume the form of outright gift.

The questions posed by modernism, the profound changes that it registered in the relations among authors, readers, publishers, critics, and a common culture, have not vanished. They reappear in contemporary debates about funding for the National Endowment for the Arts, the current crisis in academic and trade publishing, a crisis that includes the increasing erosion of meaningful distinctions between them, and the surge of unprecedented skepticism about the function and value of literary scholarship, much of it sadly justified. Whether those issues can be meaningfully assessed at a time when the public sphere has suffered massive degradation, when sound bites prevail over critical analysis and public discussions are staged as sporting events in which "winners" and "losers" receive their scores from media pundits, remains a legitimate question. But it is certain that our contribution to those debates will continue to be negligible as long as our dominant history of twentieth-century culture continues to describe modernism or the avant-garde as a mythical age of insistent subversion or pure opposition to commodity culture, futile in the long run, or fruitful only insofar as it anticipates our own more enlightened engagements with popular culture, epitomized under the rubric of postmodernism.

Modernism, in its resolute contradictoriness, may have more to tell us, even if it has less to sell us. We cannot, of course, return to the past. Upper-middle-class confidence in the integrity and sacral functions of the aesthetic is no longer as robust as it was in the age of Harriet Weaver or John Quinn, and it never will be. The institutional configurations of the arts and the media have grown more complicated and complex than they were at the century's beginning. More important, modernism itself has entered into our common culture, changing the ways in which we experience ourselves and our place in that culture. For cultural concepts, such as modernism, interact with cultural practices, exhibiting what Anthony Giddens has called the "double hermeneutic," or what Ian Hacking has termed "the looping effect," spiraling into and out of a common culture, reconstructing both that culture and themselves.[2] Although there is no straightforward way in which the accumulation of cultural knowledge leads to better or more rational modes of cultural production, one may hope that a more probing concept of modernism, one that acknowledges its institutional structures, their contradictoriness, and their ambiguous role in its vertiginous development, may help to forestall our tendency to recur to a mythical and misleading cultural genealogy of the present.

Modernism, poised between the era of journalism that had been and the age of the university that was about to be, between an elite bourgeois culture that was passing and a middlebrow ethos and aesthetics that was already arriving, between a world of timeless aesthetics and a media universe of endless, factitious fashion, was an enterprise that was perennially on the brink, always ambiguous—ambiguity that may itself account for modernism's continuous pressure on the nature of representation in art, its unremitting stress on the means by which illusions and likenesses are produced. That ambiguity replicates itself today. Looking back at modernism, we seem to scrutinize a perplexing, even haunted image of ourselves, uncertain how much that resemblance is due to likeness, how much to illusion. We are still enthralled by the modernists, and still so deeply in their debt, because they gave us so much of both.

Notes

Works frequently cited have been identified by the following abbreviations:

MANUSCRIPT COLLECTIONS

BIUL, PM.*1, 2, 3*	Bloomington, Indiana University, Lilly Library, *Pound Manuscripts 1, 2,* and *3.*
NHYB, *DP*	New Haven, Yale University, Beinecke Rare Book and Manuscript Library, The *Dial* Papers (Yale Collection of American Literature, Mss. 34)
NHYB, *PP*	New Haven, Yale University, Beinecke Rare Book and Manuscript Library, Ezra Pound Papers (Yale Collection of American Literature, Mss. 43)
PUF, *BP*	Princeton University, Firestone Library, Sylvia Beach Papers
NYPL, *QP*	New York Public Library, Manuscript Division, John Quinn Papers

BOOKS

C	Ezra Pound, *The Cantos,* tenth printing (New York: New Directions, 1986)

DMW Jane Lidderdale and Mary Nicholson, *Dear Miss Weaver: Harriet Shaw Weaver, 1876–1961* (New York: Viking Press, 1970)

EPB Donald Gallup, *Ezra Pound: A Bibliography* (Charlottesville: University Press of Virginia, 1983)

EPPP *Ezra Pound's Poetry and Prose*, 11 vols., Lea Baechler, A. Walton Litz, and James Longenbach, eds. (New York: Garland, 1991)

LOTSE 1 *Letters of T. S. Eliot*, vol. 1, *1891–1922*, Valerie Eliot, ed. (New York: Harcourt Brace, 1988)

MNY B. L. Reid, *The Man from New York: John Quinn and His Friends* (Oxford: Oxford University Press, 1968)

SLPQ *The Selected Letters of Ezra Pound to John Quinn*, Timothy Materer, ed. (New York: New Directions, 1991)

TSEB Donald Gallup, *T. S. Eliot: A Bibliography*, rev. ed. (New York: Harcourt Brace, 1969)

INTRODUCTION

1. K. J. Fielding, ed., *The Speeches of Charles Dickens* (Oxford: Clarendon Press, 1960), 154, 157.

2. Andreas Huyssen, *After the Great Divide: Modernism, Mass Culture, Postmodernism* (Bloomington: Indiana University Press, 1986), 47, 53.

3. Ibid., 61.

4. Ibid., 59.

5. These episodes are discussed in more detail in Chapter 1, where full references are given.

6. Terry Eagleton, "Capitalism, Modernism, and Postmodernism," in David Lodge, ed., *Modern Criticism and Theory: A Reader* (London: Longman, 1988), 392.

7. Stephen Greenblatt, *Renaissance Self-Fashioning: From More to Shakespeare* (Chicago: University of Chicago Press, 1980); Jane Tompkins, *Sensational Designs: The Cultural Work of American Fiction, 1790–1860* (New York: Oxford University Press), 1985.

8. Marjorie Perloff, *The Futurist Moment: Avant-Garde, Avant-Guerre, and the Language of Rupture* (Chicago: University of Chicago Press, 1986), xviii.

9. Peter Bürger, *Theory of the Avant-Garde,* trans. Michael Shaw (Minneapolis: University of Minnesota Press, 1984), 49.

10. Jürgen Habermas, *The Structural Transformation of the Public Sphere: An Inquiry into a Category of Bourgeois Society,* trans. Thomas Burger (Cambridge: MIT Press, 1989).

11. Jürgen Habermas, "Further Reflections on the Public Sphere," in Craig Calhoun, ed., *Habermas and the Public Sphere* (Cambridge: MIT Press, 1992), 437.

12. For a survey of recent debate, see Calhoun, ed., *Habermas and the Public Sphere.*

13. Jeremy Treglown, "Literary History and the *Lit. Supp.*," *Yearbook of English Studies* 16 (1986): 132–149.

14. See the excellent survey by Theodore Ziolkowski, "The Institutional Approach," in his *German Romanticism and Its Institutions* (Princeton: Princeton University Press, 1990), 3–17. See also Austin Warren, in René Wellek and Austin Warren, *Theory of Literature* (New York: Harcourt Brace), 216; Stanley Fish, *Is There a Text in This Class? The Authority*

of Interpretive Communities (Cambridge: Harvard University Press, 1980), 331–332; Harry Levin, "Literature as an Institution," *Accent* 6 (Spring 1946): 159–168; Frank Kermode, "Institutional Control of Interpretation," *Salmagundi* 43 (1979), 216; Gerald Graff, *Professing Literature: An Institutional History* (Chicago: University of Chicago Press, 1987); and Leslie Fiedler, "Literature as an Institution: The View from 1980," in Houston Baker, ed., *English Literature: Opening Up the Canon* (Baltimore: Johns Hopkins University Press, 1981), 73–91. For a more recent discussion of institutions within this tradition, see Herbert Lindenberger, *The History in Literature: On Value, Genre, Institutions* (New York: Columbia University Press, 1990), xv–xvi, 131–210.

15. Peter Bürger, *Vermittlung—Rezeption—Funktion: Ästhetische Theorie und Methodologie der Literaturwissenschaft* (Frankfurt: Suhrkamp, 1979), 182–183. See also Peter Uwe Hohendahl, *The Institution of Criticism* (Ithaca: Cornell University Press, 1982), 11–43.

16. See Ziolkowski, *German Romanticism and Its Institutions*, 10–13.

17. Several works have recently taken up some of the questions examined in this study, not to furnish an institutional portrait of modernism, but with special reference to the marketplace. See Ian Willison, Warwick Gould, and Warren Chernaik, eds., *Modernist Writers and the Marketplace* (New York: St. Martin's Press, 1996); Kevin Dettmar and Stephen Watt, eds., *Marketing Modernisms: Self-Promotion, Canonization, and Rereading* (Ann Arbor: University of Michigan Press, 1996); Joyce Piell Wexler, *Who Paid for Modernism? Art, Money, and the Fiction of Conrad, Joyce, and Lawrence* (Fayetteville: University of Arkansas Press, 1997). Especially perceptive is Paul Delany, *Islands of Money: English Literature and the Financial Culture* (forthcoming, 1999). For a viewpoint extending back to an earlier period, see William G. Rowland, Jr., *Literature and the Marketplace: Romantic Writers and Their Audiences in Great Britain and the United States* (Lincoln: University of Nebraska Press, 1996). The two classic studies on the emergence and early evolution of authorship as a profession remain A. S. Collins, *Authorship in the Days of Johnson, Being a Study of the Relation Between Author, Patron, Publisher, and Public, 1726–1780* (London: George Routledge, 1927); and, in the U.S. context, William Charvat, *The Profession of Authorship in America, 1800–1870* (Columbus: Ohio State University Press, 1968), usefully complemented by Carl F. Kaestle et al., *Literacy in the United States: Readers and Reading Since 1880* (New Haven: Yale University Press, 1991). Two indispensable works on the Victorian period are Richard Altick, *The English Common Reader* (Chicago: University of Chicago Press, 1957); and John Sutherland, *Victorian Novelists and Publishers* (London: Athlone Press, 1976). Their counterpart in the visual arts is the landmark study by Cynthia and Harrison White, *Canvasses and Careers* (New York: Wiley, 1965). More recently, see Robert Jensen, *Marketing Modernism in Fin-de-Siècle Europe* (Princeton: Princeton University Press, 1994); Michael FitzGerald, *Making Modernism: Picasso and the Creation of the Market for Twentieth-Century Art* (New York: Farrar, Straus and Giroux, 1995); and Thomas Crow, *Modern Art in the Common Culture* (New Haven: Yale University Press, 1996).

18. Quoted in Miriam Fuchs, "Poet and Patron: Hart Crane and Otto Kahn," *Book Forum* 6, no. 1 (Spring 1982): 47.

19. Huyssen, *After the Great Divide*, 160; Charles Newman, *The Post-Modern Aura: The Act of Fiction in an Age of Inflation* (Evanston, Ill.: Northwestern University Press, 1985), 27–35.

CHAPTER 1: THE CREATION OF THE AVANT-GARDE

1. Peter Bürger, *Theory of the Avant-Garde,* trans. Michael Shaw (first edition in German, 1974; Minneapolis: University of Minnesota Press, 1984), 49.

2. For the Marxist view, see David Cottington, "What the Papers Say: Politics and Ideology in Picasso's Collages of 1912," *Art Journal* 47, no. 4 (Winter 1988): 350–359, here 358. See also his "Cubism, Aestheticism, Modernism," in William Rubin, ed., *Picasso and Braque: Pioneering Cubism,* exhibition catalogue, 2 vols. (1989; New York: Museum of Modern Art, 1992), 2:58–72. For a defense of avant-garde practice, see Christine Poggi, *In Defiance of Painting* (New Haven: Yale University Press, 1992), 128, 129. For a wide-ranging collection of recent approaches to this issue, see James Naremore and Patrick Brantlinger, eds., *Modernity and Mass Culture* (London: Routledge, 1992); and for a discussion influential in criticism on the visual arts, Thomas Crow, "Modernism and Mass Culture," in Benjamin Buchloh, Serge Guilbaut, and David Solkin, eds., *Modernism and Modernity* (Halifax: Press of the Nova Scotia College of Art and Design, 1983), 215–264. Crow argues that the social function of the avant-garde was to effect "a necessary brokerage between high and low [cultures]. In its selective appropriation from fringe mass culture, the avant-garde searches out areas of social practice which retain some vivid life in an increasingly administered and rationalized society" (253).

3. See, for example, Luciano De Maria, *La nascita dell'avanguardia: Saggi sul futurismo italiano* (Venice: Marsilio editori, 1986), the title of which announces his equation of the genesis of Futurism and the birth of the avant-garde. De Maria also mentions "l'avanguardia storica europea, di cui, a mio parere, il futurismo segna la nascita effettiva" (12); he urges that "Marinetti inventò, letteralmente, il prototipo dell'avanguardia storica" (15); and he notes, "Marinetti e compagni già gettavano le basi della prima autentica, codificata avanguardia europea" (31). An equally crucial role is assigned to Marinetti and Futurism by Marjorie Perloff in *The Futurist Moment* (Chicago: University of Chicago Press, 1986). And though Peter Bürger never mentions Futurism in his *Theory of the Avant-Garde,* he does place it alongside Dada and Surrealism as "eine der historischen Avant-gardebewegungen" in his "Einleitung" to *Surrealismus* (Darmstadt: Wissenschaftliche Buchgesellschaft, 1982), 6.

4. Both theses are forcefully argued by Marjorie Perloff in *The Poetics of Indeterminacy* (1981; reprint, Evanston: Northwestern University Press, 1983), where she shows Pound as a crucial figure in "the other tradition," a turn away from a symbolist aesthetic to one of collage and juxtaposition.

5. "Ezra Pound: His Metric and Poetry," in T. S. Eliot, *To Criticize the Critic* (New York: Farrar, Straus and Giroux, 1965), 175. The essay was originally published anonymously as an independent volume by Alfred Knopf in 1917; see *TSEB,* 24, A2.

6. Eliot's arrival in London is announced in Pound to Harriet Monroe, 22 September 1914, cited in Humphrey Carpenter, *A Serious Character: The Life of Ezra Pound* (Boston: Houghton Mifflin, 1988), 258; cf. Eliot to Conrad Aiken, 30 September 1914, in *LOTSE I,* 58–59.

7. Noel Stock, *The Life of Ezra Pound* (1970; reprint, Harmondsworth: Penguin, 1974), 144. All subsequent quotations from Stock are also from this page.

8. James Wilhelm, *Ezra Pound in London and Paris: 1908–1925* (University Park: Pennsylvania State University Press, 1990), 93–94. All subsequent quotations from Wilhelm are also from these pages.

9. D. D. Paige, ed., *Selected Letters of Ezra Pound* (1950; reprint, New York: New Directions, 1971), hereafter abbreviated as *SL*. See Ezra Pound to Harriet Monroe, January 1915, 49. Paige transcribes: "I wish [Vachel] Lindsay all possible luck but we're not really pulling the same way, though we both pull against entrenched senility." He omits the sentence that follows: "In reality, he is of the race of Marinetti." See also the letter that follows, Ezra Pound to Harriet Monroe, March 1915, 55, again discussing Vachel Lindsay. Paige transcribes: "I don't say he copies Mennetti; but he is with him, and his work is futurist." The correct reading for both letters is given, albeit in translation, in the Italian edition of Pound's letters: Aldo Tagliaferri, ed., *Lettere, 1907–1958* (Milan: Feltrinelli, 1980), respectively 51 and 54.

10. A synthetic but approximate chronology—dates are given by the month only, rather than by the exact day—is given by Perloff, *The Futurist Moment*, 172–173, drawing on Cianci, "Futurism and the English Avant-Garde," and Ardizzone, "Bibliografia," both listed below in this note. Indispensable to the study of the relations between Pound and Marinetti are two bibliographies listing 240 primary sources that describe Marinetti's activities in England during 1910–1915: (1) Patrizia Ardizzone, "Il futurismo in Inghilterra: Bibliografia (1910–1915)," *Quaderno* 9 (1979, special issue on *futurismo/vorticismo*): 91–115, hereafter abbreviated as "Bib."; and (2) Valerio Gioè, "Il futurismo in Inghilterra: Bibliografia (1910–1915)—Supplemento," *Quaderno* 16 (1982): 76–83, hereafter abbreviated as "Bib. Supp." Both bibliographies are poorly organized, mingling strictly bibliographical with historical entries, and together they contain hundreds of errors in the recording of titles, authors, journal names, and page references; moreover, both include publications that have little or nothing to do with Futurism but concern Vorticism. Even so, they remain indispensable.

   Secondary studies on Pound and Marinetti are legion. See Niccolò Zapponi, "Odi e amori futuristi di Ezra Pound," *Studi americani* 18 (1972): 299–311; Niccolò Zapponi, "Dialoghi e scontri con la cultura italiana," chapter 2 in his *L'Italia di Ezra Pound* (Rome: Bulzoni editore, 1976), 77–140; Ulrich Weisstein, "Futurism in Germany and England: Two Flashes in the Pan," in *Revue des langues vivantes* 44 (1978): 467–497; Niccolò Zapponi, "Ezra Pound and Futurism," in Angela Jung and Guido Palandri, trans. and eds., *Italian Images of Ezra Pound* (Taipei, Taiwan: Mei Ya Publications, 1979), 128–138. See also the perceptive studies by Giovanni Cianci, "Futurismo e avanguardia inglese: Il primo Pound tra imagismo e vorticismo," *Quaderno* 9 (1979, special issue on *futurismo/vorticismo*): 9–66; idem, "D. H. Lawrence e il futurismo/vorticismo," *Il verri*, series 6, no. 17 (1980): 80–99; idem, "Pound e il futurismo," *Rivista di studi anglo-americani* 1 (1981): 123–131; idem, "Futurism and the English Avant-Garde: Pound Between Imagism and Vorticism," *Arbeiten aus Anglistik und Amerikanistik* 6, no. 1 (1981): 3–39, an updated and slightly revised version of the essay that appeared in *Quaderno* 9 (1979); and idem, "Catalizzazione futurista: La poetica del vorticismo," in Giovanni Cianci, ed., *Modernismo/Modernismi* (Milan: Casa editrice G. Principato, 1991), 156–174.

   For subsequent studies, see Laurette Veza, "Marinetti et le vorticisme," in Jean-Claude

Marcadé, ed., *Présence de F. T. Marinetti: Actes du colloque international tenu à l'UN-ESCO, 1976* (Lausanne: Editions l'age d'homme, 1982), 277–286; Giovanni Cianci, "Pound and Futurism," in Bradford Morrow, ed., *Blast 3* (Santa Barbara, Calif.: Black Sparrow Press, 1984), 63–67; and William C. Wees, "Futurismo, vorticismo e 'mondo moderno,'" in Renzo De Felice, ed., *Futurismo, cultura e politica* (Turin: Fondazione Giovanni Agnelli, 1988), 439–452.

11. There was one brief report about Futurism in 1910, an article entitled "Futurist Venice" by Douglas Goldring, which appeared in *The Tramp* in August 1910, 487–488. This contained excerpts from "Contro venezia passatista" and "Fondazione e manifesto del futurismo" ("Bib.," B.1; "Bib. Supp.," D.1). Goldring was the editorial assistant for the *English Review,* a journal edited by Ford Madox Ford in 1908–1910 and the first important review to publish work by Ezra Pound, in March 1909. He was also personally acquainted with Pound and, though they were not especially close, they saw one another often in 1909 and early 1910. It is thus possible that Pound was aware of Goldring's report in *The Tramp.* Significantly, Pound's earliest mention of Marinetti is a reference to his manifesto "Contro venezia passatista," a reference that appears in the last paragraph of "Patria mia. III," *New Age* 11, no. 21 (19 September 1912): 491–492; reprinted in *EPPP* 1:79. The fact is significant because that is also the manifesto cited by Goldring in his essay in *The Tramp.* But by September 1912, when Pound wrote his essay, he could easily have obtained information about this manifesto from other sources.

12. On Sackville Street and its development in 1731, see F. H. W. Sheppard, ed., *Survey of London,* vol. 23, *The Parish of St. James Westminster,* part 2, *North of Piccadilly* (London: Athlone Press, University of London, 1963), 342–352, 360 for a detailed description of number 28 Sackville Street, and plate 128 for a 1958 photograph of it.

13. See "Artists of the Future: Weird Paintings Exhibited in Paris" (photographs of five paintings, with derogatory caption), *Daily Mirror* (London), 7 February 1912, 11, cols. 1–3 ("Bib.," D.2); "Futurist Paintings" (illustrations with captions), *Sketch* (London), 14 February 1912, 166–167 ("Bib.," D.3); and G. Konody, "Futurism the Latest Art Sensation," *Illustrated London News,* 17 February 1912, 225 ("Bib.," D.4). Though published after 1 March 1912, see also "The New Crazy 'Exploding' Pictures by 'Art Anarchists'" (three photos accompanying article), *Illustrated London News,* 20 March 1912, reproduced in full in Pontus Hulten, ed., *Futurismo e futurismi* (Milan: Bompiani, 1986), 580; or in the American edition, *Futurism and Futurisms* (New York: Abbeville, 1986), 572. The article notes that "all Paris is crowding into their salon to see these strange paintings. It is the very newest expression of art, and Paris likes it."

14. Sir Philip Burne-Jones quoted in Max Rothschild, letter to the editor, dated 1 March 1912 and subtitled "Sir Philip Burne-Jones and the Futurists," *Pall Mall Gazette* (London), 4 March 1912, 8, col. 3.

15. Burne-Jones is challenged to defend his assertions by Max Rothschild in the letter cited in note 14. He replies in a letter to the editor of his own, dated 4 March 1912 and subtitled, "Sir Philip Burne-Jones and the Futurists," *Pall Mall Gazette,* 5 March 1912, 5, cols. 3–4.

16. See, for example, the headlines from the *Pall Mall Gazette* for 1 March 1912, 1, col. 1, which read: "BLACK FRIDAY. / COAL WAR BEGUN / DESPERATE SITUATION / . . . RETURN TO CHAOS." See the cartoon in the same newspaper, 7, cols. 2–4.

17. See, for example, the headlines from the *Pall Mall Gazette* for 4 March 1912, 1, col. 5, which read: "SUFFRAGISTS BREAK MORE WINDOWS / ATTACK ON DRAPERY SHOPS TO-DAY / HARRODS' STORES DAMAGED / POLICEMAN PULLED OFF HIS HORSE." Or 5 March 1912, 1, col. 5: "SUFFRAGETTISM AND ITS RESULT. / WARMEST FRIENDS DISGUSTED / . . . COUNTRY ROUSED BY ROWDYISM."

18. See, for example, *Pall Mall Gazette*, 1 March 1912, 2, cols. 3–5, which includes a photograph of Severini's *The Pan-Pan Dance at the Monico* without comment but surrounded by headlines such as, "THE FIRST OUTRAGE. MINERS SMASH TRAIN WINDOWS." Or: "INDUSTRIAL CHAOS. Over a Million Men Out To-Day." For a different but useful reading of public response to the 1912 exhibition, see Rossella Caruso, "La mostra dei futuristi a Londra nel 1912: recensioni e commenti," *Ricerche di storia dell'arte* 45 (1991): 57–64.

19. The review is reprinted in Omar Pound and A. Walton Litz, eds., *Ezra Pound and Dorothy Shakespear: Their Letters, 1909–1914* (New York: New Directions, 1984), 70.

20. On Pound's relations with Margaret Cravens see the introduction by Omar Pound and Robert Spoo, eds., in *Ezra Pound and Margaret Cravens: A Tragic Friendship, 1910–1912* (Durham, N.C.: Duke University Press, 1988).

21. Arthur Marwick, *The Deluge* (Boston: Little, Brown, 1965), 23, citing Arthur Lyon Bowley, *The Division of the Product of Industry* (Oxford: Oxford University Press, 1919), 18; and again Marwick, 20.

22. Pound to Henry Hope Shakespear, 12 March 1912, in *Ezra Pound and Dorothy Shakespear*, 87. As a point of comparison, Dorothy Shakespear notes in March 1912 that Selwyn Image, the Slade Professor of Art at Oxford, was earning £400 per annum, also in *Ezra Pound and Dorothy Shakespear*, 94.

23. Information on Pound's three lectures of 1912 is from *Ezra Pound and Dorothy Shakespear*, 89, which reproduces a lecture program, also reproduced here.

24. On Queen Anne's Gate, see Montagu H. Cox and Philip Norman, eds., *The Survey of London*, vol. 10, *The Parish of St. Margaret, Westminster*, part 1 (London: London County Council, 1926), 78–81 and 101–103; on Queen Anne's Gate numbers 30 and 32, see 128–131, along with the accompanying plates. See also Dan Cruickshank, "Queen Anne's Gate," *Georgian Group Journal* 2 (1992): 56–67. On numbers 26–32, and number 34 in particular, see Department of the Environment, *List of Buildings of Special Architectural or Historic Interest: City of Westminster, Greater London*, part 5, *Streets Q–S* (London: National Monuments Record, Crown copyright, 1987), 1333–1337. The property and building at 34 Queen Anne's Gate were sold after the death of Edward Tennant in 1920 to Sir Harrison Hughes, who owned it until 1960, when it became the home of the St. Stephen's Constitutional Club, a club for members of the Conservative Party. I am grateful to Lance Mawbry of the St. Stephen's Partnership for kindly permitting me to tour the building.

25. See Simon Blow, *Broken Blood: The Rise and Fall of the Tennant Family* (London: Faber and Faber, 1987), 74–85.

26. See ibid., 120–124; "In the Great World: Lord and Lady Glenconner," *Sketch*, 10 December 1913, 298.

27. See Blow, *Broken Blood,* 112–117. On Pamela Wyndham's parents and their house, Clouds, see the excellent study by Caroline Dakers, *Clouds: The Biography of a Country House* (New Haven: Yale University Press, 1993). Dakers also discusses Pamela in some detail, especially 160–176; she reproduces photographs and paintings of her on 124, 161, and 170. Pamela is perhaps best known to many people as the middle sitter of the three portrayed in John Singer Sargent's painting *The Wyndham Sisters,* now in the Metropolitan Museum of Art in New York. For her brother's views on Romanticism, see George Wyndham, *The Springs of Romance in the Literature of Europe* (London: Macmillan, 1910). T. S. Eliot later wrote a damning review of George Wyndham's posthumously collected essays, *Essays in Romantic Literature* (London: Macmillan, 1919), which he titled "A Romantic Patrician," in the *Athenaeum,* 2 May 1919, 265–266. Pamela Tennant's publications consist of ten books: *The Book of Peace* (London: printed at the Chiswick Press, 1900), a collection of passages from mystical works paired with poems; *Village Notes, and Some Other Papers* (London: Heinemann, 1900), a collection of prose meditations on rural themes; *Windlestraw* (London: printed at the Chiswick Press, 1905), a collection of her own poems; *The Children and the Pictures* (London: Heinemann, 1907), a work of prose fiction; *White Wallet* (London: Unwin, 1912), an anthology of poems by others; *The Sayings of the Children* (Oxford: Blackwell, 1918), a short collection of observations that her children had made, which went through at least five editions by 1924; *The Significance of the Spiritual World as Revealed to the Mind of Man in Symbols* (London: Friars printing association, 1918), a brief tract on spiritualism and mysticism, subjects that increasingly gripped her imagination after the death of her oldest son in World War I; *Edward Wyndham Tennant: A Memoir by His Mother* (New York: John Lane, 1919), her memoir of the same son; *The Earthen Vessel; A Volume Dealing with Spirit-Communication Received in the Form of Book-Tests* (London: privately printed, 1921); and *Shepherd's Crown* (Oxford: Basil Blackwell, 1924), a short collection of essays, mostly concerning communications with "the other world." American libraries catalogue her works under the name Grey, because of her later marriage to Edward Grey in 1921; British, under Tennant.

28. Pamela Wyndham Tennant to her sister and brother, quoted in Blow, *Broken Blood,* 115, 116, 117.

29. On Wilsford Manor see Clive Aslet, *The Last Country Houses* (New Haven: Yale University Press, 1982), 245–255; and Gervase Jackson-Stops, "From Craft to Art: Detmar Blow's Wiltshire Houses," *Country Life,* no. 4637 (3 July 1986): 18–23. On the further career of Detmar Blow, see Simon Blow, "Blow-by-Blow Account of a Duke's Desertion" (a review of George Ridley, *Bend'Or, Duke of Westminster*), *Spectator,* no. 8220 (25 January 1986): 22–23.

30. Detmar Blow's plans for the building are preserved at the British Architectural Library, the Drawings Collection and Heinz Gallery, Detmar Blow Papers, Roll no. 32.

31. Members of the Tennant family published two catalogues. The first is assigned sometimes to Charles Tennant, sometimes to Morland C. Agnew, *Catalogue of the Pictures Forming the Collection of Sir Charles Tennant, Bart., of 40, Grosvenor Square, and The Glen, Innerleithen* (London: privately printed, 1896). The second and much smaller catalogue is ascribed sometimes to Edward Tennant and sometimes to Pamela Tennant; it

records the thirty-seven pictures that were housed in "the private gallery": *Catalogue of Pictures in the Tennant Gallery, 34, Queen Anne's Gate, S.W., . . . Compiled From Various Sources by Various Hands* (London: privately printed, n.d. but 1910). The introduction to the catalogue, 5–12, is signed by Pamela Tennant. For further information on the Tennant collection, see also W. Roberts, "The Passing of the Tennant Collection," *Queen* 154 (18 October 1923), 470–471; and James Dugdale, "Sir Charles Tennant: The Story of a Victorian Collector," *Connoisseur* (September 1971), 3–15.

32. Joshua Reynolds's *Robert Mayne* is now in a private collection; Raeburn's *The Leslie Boy* is held in the Cincinnati Museum of Art; the location of Romney's *Portrait of Mrs. Inchbald* is not known; Reynolds's *Girl Crying* is in a private collection in England. For further information on *Girl Crying,* listed as *Doloré* in the two Tennant catalogues cited above, see Martin Postle, *Sir Joshua Reynolds: The Subject Pictures* (Cambridge: Cambridge University Press, 1995). The portrait *Lady Diana Crosby* is now at the Huntington Museum in San Marino, California. Romney's *Elizabeth, Countess of Derby* is in the Metropolitan Museum of Art, New York; Hogarth's *Peg Woffington* is in a private collection; Gainsborough's *Miss Hippisley* is in the LaSalle College Art Gallery, Philadelphia; the location of Gainsborough's *The Ladies Erne and Dillon* is not known, nor is that of Ramsay's *Lady Erskine* or Hoppner's *Mrs. Gwynn.* The "private gallery" housed still other paintings that are not recorded in the few contemporary photographs that we have: Reynolds's *Miss Ridge* (Cincinnati Art Museum), his popular *The Fortune Tellers* (Huntington Museum, San Marino, Calif.), and *Collina* (Columbus Museum of Art, Columbus, Ohio); there was also one painting by Turner, *The Burning of the Houses of Parliament,* and Hoppner's ever popular *Frankland Sisters* (National Gallery, Washington). Other paintings in the house included Bonington's *Fishmarket by Boulogne* (now in the British Art Center, New Haven, Conn.) and *Shoreline in Picardy* (now in a private collection outside London), and Turner's famous *Approach to Venice* (now in the National Gallery, Washington). I am grateful to Professor David Manning of the University of Aberdeen for his generous help in locating Reynolds's portraits.

33. Dugdale, "Sir Charles Tennant," 11.

34. Philip Burne-Jones to Pamela Wyndham Tennant, 22 May 1905, quoted in Blow, *Broken Blood,* 130. Because his father had received several commissions from Pamela's parents, Philip Burne-Jones spent a considerable amount of time with the Wyndhams while he was young, and he may have had a youthful passion for Pamela's older sister, Madeline; see Dakers, *Clouds,* 79, 83, 90, 153, 176, 180, and 213. It should be noted that in 1898 he had been commissioned to paint a portrait of Hugo Charteris, Pamela's brother-in-law, and that he was also commissioned to paint portraits of her nephew, Perf Wyndham, and his wife Sibell, the heirs of Pamela's favorite brother, George. The poem that is quoted, "Envoy to Village Notes," is found in *Windlestraw,* 63.

35. A biographical sketch of Lady Low is given in Pound and Litz, eds., *Ezra Pound and Dorothy Shakespear,* 349, and there are frequent references to her in the letters from Dorothy Shakespear to Pound during 1911–1913. On 13 July 1911 Dorothy notes "the great and fast friendship between O. [Dorothy's mother, Olivia] and Lady Low"; on 2 September she urges Ezra to visit Lady Low in Dorset, saying, "She's a blessed woman with a brain. I am duly grateful for having met her." (Pound apparently did visit her). On 26

September Dorothy terms her "our best [mutual friend] at present," and on 1 October Lady Low sends the Shakespears a cutting from the *Daily Mail* favorably reviewing Pound's *Canzoni.* See *Ezra Pound and Dorothy Shakepear,* 35, 47, 52, 66, 69–70.

36. Ezra Pound to Homer Pound, unpublished letter, 14 March 1912, Beinecke Library, Yale University, NHYB, *PP,* Box 60, Folder 2669.

37. Ezra Pound, "Psychology and Troubadours," *Quest* 4, no. 1 (October 1912), 37–53; reprinted in *EPPP* 1:83–99, here, 86.

38. Dorothy Shakespear to Pound, 19 March 1912, in *Ezra Pound and Dorothy Shakepear,* 89–90.

39. "'Futurist' Leader in London," *Daily Chronicle* (London), 20 March 1912, 1, col. 3 ("Bib.," C.3.a); "Futurism in London," *Morning Leader* (London), 21 March 1912, page not in source ("Bib.," C.3.a); and "Futurism in Literature and Art," *Times* (London), 21 March 1912, 2, col. 6 ("Bib." C.3.c). See also Richard Cork, *Vorticism and Abstract Art in the First Machine Age* (Berkeley: University of California Press, 1976), 28.

40. "A nation of sycophants" and "the long-haired gentlemen" are from the *Daily Chronicle,* 20 March 1912, 1, col. 3; "Some of his audience" is from the article in the *Times,* 21 March 1912, 2, col. 6; and "wildly applauded his outspoken derision" is from a passage recollecting the lecture by Harold Monro in his "Varia," *Poetry and Drama* 1, no. 3 (September 1913), 263.

41. Letter from F. T. Marinetti to F. B. Pratella, 12 April 1912, in Maria Drudi Gambillo and Teresa Fiori, eds., *Archivi del futurismo,* 2 vols. (Rome: De Luca, 1959–1962), 1:237–238. Richard Cork, in his *Vorticism and Abstract Art in the First Machine Age,* 26, concludes, "It would be difficult to exaggerate the impetus which Lewis's yearning for revolt must now have been given by Futurism's first concerted onslaught on London."

42. Tickets for Marinetti's lecture were advertised in the *Times,* 19 March 1912, 1, col. 6, and in the *Pall Mall Gazette,* 19 March 1912, 4, col. 3. Both advertisements listed tickets in four price categories (10s. 6d., 5s., 2s. 6d., and 1s.), and tickets could be purchased at the box office of Bechstein Hall or at the Sackville Gallery. Information on seating capacity is from Ben Weinreb and Christopher Hibbert, *The London Encylopaedia* (Bethesda, Maryland: Adler and Adler, 1986), 963 s.v. "Wigmore Hall" (the name was changed after World War I). However, one cannot assume that Marinetti attracted a full house. Recalling the Bechstein Hall lecture, in September 1913, Harold Monro described "the little Marinetti" speaking in "a huge empty hall," and at another point he noted that Marinetti spoke "to a handful of English." His account is at odds with the larger audience presupposed by the *Times* and the *Daily Chronicle,* but I may be in error in not giving sufficient weight to his testimony about the actual as opposed to the potential audience. See Harold Monro, "Varia," 263.

43. Ezra Pound, "Prefatory Note" to "The Complete Poetical Works of T. E. Hulme" (first published at the end of *Ripostes* in October 1912), in his *Personae* (New York: New Directions, revised edition 1990), 266. The chronological limits for the preparation of *Ripostes* are as follows. In an undated letter from March 1912, Pound informed his father: "The 'mss.' of 'Ripostes' has gone to publishers." The letter was evidently written sometime after 1 March, because Pound refers to the coal strike that began on that date, and not long before 19 March, since he also notes that he must "get my 'Arnaut' ready for

delivery" (Ezra Pound to Homer Pound, unpublished letter, March 1912, NHYB, *PP* 43). Most likely it was around 14 March, therefore, that Pound sent off the manuscript of *Ripostes*. It should not be assumed, however, that the original manuscript necessarily contained either the five poems by Hulme that Pound labeled "The Complete Poetical Works of T. E. Hulme," or the "Prefatory Note" that preceded them, with its mention of "les Imagistes." Since the poems and the note were printed at the very end of the volume, they may have been added after he sent off the manuscripts in mid-March. But how much later? Pound remained in London, apart from one-day excursions, from mid-March to the end of April. Probably on 1 May he left London for Paris, for Dorothy wrote to him on 3 May, "I wish I were in Paris" (*Ezra Pound and Dorothy Shakespear,* 95). At first sight, this is the latest date when Pound could still have added the text of Hulme's poems, if not the prefatory note, for while in Paris he would have had difficulty securing a text of Hulme's works. Even so, he had still not received proofs. After his arrival in Paris around 1 or 2 May, Pound stayed with the pianist Walter Morse Rummel until 26 or 27 May (see *Ezra Pound and Margaret Cravens,* 110); he then left for a walking tour in southern France, suddenly returning to Paris on 11 June after learning of Margaret Cravens's suicide (*Ezra Pound and Margaret Cravens,* 122). The proofs for *Ripostes,* meanwhile, reached Dorothy Shakespear in England on 12 June (*Ezra Pound and Dorothy Shakespear,* 111), and she immediately forwarded them to Pound in Paris. On 16 June, while still in Paris and attending to affairs occasioned by Cravens's death, he wrote that he had "just corrected" them (*Ezra Pound and Dorothy Shakespear,* 113). This date, then, would seem to have been the last when Pound might still have added the poems by Hulme, or, if they already formed part of the volume, his prefatory note to them. However, some evidence suggests that Pound received and corrected a second set of proofs for *Ripostes* some two months later, in mid-August 1912, after he had returned to London. In a letter dated [18] August 1912 to Harriet Monroe (*Selected Letters,* 9), Pound wrote, "the proofs of *Ripostes* are on my desk." If this letter is dated correctly by Paige, it can refer only to a second set of proofs, and in that case Pound could easily have added his prefatory note concerning "les Imagistes" as late as 18 August 1912. I suspect that this is indeed what happened, a suspicion partly corroborated by the chronology of his other references to Imagism. For in all of his extant correspondence, there is not a single reference to Imagism prior to this one in the letter of 18 August to Monroe. (The passage in question is quoted below.) It is also corroborated by an otherwise curious reference in the "Prefatory Note," in which Pound contrasts the "School of Images," which had supposedly led to the formation of Imagism, with more recent movements, noting that "its principles were not so interesting as those of the 'inherent dynamists' . . . yet they were probably sounder than those of a certain French school which attempted to dispense with verbs altogether." These are plainly satirical descriptions corresponding to no movement that actually existed, yet taken together the references to "dynamism" and the suppression of verbs seem to allude to the recent developments of Futurism, and in particular to Marinetti's prescription urging the elimination of all verbs except those in the infinitive, advocated in the "Technical Manifesto of Futurist Literature" published in May 1912 (F. T. Marinetti, "Manifesto tecnico della letteratura futurista," originally published in 1912 by the Direction of the Futurist Movement in Milan, as a leaflet dated 11 May; reprinted in Luciano

De Maria, ed., *Teoria e invenzione futurista,* 2d ed. [Milan: Mondadori, 1983], 46–54). If so, it further corroborates a later date for the "Prefatory Note," which would then have been added after the publication of the "Technical Manifesto." That, in turn, preceded the death of Cravens by only a few weeks. In short, the available evidence suggests that Pound did not invent Imagism until mid-June or even mid-August 1912, only *after* the controversy surrounding the Futurists and *after* the death of Margaret Cravens, which in turn suggests that his creation of Imagism was, in good part, a response to both these events.

44. Olivia Shakespear to Ezra Pound, 13 September 1912, in *Ezra Pound and Dorothy Shakespear,* 153–154.

45. See Christopher Hassall, *Edward Marsh: Patron of the Arts. A Biography* (London: Longman, 1959), 189–193. Hassall shows that Marsh came up with the idea for the Georgian anthology on 19 September 1912; that he presented it the next day to Harold Monro, editor of the *Poetry Review,* who approved; and that on 25 September he wrote several poets, including Pound, to solicit contributions. For Pound's reply, see Hassall, *Edward Marsh,* 193.

46. Ezra Pound to Harriet Monroe, 18 August 1912, *Selected Letters,* 10: "I send you all that I have on my desk—an over-elaborate post-Browning 'Imagiste' affair"; and Ezra Pound to Harriet Monroe, October 1913, *Selected Letters,* 11: "I've had luck again, and am sending you some *modern stuff* by an American, I say modern, for it is the laconic speech of the Imagistes, even if the subject is classic." These appear to be Pound's earliest references to Imagism in his extant correspondence, but as the dates in Paige's edition are notoriously unreliable, one cannot be wholly confident in saying this.

47. Ezra Pound, "Editorial Comment. Status Rerum," dated 10 December 1912, *Poetry* 1, no. 4 (January 1913), 123–127; reprinted in *EPPP* 1:111–113; all quotations here are from 112.

48. "Fine Art Gossip," *Athenaeum,* no. 4402 (9 March 1912), 289–290, here 290.

49. F. S. Flint (though actually drafted by Pound and merely rewritten by Flint), "Imagisme," *Poetry* 1, no. 6 (March 1913), 198–200, reprinted in *EPPP* 1:119; and Ezra Pound, "A Few Don'ts By An Imagiste," *Poetry* 1, no. 6 (March 1913), 200–206, reprinted in *EPPP* 1:120–122. I am grateful to Robert von Hallberg for helping to prompt my reconsideration of Imagism.

50. Pound to Glenn Hughes, unpublished letter, 26 September 1927; Glenn Hughes Collection, Humanities Research Center, University of Texas.

51. F. T. Marinetti, "Manifesto tecnico della letteratura futurista"; idem, "Risposte alle obiezioni," originally published in 1912 by the Direction of the Futurist Movement in Milan as a leaflet entitled "Supplemento al manifesto tecnico della letteratura futurista," dated 11 August, reprinted in *Teoria e invenzione futurista,* 55–62; idem, "Distruzione della sintassi—Immaginazione senza fili—Parole-in-libertà," originally published in 1913 by the Direction of the Futurist Movement in Milan, dated 11 May, reprinted in *Teoria e invenzione futurista,* 65–80; idem, "Il teatro di varietà," originally published in *Lacerba* 1, no. 19 (1 October 1913), reprinted in *Teoria e invenzione futurista,* 80–90.

52. Harold Monro, "Varia," *Poetry and Drama* 1, no. 3 (September 1913), 263–265.

53. Marinetti assumes that art must respond to its milieu and that since the mileu of modernity is defined chiefly by rapid change, art itself must also change rapidly. The

presupposition owes much to Baudelaire's famous observation, "Modernity is the transient, the fleeting, the contingent; it is one half of art, the other being the eternal and immutable," in "The Painter of Modern Life," *Baudelaire: Selected Writings on Art and Artists,* trans. E. Charvet (Harmondsworth: Penguin, 1972), 403. Marinetti's "Fondazione e manifesto del futurismo" was originally published in French in *Le Figaro* (Paris), 20 February 1909, and is reprinted in *Teoria e invenzione futurista,* 7–14.

54. "Forse videro splendere nei nostri occhi la gloriosa passione che nutriamo per l'Arte. All'arte infatti, che merita ed esige il sacrificio dei migliori, noi diamo un amore assoluto" (F. T. Marinetti, "La *Divina commedia* è un verminaio di glossatori," *Teoria e invenzione futurista,* 267); my translation.

55. *"Facciamo coraggiosamente il 'brutto' in letteratura, e uccidiamo dovunque la solennità.* Via! non prendete di quest'arie di grandi sacerdoti, nell'ascoltarmi! Bisogna sputare ogni giorno sull'*Altare dell'Arte!"* (F. T. Marinetti, "Manifesto tecnico della letteratura futurista," *Teoria e invenzione futurista,* 53–54); my translation.

56. *Times,* 18 November 1913, 5, cols. 5–6. On 6 November 1913 Pound left London to stay with William Butler Yeats at Stone Cottage in Coleman's Hatch (see Dorothy Shakespear to Ezra Pound, 5 November 1913, *Ezra Pound and Dorothy Shakespear,* 273). But on 14 November he announced, "I am coming up on Monday," or 17 November, the date of Marinetti's lecture (see Pound to Dorothy Shakespear, 14 November 1913, *Ezra Pound and Dorothy Shakespear,* 273). Marinetti's lecture would surely have interested him: it was held at the Poets' Club and its subject was "Futurism in Poetry." Harold Monro attended the event and recalled it in his essay "The Origin of Futurism; Futurism and Ourselves," *Poetry and Drama* 1, no. 4 (December 1913), 389–391, here 389. Richard Aldington also attended some of Marinetti's lectures, most likely including this one; see Richard Aldington, "M. Marinetti's Lectures," *New Freewoman,* 1 December 1913, 226.

57. F. T. Marinetti, "The Meaning of the Music Hall, By the Only Intelligible Futurist," *Daily Mail* (London), 21 November 1913, 6, col. 4. The original reads: "Il Teatro di Varietà è naturalmente antiaccademico, primitivo e ingenuo, quindi più significativo per l'imprevisto delle sue ricerche e la semplicità dei suoi mezzi . . . distrugge il Solenne, il Sacro, il Serio, il Sublime dell'Arte coll'A maiuscolo" (F. T. Marinetti, "Il teatro di varietà," *Teoria e invenzione futurista,* 86).

58. *Sketch,* no. 1111 (13 May 1914), cover page. See, for example, "FUTURIST CLOTHES. Man's Suit in Single Piece. ONE BUTTON," *Pall Mall Gazette,* 28 May 1914, 2, col. 3. The *Sketch,* in a caption to its cover photograph, notes that Marinetti "has been lecturing to very interested audiences."

59. "Futurist Music: 'Noisy Tuners' at a Rehearsal; Cracklers and Roarers," *Pall Mall Gazette,* 12 June 1914 (Friday), 1, col. 5.

60. Felix Barker, *The House That Stoll Built: The Story of the Coliseum Theatre* (London: Frederick Muller, 1957), 11.

61. Quoted in Victor Glasstone, *Victorian and Edwardian Theatres* (Cambridge: Harvard University Press, 1975), 116.

62. Victor Glasstone, *The London Coliseum* (Cambridge: Chadwyck-Healy, 1980), 17.

63. *Times,* 16 June 1914, 5, col. 4, "ART AND PRACTICE OF NOISE. Hostile Reception of Signor Marinetti."

64. I adapt this observation from Pierre Bourdieu, *Distinctions* (Cambridge: Harvard University Press, 1984), 569n.81.

65. Stage manager quoted in Barker, *The House That Stoll Built,* 186; see also Christopher R. W. Nevinson, *Paint and Prejudice* (New York: Harcourt Brace, 1938), 83. I have synthesized Nevinson's account of Marinetti's first performance with Barker's, 183–186, though they differ in several details.

66. [Wyndham Lewis and Ezra Pound], "Manifesto," *Blast* 1 (July 1914; reprint, Santa Barbara, Calif.: Black Sparrow Press, 1981), 21.

67. Solomon Eagle [John Collings Squire], "Current Literature: Books in General," *New Statesman* 3, no. 65 (4 July 1914), 406. Compare "The Futurists," *New Statesman* 3, no. 66 (11 July 1914), 426: "One can forgive a new movement for anything except being tedious: *Blast* is as tedious as an imitation of George Robey by a curate without a sense of humour. . . . to make up of the pages of *Blast* a winding-sheet in which to wrap up Futurism for burial is to do an indignity to a genuine and living artistic movement. But, after all, what is Vorticism but Futurism in an English disguise—Futurism, we might call it, bottled in England, and bottled badly? . . . the two groups differ from each other not in their aims, but in their degrees of competence."

68. Wyndham Lewis, *Blasting and Bombardiering* (1937; reprint, New York: Riverrun Press, 1982), 47.

69. Ezra Pound to Margaret Anderson, 10 May 1917, in Thomas L. Scott and Melvin J. Friedman, eds., *Pound/Little Review: The Letters of Ezra Pound to Margaret Anderson,* 46; and Ezra Pound to William Bird, 7 May 1924; BIUL, Bird Papers.

70. "Our object in opening a new gallery is to do business not only to fight against dishonest commercialism but in order to support ourselves and make others able to support themselves." Marius de Zayas to Alfred Stieglitz, 27 August 1915; Beinecke Library, Yale University, Alfred Stieglitz Archive. See also Douglas Hyland, *Marius de Zayas: Conjurer of Souls* (Lawrence, Kansas: Spencer Museum of Art, University of Kansas, 1981), 46, which urges that de Zayas sought to make a gallery that "would be a commercial venture in a way that Stieglitz's had never been." Hyland presents an excellent account of the two galleries run by de Zayas on 46–52. See also Stephen E. Lewis, "The Modern Gallery and American Commodity Culture," *Modernism/Modernity* 4, no. 3 (September 1997): 67–91.

71. De Zayas's principal clients are given in Hyland, *Marius de Zayas,* 48. Quinn's purchases in 1920 are detailed by B. L. Reid, *The Man from New York: John Quinn and His Friends* (New York: Oxford University Press, 1968), 471–472.

72. Quoted in Hyland, *Marius de Zayas,* 50.

CHAPTER 2: CONSUMING INVESTMENTS

1. Sylvia Beach, *Shakespeare and Company* (1956; reprint, Lincoln: University of Nebraska Press, 1980), 45–76, 84–98.

2. Noel Riley Fitch, *Sylvia Beach and the Lost Generation* (New York: W. W. Norton, 1983), 105.

3. Robert Bertholf, *"Ulysses" at Buffalo: A Centenary Exhibition* (Buffalo: State University of New York Press, 1982), n.p., s.v. "Case 2."

4. Melissa Banta and Oscar A. Silverman, eds., *James Joyce's Letters to Sylvia Beach: 1921– 1940* (Bloomington: Indiana University Press, 1987), 211n.12.

5. Even so elegant a writer as Richard Ellmann must labor to instill a breath of life into so moribund a form: "André Gide brought in his subscription in person, Pound brought in the subscription of Yeats, Hemingway sent in his own enthusiastically. . . . Among those who replied [to the prospectus] were the son or nephew of Bela Kun, an Anglican bishop, a chief of the Irish revolutionary movement, and Winston Churchill." Ellmann, *James Joyce* (New York: Oxford University Press, 1982), 506.

6. "The Battle of *Ulysses*" is the title of the chapter that recounts the story of the first edition in Fitch, *Sylvia Beach*, 65–92; "heroic efforts" is from A. Walton Litz, "Foreword," in Banta and Silverman, eds., *James Joyce's Letters to Sylvia Beach,* viii; the other quotations are from Bertholf, "Introduction," *"Ulysses" at Buffalo,* [1].

7. Banta and Silverman, eds., *James Joyce's Letters to Sylvia Beach,* 4.

8. The principal accounts are Beach, *Shakespeare and Company,* 45–76, 84–98; Ellmann, *James Joyce,* 499–526; Fitch, *Sylvia Beach,* 65–92; and *DMW,* 167–220.

9. *DMW,* 173. The Complete Press had refused to print the "Telemachus" episode in March 1918; the firm then consented to print the "Nestor" episode for the *Egoist* issue dated January–February 1919, but insisted on cutting material from the "Proteus" episode for the issue of March–April 1919 and finally refused to print any more. Weaver turned to the Pelican Press for subsequent issues, which contained parts of "Hades," "Scylla and Charybdis," and "Wandering Rocks," from July to December 1919. She then decided to close the *Egoist* as a serial. See *DMW,* 147, 155, 159, 163, 173–174.

10. John Rodker's nine publications in the *Little Review* were: "Night-Pieces," 4 (July 1917), 16–18; "Theatre Muêt," 4 (August 1917), 12–15; "Incidents in the Life of a Poet," 4 (January 1918), 31–35; "Notes on Novelists," 5 (August 1918), 53–56; "Books," 5 (September 1918), 47–50; "List of Books," 5 (November 1918), 31–33; "'Exiles': A Discussion of James Joyce's Play," 5 (January 1919), 20–22; "De Gourmont-Yank," 5 (March 1919), 29– 32; and "A Barbarian," 6 (December 1919), 40–42.

11. Plans for the press were under way by 6 July 1919, when Ezra Pound wrote to John Quinn suggesting that "Joyce will perhaps have to be published by the Ovid Press. Thank God the press can at least publish the suppressed parts. It will mean a huge job for Rodker if he has to print the whole novel"; Pound, *SLPQ,* 177. Under the imprint of the Ovid Press, Rodker later issued three deluxe editions: Wyndham Lewis's portfolio *Fifteen Drawings* (January 1920), Eliot's *Ara Vos Prec* (February 1920), and Pound's *Hugh Selwyn Mauberley* (June 1920), all in limited editions of 250, 264, and 250 copies, respectively. On the portfolio by Lewis, see Omar Pound and Philip Grover, *Wyndham Lewis: A Descriptive Bibliography* (Folkestone, Kent: William Dawson and Sons, 1978), 73–74; Bradford Morrow and Bernard Lafourcade, *A Bibliography of the Writings of Wyndham Lewis* (Santa Barbara, Calif.: Black Sparrow Press, 1978), 38–39; and William Ransom, *Private Presses and Their Books* (New York: R. R. Bowker, 1929), 374. On the Eliot edition, see *TSEB,* 25–27; on the Pound edition, see *EPB,* 29–31. Rodker also reports, in his correspondence with Wallace Stevens, that he published an

edition of his own poems. See Rodker to Stevens, 24 March 1920, Huntington Library, Wallace A. Stevens Collection, 1582.

12. Huntington Library, Stevens Collection, 1582.

13. James Joyce, *Letters of James Joyce,* vol. 3, ed. Richard Ellmann (New York: Viking Press, 1966), 12.

14. Rodker to Stevens, 28 July 1920, Huntington Library, Stevens Collection, 1583.

15. Joyce, *Letters of James Joyce,* vol. 3, 15; *DMW,* 174.

16. "Miss Weaver writes nobody will print it. So it will be printed, it seems, in Paris and bear Mr. John Rodker's imprint as English printer" (Joyce to Stanislaus Joyce, ibid., 17).

17. Rodker had still not seen the "Nausicaa" and "Oxen" episodes by 13 September 1920, when Joyce wrote to him in London, but at this point, the project for a complete edition of *Ulysses* may have changed into plans for a deluxe edition of only the "Nausicaa" and "Oxen" episodes, an edition that would be more manageable for Rodker and might earn money to tide Joyce over until a complete edition could be published in the future (see ibid., 21). Two weeks later, by 29 September, Rodker had finally read "Oxen" and written to Joyce in its praise. Joyce, in reply, promised to "speak . . . of your suggestion" to Huebsch, who was visiting Joyce in Paris (ibid., 23). The same day, after his meeting with Huebsch, Joyce wrote to Frank Budgen: "Huebsch my New York publisher is here. They say *Ulysses* will come out first in a private edition of 1000 copies at 150 frs each" (Joyce, *Letters of James Joyce,* vol. 1, ed. Stuart Gilbert [New York: Viking Press, 1957], 148). This is Joyce's first mention of the "private edition" discussed below, and it shows how easily the Rodker project was assimilated to the new plan.

18. For the events surrounding the case, I rely on Jackson R. Bryer, "Joyce, *Ulysses,* and the *Little Review,*" *South Atlantic Quarterly* 66 (Spring 1967): 148–164; *MNY,* 441–457; and Ellmann, *James Joyce,* 502–504.

19. Quinn to Pound, 7 December 1920, BIUL, *PM.1:*

> I adjourned it to December 13th, and on December 13th it will, because of my legal engagements, be adjourned to January. In the meantime I will make a motion to have it taken away from Special Sessions, which means a trial by three judges with conviction certain, and have it transferred to General Sessions, which means (a) presentation to the Grand Jury, (b) indictment, (c) pleading, and (d) holding it for a trial before jury, which would hang it up for a year because it will then become a bail case and not a jail case, and jail cases are tried first. Meantime the book can be (a) finished by Joyce, (b) published by Huebsch, I hope, in a limited edition, (c) the entire edition sold, and then my interest in the matter will end and the Little Review can get some other lawyer and I will bow myself out.

20. Quinn cites these four books when discussing *Ulysses* in a letter to Pound, 12 December 1920, BIUL, *PM.1.*

21. For a cursory discussion of the so-called private editions and their adoption by Liveright, see Tom Dardis, *Firebrand: The Life of Horace Liveright* (New York: Random House, 1995), 156–158. For Quinn's reading of Huneker's manuscript, see *MNY,* 553.

22. Quinn to Pound, 1 May 1921, BIUL, *PM.1:*

> Early in November a financial crash struck this country; prices dropped and a slow panic began. Enormous losses were made by banks and companies, firms and individ-

uals; failure followed failure from unexpected quarters; men's nerves were drawn to the snapping point; hysteria and irritability and worry were common, and for the last five months, now nearly six months, I have been driven from morning to night and had to work evenings, Sundays and holidays, even Christmas day and New Year's day, all day and many nights. The strain has been dreadful at times. . . . I have only been able to go through with the work that crowded on me by sacrifice of all personal interests and the neglect of my personal affairs. . . . During that time I have gone nowhere, declined all invitations, have not been to the theatre and have not had a single complete day's rest or time for play. I have not answered any book or art letters or letters to personal friends.

23. Joyce, *Letters of James Joyce,* vol. 1, 165. The transcription that Joyce made from the article in the *New York Tribune,* which he sent to Harriet Shaw Weaver, is conserved in the Beinecke Library, Yale University, James Joyce Collection, Folder 325. The article itself, titled "Mr. Sumner's Glorious Victory," appeared in the *New York Tribune,* 22 February 1922, 10. Fitch assumes, as I do, that Joyce's reference to "a bookshop"—"I was given one day in a bookshop here a cutting which the owner had received by chance from New York"—in his letter to Weaver of 3 April 1921 means Shakespeare and Company. See Fitch, *Sylvia Beach,* 77.

24. Beach to Eleanor Orbison Beach, 1 April 1921, PUF, *BP,* Box 19, Folder 21. The letter is also quoted in A. Walton Litz, "Foreword," in Banta and Silverman, eds., *James Joyce's Letters to Sylvia Beach,* viii, and in Fitch, *Sylvia Beach,* 78. Litz's and Fitch's transcriptions differ slightly; this one has been checked against the original.

25. Joyce, *Letters of James Joyce,* vol. 1, 162.

26. On Adrienne Monnier's "essentially religious" sense of vocation and her own writings articulating this, see Richard McDougall, ed. and trans., *The Very Rich Hours of Adrienne Monnier* (New York: Charles Scribner's Sons, 1976), 13. Beach's recollection is from *Shakespeare and Company,* 49.

27. The price of the private edition proposed by Quinn and Huebsch, two pounds, is mentioned in a letter from Joyce to Frank Budgen (Joyce, *Letters of James Joyce,* vol. 1, 144).

28. On Weaver's projected edition and the 150 subscribers, see *DMW,* 176; Weaver to Beach, 12 May 1921, PUF, *BP,* Box 232, Folder 2.

29. A list of Weaver's publications is given in *DMW,* 464–465. For the publications by Eliot, Joyce, and Pound, see *TSEB* and *EPB.*

30. Weaver to Beach, 21 April 1921, 27 April 1921, both PUF, *BP,* Box 232, Folder 2.

31. Weaver to Beach, 8 July 1921, PUF, *BP,* Box 232, Folder 2.

32. Beach to Holly Beach, 22 September 1921, 24 October 1921, both PUF, *BP,* Box 19, Folder 19.

33. See "Little Review in Court," *New York Times,* 15 February 1921, 4; "Greenwich Girl Editors in Court," *Chicago Herald Examiner,* 15 February 1921; "Improper Novel Costs Women $100," *New York Times,* 22 February 1921, 13; "Ulysses Finds Court Hostile as Neptune," *New York World,* 22 February 1921, 24; "'Ulysses' Adjudged 'Indecent'; Review Editors Are Fined," *New York Tribune,* 22 February 1921, 6; "Women Editors Fined for Obscene Article," *New York Daily News,* 22 February 1921, 3; "Greenwich Village Edi-

toresses Fined: Literary Effusion in Their Review Is Cause," *New York Herald,* 22 February 1921, 8; "Taste, Nor Morals Violated," *New York Times,* 23 February 1921, 12; "Mr. Sumner's Glorious Victory," *New York Tribune,* 23 February 1921, 10; and "Suppressing an Unread Book," *New York World,* 23 February 1921, 10. Robert Deming claims that "Joyce's reputation among men of letters was greatly increased by the suppression of the *Little Review* for publishing *Ulysses,*" in Robert Deming, ed., *James Joyce: The Critical Heritage* (London: Routledge and Kegan Paul, 1970), vol. 1, 17–18.

34. Beach to Holly Beach, 23 April 1921, PUF, *BP,* Box 19, Folder 2b.

35. Beach to Holly Beach, 14 May 1921, PUF, *BP,* Box 19, Folder 2b.

36. [Rosemary Carr], "Literary Adventurer. American Girl Conducts Novel Bookstore Here," *Chicago Tribune,* 28 May 1921, Paris edition, 3.

37. All circulation figures, except for the 1915 data, are from David Ayerst, *Garvin of the "Observer"* (London: Croom Helm, 1985), 70, 128, and 229. The 1915 data are taken from David Griffiths, ed., *Encyclopaedia of the British Press* (London: Macmillan, 1992), 444. "The Victorian Sabbath" is from Ayerst, *Garvin of the "Observer,"* 70.

38. [Sisley Huddleston], "Paris Week by Week," *Observer,* 17 April 1921. The essay is attributed to Huddleston by Beach in a letter to Holly Beach, 23 April 1921, PUF, *BP,* Box 19, Folder 2b: "I'm sending [you] a copy of the London Observer with a word by Sisley Huddleston on Ulysses."

39. Beach, *Shakespeare and Company,* 45–48; Banta and Silverman, eds., *James Joyce's Letters to Sylvia Beach,* viii.

40. Weaver to Beach, 12 May 1921, PUF, *BP,* Box 232, Folder 2.

41. Weaver to Beach, 24 May 1921, PUF, *BP,* Box 232, Folder 2.

42. Weaver to Beach, 19 July 1921, PUF, *BP,* Box 232, Folder 2.

43. Oddly, Beach did not inform Weaver of her change in policy, and Weaver did not learn about it until March 1922. See Weaver to Beach, 10 March 1922, PUF, *BP,* Box 133, Folder 6.

44. William Jackson's orders are in PUF, *BP,* Box 132, Folder 12.

45. Beach's sales records for *Ulysses* form an immense and extremely complex body of documentation, because each transaction typically required numerous letters between Beach and a buyer: (1) a buyer would write to Beach and inquire about the edition's cost; (2) Beach would reply by sending off a prospectus that described the edition and included an order blank; (3) buyers then returned the order blank, indicating which issue they preferred; (4) Beach then sent off a postcard advising the buyer that his or her copy was ready and would be shipped upon receipt of remittance; (5) buyers sent in their payment, often with letters speculating about the appropriate rate of exchange if they were not residing in Paris; (6) Beach at last sent off the copy. Beach tried to register the transaction's status at every point in the ongoing exchange and, though imperfectly maintained, her elaborate system provided so many points of cross-reference that she could almost always pinpoint an order's status, even if she had to check in several different places. Most of the correspondence and the order forms are now housed in PUF, *BP,* Boxes 132–133, but a small group of order forms (fifty-seven of them) are at the State University of New York at Buffalo, Capen Library, Poetry Collection, Sylvia Beach Papers, folder "Ulysses Subscriptions, 1st Edition." In addition to these materials, Beach

kept four different record books (now located in PUF, *BP*, Box 63). One contains preliminary records of all orders up to around January 1922. Around that date, Beach created the other three record books, organized by geography or by the location where the book would have to be sent (the United States, the United Kingdom, and France and the Continent). Here Beach was careful to record payments, for she had no intention of shipping copies that had not been paid for. Finally, Beach also kept the "Calepin de vente d'*Ulysses*," a running record of the first edition's sales, which she gave to Maurice Saillet, upon whose death in 1992 it was acquired by the Harry Ransom Center for Research in the Humanities, University of Texas, Austin, where it is among the Carlton Lake Collection. In the "Calepin de vente" Beach kept two more lists: one that recorded each sale when it was finally completed and a copy was sent off, in chronological order; and another that registered the name of the buyer and the copy number the buyer received, from 1 to 1,000. The list registering the names of the buyers has been published in *James Joyce: Books and Manuscripts* (New York: Glenn Horowitz Bookseller, 1996), 113–134. In short, I have collated the materials at Princeton, Buffalo, and Austin, and the foregoing remarks on sales derive from these collations.

46. Huddleston, "Ulysses," *Observer*, 5 March 1922; reprinted in Huddleston, *Articles de Paris* (London: Methuen, 1928), 40–47; also reprinted in Deming, ed., *James Joyce*, vol. 1, 213–216.

47. Pound to Homer Pound, 10 March 1922, NHYB, *PP*, Box 52, Folder 1967.

48. R. C. Armilt to James Joyce, PUF, *BP*, Box 133, Folder 2. An anonymous letter to Joyce, dated 7 March 1922 (in the same folder), reads: "I have seen a long review of your Ulysses in The Observer. Would it be possible for me to get a copy of the book by subscription. If the book is not too expensive."

49. The franc had fluctuated between 10.715 (20 April) and 12.06 to the dollar (26 June), a range of only 1.35 francs. Exchange rates for the franc and the dollar on the Paris Bourse are from Eleanor Lansing Dulles, *The French Franc, 1914–1928: The Facts and Their Interpretation* (New York: Macmillan Publishers, 1929), 463. Figures for the New York Stock Exchange are taken from the *New York Times*, 2 February 1922, 24, and 1 July 1922, 19. Figures for the London exchange are from the *Times* (London), 2 February 1922, 15, and 1 July 1922, 17.

50. Morrill Cody, *The Women of Montparnasse* (Cranbury, N.J.: Cornwall Books, 1984), 8–9.

51. Pound to John Quinn, 19 December 1921, NYPL, *QP*; the letter is omitted in *SLPQ*.

52. Pound's regular income came from the *Dial*, which paid him fifty dollars for his "Paris Letter" every other month; see *Dial* Papers, Beinecke Library, Yale University, Payment Records. Dorothy Pound's income is reported in Pound to Quinn, 4–5 July 1921, NYPL, *QP*, which is transcribed in *SLPQ*, 209–214, especially 210. In the same letter, Pound recalls his difficulties in the winter of 1921–1922, telling Quinn, "and you know how damn near a squeak I have had more than once, and even so recently as last winter" (211). He had requested that Quinn loan him $250 on 22 October 1921; see *MNY*, 492.

53. Arthur L. Bowley and Josiah Stamp, *The National Income, 1924* (Oxford: Oxford University Press, 1927), 30. The figure for income from wages per house presumes that more than one household member was at work.

54. Barbara Reynolds, *Dorothy L. Sayers: A Biography* (1993; New York: St. Martin's Griffin,

1997), 106. One might add that Inspector Parker, a fictional bachelor who aids Lord Peter Wimsey in Sayers's 1923 mystery *Whose Body?* pays one pound a week for "a Georgian but inconvenient flat at No. 12A Great Ormond Street" (Dorothy L. Sayers, *Whose Body?* [New York: Harper & Row, 1987], 54).

55. Martha Cohn Cooper, "Frank Crowninshield and *Vanity Fair*" (Ph.D. diss., University of North Carolina at Chapel Hill, 1976), 48.

56. See Roger Fry, "Art and Socialism," in his *Vision and Design,* ed. J. Bullen (Oxford: Oxford University Press, 1981), 39–54, especially his discussion on 43. On the organization of die Brücke, see Jill Lloyd, *German Expressionism: Primitivism and Modernity* (New Haven: Yale University Press, 1991), 16–18. For other discussions of the question by contemporaries, see A. Halbe, "Gedanken und Vorschläge zur Durchführung einer wirtschaftlichen Organisation der Künstlerschaft," *Werkstatt der Kunst* 38 (1913): 523–525, and in the English context, see the unsigned essay "The Angels Club," *New Freewoman,* 1 October 1913. The essay is ascribed to Pound by *DMW,* 98, but her attribution has not been accepted by others. For Pound's own views, see his interview with John Cournos, "Bad Poetry Due to Lack of Money. Ezra Pound, Idaho Singer, Calls for Subsidies, and a Wandering Minstrelsy Life," *Boston Evening Transcript,* 6 September 1913, sec. 3, 6, cols. 3–5.

57. Useful overviews of the Bel Esprit project are given by Humphrey Carpenter, *A Serious Character: The Life of Ezra Pound* (Boston: Houghton Mifflin, 1988), 409–412, and *SLPQ,* 8–10. All quotations are from Pound, "Paris Letter," *Dial* 73 (November 1922): 549–554, reprinted in *EPPP,* 4:261.

58. Beach's records of her transactions with the Sunwise Turn are in PUF, *BP,* Box 132, Folder 2, and Box 133, Folder 3.

59. The principal sources for the history of the Sunwise Turn are Madge Jenison, *The Sunwise Turn: A Human Comedy of Bookselling* (New York: E. P. Dutton, 1923); Harold Loeb, *The Way It Was* (New York: Criterion Books, 1959), especially chapters 2 and 3; and "Obituary Notes: Madge Jenison," *Publisher's Weekly* 178 (4 July 1960): 167–168.

60. Jenison, *The Sunwise Turn,* 19.

61. "Oxen of the Sun" opens with a triple invocation for luck and fertility, beginning with this Gaelic word: "Deshil Holles Eamus. Deshil Holles Eamus. Deshil Holles Eamus" (Joyce, *Ulysses,* ed. Hans Walter Gabler et al. [New York and London: Garland Publishing, 1984], episode 14, line 1). Don Gifford, with Robert J. Seidman, writes, "'Deshil' after the Irish *deasil, deisiol:* turning to the right, clockwise, sunwise; a ritual gesture to attract good fortune, and an act of consecration when repeated three times" (*"Ulysses" Annotated: Notes for James Joyce's "Ulysses,"* rev. ed. [Berkeley: University of California Press, 1988], 408).

62. Jenison, *The Sunwise Turn,* 19–20.

63. "We were to conduct," ibid., 19; "a burning orange," ibid., 17, 24; "beautiful pieces," ibid., 21.

64. "We would be safe," ibid., 8; "How few people there are," ibid., 8–9 (emphasis added).

65. Ibid., 158.

66. Rodker advised Stevens that the owners of the Sunwise Turn "are good customers . . . and they are interested in what I am doing" (Rodker to Stevens, 24 March 1920,

Huntington Library, Stevens Collection, 1582). Loeb recounts his journey to London and Dublin for the purpose "of replenishing our stock of rarities," especially signed first editions, in *The Way It Was*, 41.

67. Jenison, *The Sunwise Turn*, 84–85.

68. Sales figures, ibid., 35; new location, ibid., 139–140; space more than double, Loeb, *The Way It Was*, 34; foot traffic triple, Jenison, *The Sunwise Turn*, 140; volumes issued, Loeb, *The Way it Was*, 34–35.

69. Jenison, *The Sunwise Turn*, 46.

70. Loeb, *The Was It Was*, 36.

71. PUF, *BP*, Box 63, Record Books: record book entitled "France Switzerland Italy Holland [and so forth]" s.v. "G." The copy number is registered in the "Calepin de vente d' *Ulysses*," conserved in the Maurice Saillet Papers of the Carlton Lake Collection at the Harry Ransom Humanities Research Center, University of Texas at Austin. Peggy Guggenheim's subscription form is found in the Capen Library, Poetry Collection, Beach Papers, Folder "Ulysses Subscriptions, 1st Edition."

72. Joyce, *Letters of James Joyce*, vol. 1, 144.

73. Loeb, *The Way It Was*, 52–53.

74. Knopf "used to come ocasionally and buy royally," Jenison, *The Sunwise Turn*, 53. Alfred Knopf's collection is preserved in its entirety at the University of Texas at Austin, Harry Ransom Humanities Research Center, and his copy of *Ulysses* (numbered 454) is part of the Alfred Knopf Collection. But Beach's record books show that he purchased two copies, the second of which is not identified. See PUF, *BP*, Box 63, Record Books: record book entitled "United States," s.v. "K." Also at the back of this volume, see two loose-leaf pages labeled "PAID USA," which record that Knopf had paid 240 francs, or the price of two copies (at a 20 percent discount for "members of the trade"). See also the record book entitled "England, Ireland, Scotland," with a loose-leaf page labeled "Copies to be Sent to U.S.A.," which also shows that Knopf purchased 2 copies.

75. "Stopped about eight," Jenison, *The Sunwise Turn*, 111. Huebsch purchases: PUF, *BP*, Box 63, Record Book: "United Kingdom." See the loose-leaf page labeled "Send to Braverman," which records that three copies of the 150-franc edition were to be sent to Huebsch. Also in the Box 63 record book entitled "U.S.A." is a notation that three copies were to be sent to Huebsch and that his payment by check was received on 28 February. The untitled record book in Box 63 shows that Huebsch had earlier been "notified" that his copies were ready. Huebsch's name is recorded in the day-to-day sales list of the daybook in the University of Texas collection, though not in the copy-by-copy list, which makes it impossible to identify which copies he received.

76. Loeb records his first meeting with Leon Fleischmann in *The Way It Was*, 42. Fleischmann's order form is in the PUF, *BP*, Box 132, Folder 7, and it indicates that he was living at 38, rue de Penthièvre, Paris; in the Record Book entitled "France" (Box 63), Fleischmann is reported to have "paid Feb. 8" and to have received copy number 254. His purchase is also recorded in the "Calepin de vente" at the University of Texas.

77. Mary Mowbray Clarke to Beach, undated letter accompanying a check dated 8 February 1922, PUF, *BP*, Box 133, Folder 3.

78. See Shane Leslie, "Ulysses," *Quarterly Review* 238 (October 1922), 219–234; partially reprinted in Deming, ed., *James Joyce,* vol. 1, 206, 210.

79. See "A New Ulysses," *Evening News* (London), 8 April 1922, 4; reprinted in Deming, ed., *James Joyce,* vol. 1, 193.

80. "Domini Canis" [Shane Leslie], "Ulysses," *Dublin Review* 171 (September 1922), 112; reprinted in Deming, ed., *James Joyce,* vol. 1, 201.

81. John Quinn to Beach, 27 March 1922, Capen Library, Poetry Collection, Beach Papers, Folder "Ulysses Subscriptions, 1st Edition."

82. "'Ulysses' is sold out" (Beach to Harriet Shaw Weaver, 18 June 1922, British Library, Harriet Shaw Weaver Papers). "But Adrienne Monnier ('La Maison des Amis des Livres,' 7, rue de l'Odéon) took over a number [of copies] and is beginning to sell them at Fr 500 (edition at Fr 150)" (Beach to Weaver, 26 June 1922, British Library, Harriet Shaw Weaver Papers).

83. On the early August price, see Mitchell Kennerley to Beach, 4 August 1922, PUF, *BP,* Box 132, Folder 5; the London price on 12 August is in Kennerly to Quinn, reported in *MNY,* 533.

84. Joyce, *Letters of James Joyce,* vol. 1, 190.

85. Weaver to Beach, 17 March 1922, PUF, *BP,* Box 232, Folder 3.

86. Pound to Alice Corbin Henderson, 12 March 1922, in Ira B. Nadel, ed., *The Letters of Ezra Pound to Alice Corbin Henderson* (Austin: University of Texas Press, 1993), 224.

87. Weaver to Beach, 20 May 1922, PUF, *BP,* Box 232, Folder 3. Weaver urges this still more insistently in another letter, on 16 June 1922, held in the same location. Five weeks later, Beach replied: "I did not hold back any copies for speculation for fear that the public might misinterpret it. But Adrienne Monnier ('La Maison des Amis des Livres,' 7, rue de l'Odéon) took over a number [of copies] and is beginning to sell them at Fr 500 (edition at Fr 150) and will give the proceeds to Mr. Joyce. Perhaps you will give that address to people who inquire where they can obtain 'Ulysses.' I always tell them that Adrienne Monnier among other booksellers subscribed for a good many copies and might have some left" (Beach to Weaver, 26 June 1922, British Library, Harriet Shaw Weaver Papers).

88. Beach, *Shakespeare and Company,* 183.

89. Pound to Homer and Isabel Pound, 11 May 1921, NHYB, *PP,* Box 52, Folder 1966.

90. George Rehm, "Review of *Ulysses,*" *Chicago Tribune,* 13 February 1922, Paris edition, 2; reprinted in Deming, ed., *James Joyce,* vol. 1, 213.

91. Diana Crane, *The Transformations of the Avant-Garde: The New York Art World, 1940–1985* (Chicago: University of Chicago Press, 1987), 112.

92. Monnier in McDougall, ed. and trans., *The Very Rich Hours of Adrienne Monnier,* 141.

93. Robert Louis Stevenson, quoted in Jenni Calder, *Robert Louis Stevenson: A Life Study* (Oxford: Oxford University Press, 1980), 172.

94. Pound to Quinn, 4–5 July 1922, in *SLPQ,* 213.

95. Weaver to Beach, 11 April 1922, PUF, *BP,* Box 232, Folder 3.

CHAPTER 3: THE PRICE OF MODERNISM

1. The quotations are from Joyce's *Ulysses,* Eliot's "Gerontion," and Pound's *Guide to Kulchur.*

2. Richard Ellmann and Charles Feidelson, Jr., eds., *The Modern Tradition: Backgrounds of Modern Literature* (New York: Oxford University Press, 1965), vi.

3. For the English publication, see T. S. Eliot to Henry Ware Eliot, 11 October 1922: "The *Criterion* is due to appear next Monday [16 October]," in *LOTSE 1*, 580. See also Eliot to Richard Cobden-Sanderson, 16 October 1922, in *LOTSE 1*, 582. The exact date of the American publication in the *Dial* is less clear. "We are to publish the text of the poem, without the notes, in the November Dial, which will be published about October 20th" (carbon copy of Gilbert Seldes to Horace Liveright, 7 September 1922, NHYB, *DP,* Mss. 34, Box 41, Folder 1153). With a delay of perhaps one or two days, the *Dial* apparently met its schedule: Burton Rascoe reported that he received his copy of the November issue on Thursday, 26 October 1922 (see Burton Rascoe, "A Bookman's Day Book," *New York Tribune,* 5 November 1922, Section V, 8). More mystery surrounds the exact date of the Liveright release. In a letter to Seldes of 12 September, Liveright confirmed that his firm was "not to publish The Waste Land prior to its appearance in The Dial," and speculated, "I don't think that we'll publish it before January" (NHYB, *DP,* Mss. 34, Box 41, Folder 1153). However, it is clear that the book had already been typeset in August, for Eliot had received and corrected the proofs by 15 September (see *LOTSE 1,* 570), and by late October the volume must have needed only binding. Apparently Liveright hastened to release it on 15 December in order to capitalize on the publicity generated by the announcement of the Dial Award in its December issue (presumably released around 20 November). For the date, see *TSEB*, A6, 29–32. For an earlier study on *The Waste Land*'s publication, see Daniel Woodward, "Notes on the Publishing History and Text of *The Waste Land,*" *Papers of the Bibliographical Society of America* 58 (1964): 252–269.

4. On Bishop see Elizabeth Carroll Spindler, *John Peale Bishop* (Morgantown: West Virginia University Library, 1980), chapters 5–7. It should be noted that Spindler often errs on points of detail, especially in transcribing letters. See below, note 7, for examples.

5. Seldes to Scofield Thayer, cable of 6 March 1922 (NHYB, *DP,* Box 40, Folder 1138). Thayer to Seldes, cable of 9 March 1922, and Seldes to Thayer, letter of 11 March 1922 (NHYB, *DP,* Box 40, 1139).

6. Ezra Pound to Jeanne Foster, 6 May 1922 (Harvard University, Houghton Library, bMS Am 1635). On Foster and Quinn, see *MNY,* 313, 367 (her background and their meeting in 1918), 464–465, 579 (her poetry), and 549 (her work for *Vanity Fair*). On Quinn's own work for *Vanity Fair* and his relations with its editor, Frank Crowninshield, see *MNY,* 276–277, 302–304, and 373. For a Foster contribution to *Vanity Fair* that was inspired by Pound, see "New Sculptures by Constantin Brancusi," *Vanity Fair* 18 (May 1922), 68. On her relations with Bishop, see Pound to Jeanne Foster, [20 April] 1922 (Harvard University, Houghton Library, bMS Am 1635).

7. John Peale Bishop to Edmund Wilson, 5 August 1922 (NHYB, Edmund Wilson Papers, Series 2). The letter is reported by Spindler, *John Peale Bishop,* 68–69, though with numerous errors. Whereas Bishop states that he met Pound extended on a "bright green couch swathed in a hieratic bathrobe," Spindler reports him on "a *high* green couch swathed in a *heraldric* bathrobe"—curious garb indeed. And whereas Bishop describes the bathrobe as "made of a maiden aunt's shit-brown blanket," Spindler fabricates "a maiden aunt's *shirt*-brown blanket" (68; all emphases added). Spindler also omits the three

sentences from "Here's the thing . . ." to "written in English since 1900." It is important to note that Bishop was apparently acting in collaboration with Edmund Wilson in his effort to purchase *The Waste Land,* a point elaborated below.

8. Pound himself was conscious of the dilemma presented by his role as impresario and its effects on his literary reputation. Consider his remarks to Margaret Anderson in 1921: "Point I never can seem to get you to take is that I have done more log rolling and attending to other people's affairs, Joyce, Lewis, Gaudier, etc. (don't regret it). But I am in my own small way, a writer myself, and as before stated I shd. like (and won't in any case get) the chance of being considered as the author of my own poems rather than as a literary politician and a very active stage manager of rising talent." See Pound to Margaret Anderson, [22? April 1921], *Pound/The Little Review: The Letters of Ezra Pound to Margaret Anderson,* Thomas L. Scott and Melvin J. Riedman, eds. (New York: New Directions, 1988), 266.

9. Pound to Felix Schelling, 8–9 July 1922, in Ezra Pound, *Selected Letters, 1907–1941,* D. D. Paige, ed. (New York: New Directions, 1971), 180.

10. It should be stressed that Pound did not at this time have a copy of the manuscript and so could not lend it to Bishop. One week before their meeting of 3 August, on 27 July, Pound had written to Eliot requesting a copy of the manuscript precisely because he had none available to show James Sibley Watson, Jr., who was then visiting Pound and wished to read it. This can be inferred from Eliot's reply of 28 July, when he stated that he had only one copy to hand but would make another and send it as soon as he could (see *LOTSE I,* 552). Equally important, the typescipt did not arrive until 14 August, or seven days after Bishop's departure, as reported by Watson to Thayer when he sent it on to him in Vienna (James Sibley Watson to Thayer, 16 August 1922, NHYB, *DP,* Box 44, Folder 1260).

11. The dates of Eliot's arrival and departure are inferred from Vivien Eliot to Mary Hutchinson, 12 January 1922, in *LOTSE I,* 501. She reports that "Tom has been here ten days," implying that he arrived on 2 January; and she states that "he will be back [in London] on Monday," 17 January 1922, suggesting that he would leave the day before, or 16 January. The new dates also make clear that all of Pound's editorial interventions occurred between 2 and 16 January 1922. Further, as scholars have previously suspected, these consisted principally of two editorial sessions. This hypothesis is confirmed by Eliot's letter of 20 January 1922 to Scofield Thayer, in which he reports that his poem "will have been three times through the sieve by Pound as well as myself" (*LOTSE I,* 503). In other words, in addition to the two times that Pound had already gone over the poem while the two men were in Paris, Eliot was planning to send it to him for yet a third time. Eliot probably sent the poem to Pound on 19 or 20 January, at roughly the same time he was writing to Thayer, and in response Pound wrote his letter dated "24 Saturnus," or 24 January 1922 (mistakenly assigned to 24 December 1921 by Valerie Eliot, and printed in *LOTSE I,* 497–498).

12. On *Instigations,* see *EPB,* A18. For Liveright's acceptance of *Poems, 1918–1921,* see Liveright to Pound, 13 September 1920, BIUL, *PM.2,* Liveright. For his helpful role in Pound's personal finances in 1921, see Lawrence S. Rainey, *Ezra Pound and The Monument of Culture* (Chicago: University of Chicago Press, 1991).

13. Copy of Liveright to John Quinn, 24 March 1922, BIUL, *PM.1,* Quinn:

I am attaching to this letter a card which James Joyce gave me in Paris one evening when I had dinner with him. . . . Ezra Pound and T.S. Eliot had dinner with us that night and as I am publishing Ezra Pound, and I'm about to publish Eliot, providing that Knopf has no legal claim on his next book, I think Joyce belongs in the Boni and Liveright fold.

I saw Pound each day during the six days I was in Paris, and I made a little arrangement with him that will take care of his rent over there for the next two years anyhow.

Liveright's contract with Pound is dated 4 January 1922, and this is also the date he apparently left Paris. He refers to his departure in a postcard from London to Pound, dated 11 January 1922, where he reports that he met May Sinclair "last Thursday," 5 January 1922; presumably, therefore, he left Paris on 4 January. If so, and if he stayed "six days in Paris" (as he reports), then he must have arrived there on 29 or 30 December 1921. Since Eliot himself did not arrive in Paris until 2 January, the dinner could have occurred only on the evenings of 2 or 3 January. The latter date is more likely, as Eliot would have been tired after arriving from Lausanne on 2 January, and as some time must be allowed for plans to have been formulated and accepted by all the parties. There are also three other references to the dinner. Eliot reports on his offer from Liveright in a letter to Alfred A. Knopf, dated 3 April 1922, in which he explains that "Mr. Liveright, whom I met in Paris," has made an offer for the poem (see *LOTSE 1*, 519). Pound also refers to the dinner in a letter to Jeanne Foster, dated 5 April 1922: "Liveright saw the right people in Paris. . . . He saw Joyce and Eliot with me" (see Pound to Jeanne Foster, 5 April 1922, Harvard University, Houghton Library, bMS Am 1635). Finally, Eliot reports the meeting again in a letter to John Quinn, dated 25 June: "Pound introduced me to Liveright in Paris, and Liveright made me the offer" (see *LOTSE 1*, 530).

14. Pound to Jeanne Foster, 5 April 1922.

15. Pound to Quinn, 20 June 1920, NYPL, *QP*, Box 34, Folder 4.

16. Liveright to Pound, 11 January 1922, NHYB, *BP*, Folder 23. It is Liveright's concern with the length of the poem that explains Eliot's repeated proposals designed to make the book longer by adding as prefatory material to *The Waste Land:* (1) three minor pieces, a suggestion that Pound rejected on 24 January, (2) a reprint of "Gerontion," an idea advanced to Pound in a letter circa 26 January (assigned to "24? January" by Valerie Eliot), and (3) one or two poems by Pound, also advanced in the same letter of circa 26 January to Pound. In addition, however, Liveright was nervous about its publication in periodical form, and whether it would be printed in a single issue: "And does it *all* appear in *one* issue of the Dial—please let me know." This concern prompted Eliot to worry about the same question, as emerges in his letter offering the poem to the *Dial* on 20 January 1922: "It could easily go into 4 issues if you like, but not more" (T. S. Eliot to Scofield Thayer, 20 January 1922, NHYB, *DP*, Box 31, Folder 810). Liveright may have communicated his concerns directly to Eliot after he arrived in London on 17 January, for Liveright did not depart for the United States until 28 January and could easily have met or contacted the poet until then. Surely this explains Eliot's anxiety in his letters to Thayer (20 January) and Pound (circa 26 January) on precisely those matters raised earlier in Liveright's note of 11 January to Pound.

17. See Liveright to Pound, 12 October 1922, NHYB, *BP,* Folder 23: "It doesn't seem that we've found the right thing yet, does it? . . . And if Yeats insists on sticking to Macmillan, and I firmly believe that Yeats has more to do with it than Watt [his agent] because I did have a long talk with Watt and he seemed inclined to let me have a look-in,—well, all the worse for Yeats."

18. Pound to Thayer, 18 February 1922, NHYB, *DP,* Box 38, Folder 1070; Thayer to Pound, 5 March 1922, and Pound to Thayer, 9–10 March 1922, NHYB, *DP,* Box 38, Folder 1071.

19. Thayer's marginalia on Eliot's letter of 20 January 1922 (NHYB, *DP,* Box 31, Folder 810) record his diligent calculations of the poem's price at normal rates: if typeset at thirty-five lines per page, the poem would come to slightly less than twelve pages, yielding a price of $120; if typeset at forty lines per page, it would come to eleven and a quarter pages, yielding a price slightly over $110. Summarizing his results, Thayer firmly concludes: "12 pp. $120." His offer of $150, then, was already 25 percent higher than normal rates.

20. It must be stressed that there is no straightforward procedure that would enable us to establish an exact value in current dollars for a specific income from 1922. One can make an estimate based on the consumer price index, which by 1986 had risen to 5.79 times its level in 1922. However, this may produce misleading figures, insofar as it fails to indicate the relative position of a given income within the larger economy. If, for example, we assume that the average per capita income was $735 in 1922 and multiply this by 5.79, it yields a 1986 average per capita income of $4,256. In reality, however, the national income per capita in 1986 was more than three times as high: $14,166. The reason for this discrepancy is that the average person enjoys more wealth today than he did in 1922, a fact that must also be taken into account when attempting to estimate an equivalent income figure. A better approach, then, is to take the given sum as a percentage of national income per capita. In that case, the offer of $150 was 20 percent of the national income per capita of $750 (hereafter the figure of $735 is rounded to $750), and the equivalent figure in 1986 dollars would be $2,833. Again, these figures are offered as rough estimates, not precise equivalents. It is impossible to be more exact because it was not until the 1940s that the minimum income requirement for annual tax returns was lowered enough to facilitate accurate nationwide estimates of income distribution for families and individuals. Prior to then, higher minimums meant that information was available for only a small fraction of the population, those with the highest incomes. For various estimates of national income per capita, see Wesley C. Mitchell, Willford I. King, et al., *Income in the United States: Its Amount and Distribution, 1909–1919* (New York: Harcourt, Brace, 1921), with relevant figures on 13, 76, and 144–147; they concluded that income per capita in 1918 and 1919 totaled $586 and $629, respectively. See also *Historical Statistics of the United States: Colonial Times to 1970, Part 1* (Washington: Department of Commerce, 1976), 166–167 and 284 ff.; it reports that the average annual earnings of employees in the educational services in 1922 were $1,109. See also Robert F. Martin, *National Income in the United States, 1799–1938* (New York: National Industrial Conference Board, 1941), 7; and Simon Kuznets, *National Income and Its Composition, 1919–1938,* vol. 1 (New York: National Bureau of Economic Research, 1941). For help in considering these economic questions, I am grateful to Lance Davis.

21. Eliot to Thayer, 16 March 1922, NHYB, *DP,* Box 31, Folder 810.

22. Eliot to Pound, 12 March 1922, *LOTSE 1*, 507.

23. Thayer visited Pound for the first time on 12 July 1921. Pound's initial contract to serve as writer and talent scout for the *Dial* had expired twelve days earlier, and Thayer had advised him that it would not be renewed. When the two met for a second time on 13 July, however, the contract was renewed, though only in part: Pound would continue to write for the *Dial* but not serve as talent scout, and he would receive roughly half his former salary. These meetings were only part of a series that continued throughout the month: 12 July, 13 July, circa 20 July, 26 July, and 28 July. For the meetings, see Pound to Dorothy Shakespear Pound, 12 July, 14 July, 21 July, 26 July, 30 July 1921, BIUL, *PM.3, 1921*. On the contracts, negotiations, and the economic background to Pound's finances, see Lawrence S. Rainey, "The Earliest Manuscripts of the Malatesta Cantos by Ezra Pound" (Ph.D. diss., University of Chicago, 1986), 25–51, and especially 43–46.

24. Pound to Thayer, 23 April 1922, NHYB, *DP*, Box 38, Folder 1072.

25. Pound to Thayer, 6 May 1922, NHYB, *DP*, Box 38, Folder 1073.

26. The visit is mentioned in Eliot to Sidney Schiff, attributed to "early June 1922" by Valerie Eliot in *LOTSE 1*, 528: "I also went to Verona and saw Pound." On Pound's travels in 1922 see Rainey, "The Earliest Manuscripts of the Malatesta Cantos by Ezra Pound," 70–91, especially 85–88. His meeting with Eliot is rehearsed in various drafts for the Malatesta Cantos, in particular: Draft B, lines 3–4, transcribed in ibid., 406–407; Draft C1, lines 82–85, transcribed in ibid., 482–488; and Draft C3, lines 61–100, transcribed in ibid., 566–571, with annotations for specific passages. For Pound's later reminiscences, see Cantos 29 and 78.

27. Eliot to Pound, 12 March 1922, *LOTSE 1*, 508. Eliot mentions the *Little Review* only twice in his correspondence for 1922, both times in letters to Pound. Clearly he considered the journal to be largely Pound's.

28. Pound to Dorothy Shakespear Pound, 21 July 1922, BIUL, *PM.3, 1922*.

29. Thayer to Seldes, 20 July 1922, NHYB, *DP*, Box 40, Folder 1148. Thayer reports that Watson "is present as I dictate," leaving no doubt that Watson departed within hours of his meeting with Pound on 19 July (date of meeting from Pound to Dorothy Shakespear Pound, 21 July 1922).

30. Thayer to Eliot, 5 October 1922, NHYB, *DP*, Box 31, Folder 810: "I have been very glad to learn from New York that the suggestion I made to Mr. Watson while he was with me in Berlin last July has borne fruit and that we are despite your asperity to have the pleasure of recognizing publicly your contribution to contemporary letters."

31. Pound to Dorothy Shakespear Pound, 29 July 1922, BIUL, *PM.3*.

32. Angle brackets indicate handwritten insertion. Watson to Thayer, 29 July 1922, NHYB, *DP*, Box 44, Folder 1260.

33. Eliot to Pound, 28 July 1922, *LOTSE 1*, 552.

34. Angle brackets indicate handwritten insertion. Watson to Thayer, 16 August 1922, NHYB, *DP*, Box 44, Folder 1260.

35. Eliot to Watson, 15 August 1922, *LOTSE 1*, 560.

36. Watson to Thayer, 19 August 1922, NHYB, *DP*, Box 44, Folder 1260.

37. Eliot to Quinn, 21 August 1922, *LOTSE 1*, 564. Also cited in Valerie Eliot, ed., *T. S. Eliot, The Waste Land. A Facsimile* (New York: Harcourt, Brace, 1971), xxiv.

38. Eliot to Pound, 30 August 1922, *LOTSE 1,* 567; punctuation here reproduces the original.

39. Eliot to Watson, 21 August 1922, *LOTSE 1,* 564–565; Seldes to Thayer, 31 August 1922, NHYB, *DP,* Box 40, Folder 1151.

40. Liveright to Pound, 5 February 1922, BIUL, *PM.1,* Liveright.

41. "A Group of Poems by T. S. Eliot: A Selection from the Dramatic Lyrics of a Much Discussed American Poet," *Vanity Fair* 20, no. 4 (June 1923), 67. The publication is not mentioned in *EPB* because Gallup's policy is to exclude reprints of poems that have previously appeared in book form. The other articles by Eliot appeared in *Vanity Fair* 20, no. 5 (July 1923), 51, 98; 21, no. 3 (November 1923), 44, 118; and 21, no. 6 (February 1924), 29, 98.

42. On *The Egoist,* see *DMW.*

43. On the *Little Review,* see Frank Luther Mott, *A History of American Magazines,* vol. 5, *Sketches of Twenty-one Magazines, 1905–1930* (Cambridge: Harvard University Press, 1968), 166–178. Mott considers it "unlikely that the circulation ever rose to much over a thousand" (171). His figure is offered as a correction to the earlier estimate of 2,000 given by Frederick J. Hoffman et al., *The Little Magazine: A History and Bibliography* (Princeton: Princeton University Press, 1946), 57. My figures are from Pound to Quinn, 8 February 1917, NYPL, *QP.* For the *Egoist,* see *DMW,* 460; Jane Lidderdale reports that its largest circulation was 400 copies per issue, with about 268 by subscription, during the first six months of its life (1913). "Then it went into a long decline, with a sharp drop in November 1916 when the long-term subscriptions ran out; and the circulation never rose again above 200."

44. In the second half of 1915 the *Egoist* earned £37 in sales and subscriptions, and one surmises that its advertising revenues were around £5 (see *DMW,* 99). In *Sketches of Twenty-one Magazines,* Mott estimates that advertising revenues for the *Little Review* "seldom or never exceeded $500 a year" (171); sales and subscriptions probably earned around $4,000 in 1917, according to my estimate.

    The "revolution" in the magazine industry is usually dated to 1893, when several magazines dramatically dropped their prices and achieved unprecedented circulation rates; the price of a magazine was now less than the cost of its production, and the difference was made up with expanded revenues from advertisers. The most perceptive discussion of this transformation appears in Richard Ohmann, *Selling Culture: Magazines, Markets, and Class at the Turn of the Century* (London: Verso, 1996), 24–38.

45. All figures are from the annual financial reports of the *Dial,* in NHYB, *DP,* Box 9, Folders 327–332.

46. For the *Little Review* figure, see Mott, *Sketches of Twenty-one Magazines,* 171, and *MNY,* 343. The four donors were John Quinn, Otto Kahn, Mrs. James Byrne, and Max Pam. Quinn's patronage included a standing subsidy of $750 per year, in addition to his $400 gift as part of the syndicate. For the *Egoist,* see *DMW,* 459. Weaver's contributions were respectively £251, £342, £234, and £185.

47. Lewis appeared in the *Little Review* of November 1918 and the *Dial* of August 1921. Zadkine appeared in the *Little Review* of December 1918 and the *Dial* of October 1921.

48. Thayer to Seldes, 28 November 1922, NHYB, *DP,* Box 41, Folder 1157.

49. See [Scofield Thayer], "Comment," *Dial* 73, no. 1 (July 1922), 119. Springarn's major

essays are collected in Joel Springarn, *Creative Criticism: Essays on the Unity of Genius and Taste* (New York: Henry Holt, 1917). The book is dedicated "to my friend Benedetto Croce, the most original of all modern thinkers on Art," and it reports that the central essay, "The New Criticism," was originally delivered as a lecture at Columbia University in 1910 (iii). For Springarn's influence on the *Dial,* see William Wasserstrom, *The Time of the Dial* (Syracuse: Syracuse University Press, 1963), 17–19. See also Nicholas Joost, *Scofield Thayer and the Dial* (Carbondale: Southern Illinois University Press, 1964); and Nicholas Joost, *The Dial, 1912–1920* (Barre, Mass.: Barre Publishers, 1967).

50. Eliot to Thayer, 1 January 1921, *LOTSE 1,* 429.

51. Thayer to Seldes, 12 October 1922, NHYB, *DP,* Box 41, Folder 1153. The practice was a regular one at the *Dial,* and newspaper clippings from 1920–1929 fill three boxes; NHYB, *DP,* Boxes 16, 17, 18.

52. On *Vanity Fair,* see Martha Cohn Cooper, "Frank Crowninshield and *Vanity Fair*" (Ph.D. diss., University of North Carolina, 1976); Kitty Hoffman, "A History of *Vanity Fair:* A Modernist Journal in America" (Ph.D. diss., University of Toronto, 1980); and Cynthia L. Ward, "*Vanity Fair* Magazine and the Modern Style, 1914–1936 (New York City)" (Ph.D. diss., State University of New York at Stony Brook, 1983). Also useful is Caroline Seebohm, *The Man Who Was Vogue: The Life and Times of Condé Nast* (New York: Viking, 1982). For a useful survey of the magazine market and industry see Theodore Peterson, *Magazines in the Twentieth Century* (Urbana: University of Illinois Press, 1964). For Nast's strategy of market segmentation see Cohn Cooper, "Frank Crowninshield and *Vanity Fair,*" 38.

53. Thayer to Mrs. Edward D. Thayer, 16 December 1922, NHYB, *DP,* Box 43, 1922; Thayer to Seldes, 26 December 1922, NHYB, *DP,* Box 441 Folder 1159; Thayer to Seldes, 18 January, 28 May, and 8 June 1923, NHYB, *DP,* Box 41, Folders 1160, 1166, 1167. "I was recently sent a copy of *Vanity Fair* and was interested to see how many of my friends are now writing for that paper. In the number for December I find the names of Kenneth MacGowan, Henry McBride, Kenneth Burke, Gilbert Seldes and of my acquaintance Miss Millay" (Thayer to Mrs. Edward D. Thayer, 16 December 1922). Thayer also complains that "Mr. Burke's review [in the *Dial*] interested me, but I do not find it so good as his recent article developing more or less the same theme in Vanity Fair" (Thayer to Seldes, 26 December 1922).

54. As a point of comparison, the two leading weeklies, *Collier's* and the *Saturday Evening Post,* had circulations of 1 million and 2.1 million, respectively. For the advertising revenues of *Vanity Fair,* I rely on Peterson, *Magazines in the Twentieth Century,* 271. For the circulation figures of all the journals discussed here, *N. W. Ayer & Son's American Newspaper Anuual and Directory* (Philadelphia: N. W Ayer & Son's, 1922), 1224–1226, reports figures from the Audit Bureau of Circulation. On advertising as "an integral part of the magazine" (that is, *Vanity Fair*), see Cohn Cooper, "Frank Crowninshield and *Vanity Fair,*" 42.

55. B. L. Reid, *The Man from New York: John Quinn and His Friends* (New York: Oxford University Press, 1968), 594.

56. Less is known about Thayer's collecting; but see Joost, *Scofield Thayer,* 23–36.

57. See Nicholas Fox Weber, *Patron Saints: Five Rebels Who Opened America to a New Art*

(New York: Knopf, 1992), 56; and *The Frank Crowninshield Collection of Modern French Art,* Auction Catalogue, Parke-Bernet Galleries (20–21 October 1943).

58. Ward, "*Vanity Fair* Magazine and the Modern Style," 91–92, 100–101; see Alfred H. Barr, Jr., "An American Museum of Modern Art," *Vanity Fair* 33 (November 1929), 79, 136.

59. John Quinn, "Jacob Epstein, Sculptor," *Vanity Fair* 9 (1917), 76, 114; and "James Joyce, A New Irish Novelist," *Vanity Fair* 8 (1917), 49, 128; see Reid, *Man From New York,* 580–590; on Gregg and *Vanity Fair,* see Ward, "*Vanity Fair* Magazine and the Modern Style," 91.

60. See Peter Bürger, *Theory of the Avant-Garde,* trans. Michael Shaw (Minneapolis: University of Minnesota Press, 1984); Andreas Huyssen, *After the Great Divide* (Bloomington: Indiana University Press, 1986); and Marjorie Perloff, *The Poetics of Indeterminacy* (Princeton: Princeton University Press, 1981; reprint, Evanston: Northwestern University Press, 1983). See also Charles Russell: *Poets, Prophets, and Revolutionaries: The Literary Avant-Garde from Rimbaud Through Postmodernism* (Oxford: Oxford University Press, 1985).

61. See Walker Gilmore, *Horace Liveright: Publisher of the Twenties* (New York: David Lewis, 1970), 38. A normal budget would have been 12 to 15 cents per copy; Liveright spent 25 cents per copy. Gilmore draws his information from interviews with Manuel Komroff, a former Liveright employee.

62. On the multiple collected editions of Tennyson, see June Steffensen Hagen, *Tennyson and His Publishers* (University Park: Pennsylvania State University Press, 1979), 149–150. See also her entire study on the emergence of this practice and Tennyson's use of it throughout his later career.

63. See Liam Miller, *The Dun Emer Press, Later the Cuala Press* (Dublin: Dolmen Press, 1973).

64. See John Dreyfus, *Bruce Rogers and American Typography* (Cambridge: Cambridge University Press, 1959).

65. Conrad Aiken to Maurice Firuski, 15 February 1922, Chapin Library, Williams College, T. S. Eliot Collection. I wish to thank Robert L. Volz, Rare Book Custodian, for his kindness in drawing this letter to my attention.

66. T. S. Eliot to Maurice Firuski, 26 February 1922, Chapin Library, Williams College, T. S. Eliot Collection. Mention of this letter is made by Valerie Eliot in *LOTSE 1,* 515n.1. I am grateful to Mrs. Eliot for permission to quote this letter in its entirety, and for her kindness in responding to my inquiries. The letter from T. S. Eliot to Edmund Wilson quoted below is also printed by permission of Mrs. Eliot, and both are copyrighted by her.

67. T. S. Eliot to Ezra Pound, 12 March 1922, *LOTSE 1,* 507.

68. T. S. Eliot to Edmund Wilson, 14 August 1922, Beinecke Library, Yale University, Edmund Wilson Papers.

69. For the wages of Crowninshield's executive secretary, Jeanne Ballot, who earned $22 per week, or $1,144 per year, see Cohn Cooper, "Frank Crowninshield and *Vanity Fair,*" 48. The $2,000 paid to Eliot in the form of the Dial Award was a remarkable figure: the highest sum *Vanity Fair* ever paid was $100, to F. Scott Fitzgerald in 1925 for a short story.

CHAPTER 4: FROM THE PATRON TO *IL DUCE*

1. On Joyce, see Jane Lidderdale and Mary Nicholson, *Dear Miss Weaver: Harriet Shaw Weaver, 1876–1961* (New York: Viking Press, 1970), 157, 224; on Eliot, see Peter Ackroyd, *T. S. Eliot: A Life* (New York: Simon and Schuster, 1984), 110.

2. *C,* Canto 10, 47; Canto 11, 48.

3. The following discussion of Sigismondo is taken, with minor changes, from my previous book, *Ezra Pound and the Monument of Culture: Text, History, and the Malatesta Cantos* (Chicago: University of Chicago Press, 1991). On Sigismondo Malatesta, see Philip J. Jones, *The Malatesta of Rimini and the Papal State: A Political History* (Cambridge: Cambridge University Press, 1974), chap. 7. Also important is a collection of essays by Philip J. Jones et al., *Studi malatestiani* (Rome: Istituto storico italiano per il medioevo, 1978), which includes an essay by Jones, "Le signorie di Sigismondo Malatesta," 5–20. The best biography is still that of Francesco Gaetano Battaglini, "Della vita e de' fatti di Sigismondo Pandolfo Malatesta Signor di Rimino, Commentario," in *Basini Parmensis poetae opera praestantiora nunc primum edita et opportunis commentariis illustrata* (Rimini: Ex typographia Albertiniana, 1794), 2:257–699.

4. See, for example, Nikolaus Pevsner, *Outline of European Architecture,* 7th ed. (Harmondsworth: Penguin, 1963), 189–190. The most complete account of the church's construction is furnished by Corrado Ricci, *Il tempio malatestiano* (Rome-Milan: Bestetti & Tumminelli, n.d. [but 1924]; reprint, Rimini: Bruno Ghigi Editore, 1974). See also Rudolf Wittkower, *Architectural Principles in the Age of Humanism* (New York: W. W. Norton, 1971; 1st ed., 1949), 1–41. On the iconography of the sculptural decorations, see Charles Mitchell, "Il tempio malatestiano," in Jones et al., *Studi malatestiani,* 71–104. And for the viewpoint of more recent architectural history, see Franco Borsi, *Leon Battista Alberti: L'opera completa* (Milan: Electa Editrice, 1980).

5. On this later stage in his career, see Giovanni Soranzo, *Pio II e la politica italiana nella lotta contro i Malatesti, 1457–1463* (Padua: Fratelli Drucker, 1911).

6. See Gioacchino Paparelli, *Enea Silvio Piccolomini: L'umanesimo sul soglio di Pietro,* 2d ed. (Ravenna: Longo Editore, 1978), 175.

7. See, for example, Giorgio Vasari, *Le vite de' più eccellenti pittori, scultori e architettori* (Novara: Istituto geografico De Agostini, 1967; 1st ed., 1550), vol. 2, 138, 358–359, 414.

8. For the first mention of this notion in 1718, see Giuseppe Garuffi, "Lettera apologetica, scritta all'Illustrissimo Signor Carlo-Francesco Marcheselli, Nobile Riminese, dal Signor Arciprete D. Giuseppe Malatesta Garuffi, in difesa del Tempio famosissimo di san Francesco, eretto in Rimini da Sigismondo-Pandolfo Maltesta in tempo, che teneva il dominio di detta città," in *Giornale de' letterati d'Italia* 30 (1718), 181. For the discussion in 1756 see Gianmaria Mazzuchelli, *Notizie intorno ad Isotta da Rimino,* 2d ed. (Brescia: Dalle stampe di Giambattista Bossini, 1759; 1st ed. 1756), 32, 38–39; as well as Giovanbattista Costa, "Il Tempio di S. Francesco di Rimino, o sia descrizione delle cose più notabili in esso contenute," in Giuseppe Rocchi, ed., *Miscellanei di varia lettura,* vol. 5 (Lucca, 1765), 88. For the discussion in 1789 see Francesco Gaetano Battaglini, *Memorie istoriche di Rimino e de' suoi signori artatamente scritte ad illustrare la zecca e la moneta riminese,* Guid'Antonio Zanetti, ed. (Bologna: Nella stamperia di Lelio dalla Volpe, 1789; reprint,

Rimini: Bruno Ghighi, 1976), 38–39n.60. For fuller discussion of this debate and its effects on Pound, see Rainey, *Ezra Pound and the Monument of Culture*, 186–209.

9. Jacob Burckhardt, *The Civilization of the Renaissance in Italy*, trans. S. G. C. Middlemore (New York: Harper & Row, 1958), 235 for all quotations to this point.

10. Ibid., 50.

11. John Addington Symonds, *Sketches and Studies in Italy and Greece*, 2d series (London: Smith, Elder, 1898; 1st ed. 1874), 103, 20; and John Addington Symonds, *The Renaissance in Italy*, vol. 1, *The Age of the Despots* (New York: Henry Holt, 1888; 1st ed., 1876), 428n.1.

12. Charles Yriarte, *Un Condottiere au XVe siècle. Rimini: Etudes sur les lettres et les arts à la cour des Malatesta* (Paris: Jules Rothschild, 1882), 218–219, 138, 218, 198.

13. Pasquale Villari, "Rimini," in *Encylopaedia Britannica*, vol. 20 (Edinburgh: A. & C. Black, 1886), 555–560, here 558; and *Encylopaedia Britannica*, vol. 23 (Cambridge: Cambridge University Press, 1911), 344–347, here 346.

14. See Karl Baedeker, *Italy: Handbook for Travelers*, 13th rev. ed., vol. 2, *Second Part: Central Italy and Rome* (Leipzig: Baedeker, 1900), 104. See also the same author and title, 1908 edition, 98. See Edward Hutton, *Sigismondo Pandolfo Malatesta—Lord of Rimini: A Study of a XV Century Despot* (London: J. M. Dent, 1906), 296, 295–296, and 207–215.

15. Giovanni Soranzo, "La sigla SI di Sigismondo Pandolfo Malatesta," *La Romagna* 6 (1909): 306–324. Aldo Francesco Massèra, "I poeti isottei," *Giornale storico della letteratura italiana* 57 (1911): 1–32.

16. Edward Hutton, *The Cities of Romagna and the Marches* (London: Methuen, 1913); and Luigi Orsini, *Il tempio malatestiano* (Florence: Fratelli Alinari, 1915; reprint, 1927), v, vi.

17. See Ricci, *Il tempio malatestiano*, 315–319.

18. See Anthony Giddens, *The Consequences of Modernity* (Stanford: Stanford University Press, 1990), 21–27.

19. Friedrich Nietzsche, *Menschliches, Allzumenschliches I*, no. 237, in Giorgio Colli and Mazzini Montinari, eds., *Sämtliche Werke: Kritische Studienausgabe* (Munich-Berlin: DTV and de Gruyter, 1980), vol. 2, 199. For the English edition contemporary with Pound, see Friedrich Nietzsche, *Complete Works*, ed. Oskar Ludwig Levy (New York: Russell & Russell, reprint of 1909–1911 ed.), vol. 6, 220–221.

20. Antonio Beltramelli, *I canti di Fauno* (Naples: Editore Francesco Perrella, 1908); *Un tempio d'amore* (Palermo: Remo Sandron, 1912), 40, 43–44.

21. Antonio Beltramelli, *L'uomo nuovo* (Rome-Milan: Monadori, 1923), 55, 56–57.

22. On Beltramelli's career, see R. Bertacchini, "Beltramelli, Antonio," in *Dizionario biografico degli italiani*, vol. 8 (Rome: Istituto della Enciclopedia Italiana, 1966), 56–60. On his participation in the convention, see Emilio R. Papa, *Fascismo e cultura* (Venice-Padua: Marsilio, 1974), 161–162 for signers of the manifesto, and 165 for the manifesto itself. For the regime's tributes to Beltramelli upon his death, see *Il Popolo d'Italia* (Milan), 16 March 1930, 3; this newspaper was founded by Mussolini and edited by his brother Arnoldo after 1922; Arnoldo's obituary notice for Beltramelli appears on the same page.

23. Beltramelli's letters to Ricci, documenting their collaboration in 1907, are transcribed in Rainey, *Ezra Pound and the Monument of Culture*, 324n.114.

24. For Ricci's life, see Rainey, *Ezra Pound and the Monument of Culture,* 193–194 and the relevant notes indicating sources.

25. On Pound's notes from Symonds, his purchase of the Baedeker, and his reading of Beltramelli in June 1922, see Rainey, *Ezra Pound and the Monument of Culture,* 117–118, 290n.105, 29–31.

26. Pound's copy of Yriarte is held at Yale University, the Beinecke Rare Book and Manuscript Library, call number ZA P865 +Zv 882y; the various notes, calling cards, and newspaper clippings that he kept inside the volume have the call number Uncat. Za file 204. Quotations and discussions of his marginalia in Yriarte appear in Rainey, *Ezra Pound and the Monument of Culture,* 30, 41–42, 121–122, 154, 163–164, 176, 182, 189–190, 316n.87, and 319n.106, with reproductions on 164, 175, and 319n.106; and Daniel Bornstein, "The Poet as Historian: Researching the Malatesta Cantos," *Paideuma* 10 (1981): 283–291. See Soranzo, *Pio II e la politica italiana.* For Pound's purchase of Soranzo's book and its immediate influence on his drafts, and for his work in the Bibliothèque Nationale, see Rainey, *Ezra Pound and the Monument of Culture,* 103–104.

27. On his meeting with Ricci, see Rainey, *Ezra Pound and the Monument of Culture,* 191–197.

28. For his efforts to contact Santi Muratori, see Ezra Pound to Dorothy Shakespear Pound, 28 March 1923, BIUL, *PM.2,* 1923; for his interest in contacting Soranzo, see Ezra Pound to Isabel Pound, 24 February 1923, NHYB, *PP,* 43, Box 52, folder 1968.

29. For drafts connecting Malatestan Rimini with the culture of Provence, see Rainey, *Ezra Pound and the Monument of Culture,* 37–42.

30. On his life, see A. S. Strnad, "Broglio, Gaspare," in *Dizionario biografico degli italiani,* vol. 14 (Rome: Istituto della Enciclopedia Italiana, 1972), 437–439. Giovanni Soranzo, *Pio II e la politica italiana,* 11. Soranzo argues that Broglio was "al corrente delle pratiche diplomatiche, delle imprese, delle condizioni politiche ed economiche del suo signore"; his chronicle is "importantissima, perchè spesso verte intorno a fatti, dei quali egli si dice testimone oculare e che invano si recercano nelle altre cronache o nelle carte degli archivi."

31. On the background of the battle and the many sources describing it, see Jones, *The Malatesta of Rimini,* 230; and Soranzo, *Pio II e la politica italiana,* 247–250. The passage in Broglio's original manuscript is in his *Cronaca universale,* Rimini, Biblioteca Civica Gambalunga, ms. SC-MS 1161 (formerly D.III.48), fol. 246^r according to the modern enumeration, fol. 273^r according to the older one. The work has been partially published as Gaspare Broglio Tartaglia, *Cronaca malatestiana del secolo XV (dalla Cronaca Universale),* ed. Antonio G. Luciani (Rimini: Bruno Ghigi Editore, 1982), but this edition contains only excerpts and omits the passage in question. All transcriptions and translations are mine.

32. For Pound's visit to Rimini, see Ezra Pound to Dorothy Pound, 21 March 1923, BIUL, *PM.3.* See also Ezra Pound to Agnes Bedford, 25 March 1923, BIUL, *PM.2,* Bedford, 1923. See Ezra Pound to Ernest Hemingway, 26 March 1923, Boston, Kennedy Library, Hemingway Collection, E. Pound. See Ezra Pound to James Sibley Watson, Jr., 26 March 1923, New York Public Library, Berg Collection; and Ezra Pound to Dorothy Pound, 28 March 1923, BIUL, *PM.3.*

33. See also Lawrence Rainey, "'All I Want You to Do Is to Follow the Orders,'" in Lawrence Rainey, ed., *A Poem Containing History: The Text of Ezra Pound's "Cantos"* (Ann Arbor: University of Michigan Press, 1996), 63–114.

34. Pound's final typescript is in Yale University, Beinecke Library, William Bird Papers, Series 2, Item 37. On the three printings see *EPB,* 269, C652; 37–30, A26; and 45–47, A31.

35. "Medieval History Condensed in Verse. Ezra Pound Writing Results of Research in Italy," *New York Herald,* 29 April 1923, sec. 2, p. 3, col. 6.

36. Pound gives a footnote citing Yriarte, *Un Condottiere,* in *C,* Canto 10, 44; and he corrects Yriarte's transcription of a document in Italian (*C,* Canto 8, 28), altering Yriarte's *gettata via* to *buttato via* to make it accord with the original manuscript housed in Florence.

37. Donald Davie, *Ezra Pound: Poet as Sculptor* (New York: Oxford University Press, 1968), 126.

38. Ezra Pound, untitled notes, NHYB, *PP,* Box 65, Folder 2538.

39. Ibid.

40. Ezra Pound, "Fascism or the Direction of the Will," NHYB, *PP,* Box 89, Folder 3359. The essay's date is inferred from Pound's references to having written *Jefferson and/or Mussolini* two months earlier in February 1933. The title alludes to Dante's letter to Can Grande. Pound, of course, also used the phrase to define his aims in *The Cantos,* implicitly urging a common program shared by his poem and Fascism.

41. Pound, revised version of "Fascism or the Direction of the Will," NHYB, *PP,* Box 89, Folder 3360.

42. Giovanni Gentile, "The Philosophic Basis of Fascism," *Foreign Affairs* 6 (1927–1928): 290–304.

43. All quotations are from Pound, "Fascism or the Direction of the Will."

44. Emilio Gentile, "The Conquest of Modernity: From Modernist Nationalism to Fascism," *Modernism/Modernity* 1, no. 3 (September 1994): 55–87, here 73.

45. G. Gentile, "The Philosophic Basis of Fascism," 296.

46. Benito Mussolini, "Discorso a Napoli," 24 October 1922, quoted in E. Gentile, "The Conquest of Modernity," 73.

47. Emilio Gentile, "Fascism as Political Religion," *Journal of Contemporary History* 25 (1990): 229–251, quotation 238.

48. Ezra Pound to Dorothy Shakespear Pound, 13 March 1923, BIUL, *PM.3,* 1923.

49. Ezra Pound to Dorothy Pound, "Wednesday" [21 March 1923], BIUL, *PM.3,* 1923. Pound's postcards to Dorothy show him in San Marino on 13–14 March, Pennabilli on 15 March, Fano on 16–17 March, Pesaro on 18–19 March, and Urbino on 19–20 March 1923.

50. My account of the life of Averardo Marchetti is based on photocopies of his birth, marriage, and death certificates, as well as the birth certificate of his first son and the death certificate of his wife, all from the Anagrafe of Forlì. These materials were kindly furnished to me by Dr. Paola Delbianco of the Biblioteca civica Gambalunga, together with her letter of 26 October 1988, and include: her own two-page typescript entitled "Averardo Marchetti," including information from her interview with Averardo's son, Federico Marchetti; a clipping from *L'Opinione* (Philadelphia), 8 December 1917; a

photocopy of *La testa di ponte* (Rimini), 6 June 1925, p. 1; and a photocopy of the title page from the copy of *Lustra* that Ezra Pound gave to Averardo Marchetti in 1923, now in the possession of his grandson Averardo. These materials are discussed at more length below. I am deeply grateful to Dr. Delbianco and the library's director, Dr. Piero Meldini, for their generous assistance in locating and forwarding these materials.

51. Max Gallo, *Mussolini's Italy,* trans. Charles Lam Markmann (New York: Macmillan, 1973; 1st ed., 1964), 127.

52. On Arpinati's campaign, see Liliano Faezna, "Primi passi del fascio riminese," *Storie e storia* 2 (October 1979) 45–61, especially 53–54.

53. Niccolò Matteini, *Rimini negli ultimi due secoli* (Santarcangelo di Romagna: Maggioli, 1977), 380, 382. Matteini cites a manifesto published by the administration upon its resignation: "La lunga aspra lotta sostenuta per circa 20 mesi contro ogni sorta di difficoltà, di contrasti, diffidenze—dall'eredità finanziaria disastrosa all'assenteismo degli Istituti di Credito locale, alla resistenza dei contribuenti, alle more degli uffici e dei poteri di stato—è culminata oggi nella violenza contro le persone degli amminstratori." From Matteini, too, comes the information regarding the appointment of Dr. Marcialis. His calling card, evidently given to Pound when they met in 1923, is preserved among the papers that Pound kept in his copy of Yriarte's *Un Condottiere,* now in the Beinecke Library (see note 26 above).

54. Dottor Luigi Marcialis, *Relazione in merito alla gestione straordinaria, 6 febbraio–9 novembre 1923* (Rimini: Comune di Rimini, but printed in Santarcangelo di Romagna, typographia Fratelli Giorgetti, 1923), [5].

55. Ezra Pound to Dorothy Pound, "Ravenna, Wednesday night" [28 March 1923], BIUL, *PM.3,* 1923.

56. On Nancy Cox-McCormack, the only published study is in Lawrence Rainey, "Ezra Pound in the Paris Years," *Sewanee Review* 102 (1994): 93–95. In the account here I also draw on her unpublished papers and memoirs at Amherst, Smith College, the Sophia Smith Collection, Nancy Cox-McCormack Papers; hereafter this is abbreviated CMP, followed by the box and folder numbers.

57. Nancy Cox-McCormack, unpublished memoir titled "Two Letters of Reminiscence Covering My Decade in Chicago, 1911–1920," CMP, Box 1, Folder 9, ts. 5.

58. Ibid., ts. 9.

59. The life-mask is conserved at the Beinecke Rare Book and Manuscript Library of Yale University, call number 1980 152; the portrait bust is at the State University of New York at Buffalo, Poetry and Rare Books Collection, without call number.

60. See Ezra Pound to Nancy Cox-McCormack, circa 30 January 1923, in which Pound inquires about the price of a room at her *pensione;* State University of New York at Buffalo, the Poetry/Rare Books Collection, Nancy Cox-McCormack Papers, B745, Folder 13. See also Ezra Pound to Nancy Cox-McCormack, 3 February 1923, B745, Folder 10, in which he specifies the room that he wants when he comes to Rome.

61. All quotations are from Nancy Cox-McCormack, unpublished typescript titled "Mussolini" (her memoirs of him), CMP, Box 7, Folder 2. The typescript is signed by Cox-McCormack and dated 1939. It was evidently intended to form part of a larger project, her autobiography, and a canceled heading on the first page of the manuscript reads

"PART TWO / Chapters 7–18." As it now stands, the typescript consists of two blocks of material. The first is given the title, in typescript, "Fascist Thunder," with an additional title added by hand, "Mussolini, 1922 fall," and its pages are numbered 141–156. The second is given the title, in typescript, "Man from Romagna," also with an additional title added by hand, "Mussolini, early 1923," and the pages of this section are numbered 239–283. The quotations given here are from typescript pages numbered 152–153 and 155. Further references to these memoirs will cite the abbreviated titles "Mussolini 1" and "Mussolini 2," followed by page references.

62. All quotations are from Nancy Cox-McCormack, unpublished typescript titled "An Italian Memoir, Incorporating the Story of Lauro de Bosis" (her experiences with the de Bosis family), CMP, Box 8, Folder 1, ts. 19. The memoir was apparently written between 1954 and 1960.

63. For Cox-McCormack's introduction to Boni, see her unpublished "An Italian Memoir," ts. 24–25. See also her published essay, "Giacomo Boni. Humanist—Archaeologyist of the Roman Forum and the Palatine," *Art and Archaeology* 28, no. 1–2 (July–August, 1929), 35–44.

64. For her meetings with Mowrer and Santa, see Cox-McCormack, "An Italian Memoir," 20. See carbon of letter from Vittorio de Santa to Benito Mussolini, 3 January 1923, CMP, Box 7, Folder 2.

65. CMP, "Mussolini 2," 247–250 for her remarks on Judson and Lidia Rismondo; 255 for her attendance at the American Chamber of Commerce; 251–253 for her first meeting with Mussolini in late April; and 257–258 for her second meeting with him in early May 1923. Her bust of Mussolini is conserved at the Herbert F. Johnson Museum of Art, Cornell University, Ithaca, New York. Another copy of the bust, formerly held in the Philadelphia Museum of Art, was "deaccessioned" some time in the past. The bust bears an inscription date, 1 July 1923. Cox-McCormack reports that her second and crucial interview with Mussolini took place in early May, in "Mussolini 2," 257, and that she began the first of ten sittings with him "the next day," 258.

66. Nancy Cox-McCormack, "Gifted Sculptor Gives Vivid Pen Picture of Mussolini," newspaper clipping from unidentified source, dated October 1923, in CMP, Box 1, Folder 10.

67. Nancy Cox-McCormack, "Preface" to Benito Mussolini, *My Diary* (Boston: Small Maynard, 1925), ix. An echo of her view that Mussolini was "much an artist" can be heard in Pound's assessment of him: "Take him as anything but an artist and you will get muddled with contradictions" (Ezra Pound, *Jefferson and/or Mussolini* [New York: Liveright, 1970; 1st ed. 1935], 34).

68. Rainey, *Ezra Pound and the Monument of Culture,* 191–193.

69. Ezra Pound to Nancy Cox-McCormack, 28 March 1923, State University of New York at Buffalo, the Poetry/Rare Books Collection, Nancy Cox-McCormack Papers, B745, Folder 5.

70. The mistakes in *al* and *del,* which should read *all'* and *dell',* will be noted by some observers. The copy is still in the possession of Federico Marchetti in Rimini. I am grateful to Dr. Paola Delbianco for obtaining a photocopy of the dedicatory inscription for me.

71. In French and Italian printing, Roman numerals are conventionally followed by a period; the title remains *A Draft of XVI. Cantos* to this day because it was first printed in France.

72. The text, in Italian with an English translation, is given in Rainey, "'All I Want You to Do Is to Follow the Orders,'" 105–106.

73. Ezra Pound to William Bird, 24 August 1925, BIUL, William Bird Papers, Letters to William Bird.

74. Pound, *Jefferson and/or Mussolini*, 26–27.

75. Ezra Pound to Dorothy Shakespear, "Wednesday" [16 August 1922] Dorothy Shakespear to Ezra Pound, 20 August 1922; and Ezra Pound to Dorothy Shakespear, "Friday" [25 August 1922]; all in BIUL, *PM.3*.

76. Pound reports his attending Steffens's lecture of 29 October 1922 in Ezra Pound to Homer Pound, 30 October 1922, NHYB, *PP*, Box 52, Folder 1967. For Steffens's views on the Lausanne conference, see his letters of 25 and 30 November 1922, in *The Letters of Lincoln Steffens*, ed. Ella Winter and Granville Hicks (New York: Harcourt Brace, 1938). Steffens's views on Mussolini, which were published in the *Los Angeles Times* of 23 December 1922, are quoted from Justin Kaplan, *Lincoln Steffens: A Biography* (New York: Simon and Schuster, 1974), 259. Quotations from *The Autobiography of Lincoln Steffens* (New York: Harcourt Brace, 1931), 816, 817, 819.

77. Mary Colum, *Life and the Dream* (Garden City, N.Y.: Doubleday, 1947), 307–308.

78. Ezra Pound to Nancy Cox-McCormack, 15 August 1923, State University of New York at Buffalo, Poetry Collection, B745, Folder 16.

79. See Angelo Battaglini, "Della corte letteraria di Sigismondo Pandolfo Malatesta signor di Rimino commentario," in Francesco Gaetano Battaglini, ed., *Basini Parmensis poetae opera praestantiora nunc primum edita et opportunis commentariis illustrata* (Rimini: Ex typographia Albertiniana, 1794), 2:1–257.

80. Ezra Pound to Nancy Cox-McCormack, circa 5 January 1924, Tennessee State Library and Archives, Manuscript Section, Nancy Cox-McCormack Papers, Accession no. 413. I have capitalized "Rome" in the second paragraph.

81. Ezra Pound to Nancy Cox-McCormack, 13 January 1924, State University of New York at Buffalo, Poetry Collection, B745, Folder 15.

82. Ezra Pound to Nancy Cox-McCormack, 28 January 1924, State University of New York at Buffalo, Poetry Collection, B745, Folder 17.

83. Timothy Redman, "An Epic Is a Hypertext Containing Poetry," in Rainey, ed., *A Poem Containing History*, 125; and Timothy Redman, *Ezra Pound and Italian Fascism* (Cambridge: Cambridge University Press, 1990), 156–157.

84. Benito Mussolini, "The General Strike and Violence" (Lo sciopero general e la violenza), a review of Georges Sorel's *Considerazioni sulla violenza* (Bari: Laterza, 1908), known in English as *Reflections on Violence;* the review was first published in *Il Popolo d'Italia*, no. 2736, 25 June 1909, 10, and reprinted in Enzo Santarelli, ed., *Scritti politici di Benito Mussolini* (Milan: Giangiacomo Feltrinelli Editore, 1979), 115–120. See also Mussolini's "Syndicalist Theory" (La teoria sindicalista), a review of Giuseppe Prezzonlini's *La teoria sindicalista* (Naples: Editore Francesco Perrella, 1909), first published in *Il Popolo d'Italia*, no. 2713 (27 May 1909), 10, and reprinted in Santarelli, *Scritti politici di Benito Mussolini*, 109–114.

85. Pound, revised version of "Fascism or the Direction of the Will," NHYB, *PP,* Box 89, Folder 3360, ts. 2.
86. Pound, draft of Canto 41, NHYB, *PP,* Box 66, Folder 2548.

CHAPTER 5: PATRONAGE AND THE POETICS OF THE COTERIE

Epigraph: *LOTSE 1,* 488.

1. See Leslie Fiedler and Houston A. Baker, eds., *Opening Up the Canon: Selected Papers from the English Institute* (Baltimore: Johns Hopkins University Press, 1981); Robert von Hallberg, ed., *Canons* (Chicago: University of Chicago Press, 1984); Allan Bloom, *The Closing of the American Mind* (New York: Simon and Schuster, 1987); E. D. Hirsch, *Cultural Literacy: What Every American Should Know* (Boston: Houghton Mifflin, 1987).
2. Inevitably this account oversimplifies the evolution of the modernist poetic canon, especially in slighting asymmetries in the reception histories of Pound and Stevens. For fuller accounts, see Hugh Kenner, "The Making of the Modernist Canon," in von Hallberg, ed., *Canons,* 363–376; and Marjorie Perloff, "Pound/Stevens: Whose Era?" in *The Dance of the Intellect: Studies in the Poetry of the Pound Tradition* (Cambridge: Cambridge University Press, 1985), 1–32. Also slighted is the limited revival of interest in H.D. that occurred in the 1960s, perhaps best represented by the late Robert Duncan; this revival owed much to H.D.'s association with Pound and Williams, poets whose work was an alternative to the more canonical figures of Eliot and Yeats.
3. Michael King, "Introduction," in Michael King, ed., *H.D.: Woman and Poet* (Orono, Maine: National Poetry Foundation, 1986), 16.
4. Susan Stanford Friedman, "Hilda Doolittle (H.D.)," in *Dictionary of Literary Biography: Modern American Poets,* vol. 45 (Detroit: Gale Research, 1986), 144–145.
5. Albert Gelpi, "Re-membering the Mother: A Reading of H.D.'s *Trilogy,*" in King, ed., *H.D.,* 174.
6. Alicia Ostriker, blurb on back cover of Louis Martz, ed., *H.D.: Selected Poems* (New York: New Directions, 1988).
7. Susan Stanford Friedman, "Modernism of the 'Scattered Remnant': Race and Politics in the Development of H.D.'s Modernist Fiction," in King, ed., *H.D.,* 116. "The reactionary center," obviously, is a contradiction in terms. Elsewhere, Friedman argues for "how important issues of racial discrimination and Afro-American culture were to the formation of her postwar modernist vision," and claims that "H.D.'s particular emphasis grew out of her perspective as a woman" (Friedman, "Hilda Doolittle," 132; ibid., 117).
8. Quoted by Jackson R. Bryer, "H.D.: A Note on Her Critical Reputation," *Contemporary Literature* 10, no. 4 (Autumn 1969), 627. See Bryer's entire study for a survey of H.D.'s reception through 1969. See also Susan Stanford Friedman, "Who Buried H.D.? A Poet, Her Critics, and Her Place in 'The Literary Tradition,'" *College English* 36 (March 1975): 801–814; Friedman's reception history of H.D. largely coincides with that of Bryer. In 1975 it was safe to say that "the more difficult epic poetry" of H.D. was "largely unread" and "seldom studied or taught" (801). Especially relevant are her comments (804) concerning the continued neglect of H.D.'s work between the time of Bryer's article in 1969 and her own in 1975.

9. The "accessible canon" refers to works that have been recently reprinted and so are available to a readership. I adopt the term from Alastair Fowler, *Kinds of Literature: An Introduction to the Theory of Genres and Modes* (Cambridge: Harvard University Press, 1982), 214–215. Fowler goes on to distinguish this from "selective canons," which are an outcome of systematic preferences exercised within the accessible canon, and to argue that the "selective canons with [the] most institutional force" are "formal curricula."

10. Some of the texts included in the *Selected Poems* as independent poems were actually portions of larger works wrested from their context. Thus "Heat" was actually the second part of a longer poem, "Garden"; "And Pergamos" was part of H.D.'s translation "From the Iphigenia in Aulis of Euripides." There is no complete or reliable bibliography of H.D.'s works, though a very useful checklist was assembled in 1969; see Jackson R. Bryer and Pamela Roblyer, "H.D.: A Preliminary Checklist," *Contemporary Literature* 10, no. 4 (Autumn 1969): 632–675. A useful supplement, restricted to H.D.'s periodical publications but intended as part of a complete bibliography in progress, appears in Michael Boughn, "The Bibliographic Record of H.D.'s Contributions to Periodicals," *Sagetrieb* 6, no. 2 (1987): 71–94.

11. Friedman errs in reporting that all these were "unpublished," in Friedman, "Hilda Doolittle," 146. All but six or seven of the poems had been previously published in periodicals; they were uncollected, not unpublished.

12. Works by H.D. published between 1980 and 1990 are: *Hedylus* (Redding Ridge, Conn.: Black Swan, 1980), first published in 1928; *Hermione* (New York: New Directions, 1981), not published during H.D.'s lifetime; *The Gift* (New York: New Directions, 1982), not published during H.D.'s lifetime; *Notes on Thought and Vision* (San Francisco: City Lights, 1982), not published during H.D.'s lifetime; *Collected Poems, 1912–1944,* edited by Louis Martz (New York: New Directions, 1983), with two hundred pages of previously uncollected or unpublished poems; *Bid Me to Live* (Redding Ridge, Conn.: Black Swan, 1983), first published in 1960; *Ion: A Play After Euripides* (Redding Ridge, Conn.: Black Swan, 1983), first published in 1937; *Tribute to Freud* (New York: New Directions, 1984), published in 1956 and 1974; *Hippolytus Temporizes* (Redding Ridge, Conn.: Black Swan, 1985), first published in 1927; *Nights* (New York: New Directions, 1986), first published in 1935; *The Hedgehog* (New York: New Directions, 1988), first published in 1936; *Selected Poems,* edited by Louis Martz (New York: New Directions, 1988), not published during H.D.'s lifetime; *By Avon River* (Redding Ridge, Conn.: Black Swan, 1990), first published in 1949. It should be noted that still more volumes by H.D. have appeared since 1990: *Asphodel,* edited by Robert Spoo (Durham, N.C.: Duke University Press, 1992); *Paint It Today,* edited by Cassandra Laity (New York: New York University Press, 1992); and *Richard Aldington and H.D.: The Early Years in Letters,* edited by Caroline Zilboorg, (Bloomington: Indiana University Press, 1992). The correspondence between H.D. and Bryher during the period of H.D.'s analysis with Freud is being edited by Susan Stanford Friedman, and the correspondence between H.D. and Norman Holmes Pearson is being edited by Louis Silverstein.

13. Rachel Blau Duplessis, *H.D.: The Career of That Struggle* (Bloomington: University of Indiana Press, 1986), 137; and Susan Stanford Friedman, *Psyche Reborn: The Emergence of H.D.* (Bloomington: University of Indiana Press, 1981), 44. See also Susan Stanford

Friedman, *Penelope's Web: Gender, Modernity, H.D.'s Fiction* (Cambridge: Cambridge University Press, 1990). The biographies are Janice S. Robinson, *H.D.: The Life and Work of an American Poet* (Boston: Houghton Mifflin, 1982), and Barbara Guest, *Herself Defined: The Poet H.D. and Her World* (Garden City: Doubleday, 1984).

14. An overview of the publication of H.D.'s works is given by Susan Stanford Friedman, "H.D. Chronology: Composition and Publication of Volumes," *Sagetrieb* 6, no. 2 (1987): 51–55.

15. Perdita Schaffner, "Introduction" to H.D., *The Hedgehog* (New York: New Directions, 1988), ix.

16. On the Cuala Press, see Liam Miller, *The Dun Emer Press, Later the Cuala Press* (Dublin: Dolmen Press, 1973), and on Elkin Mathews see the excellent study by James G. Nelson, *Elkin Mathews: Publisher to Yeats, Joyce, Pound* (Madison: University of Wisconsin Press, 1989). For Rodker see the discussion here in Chapter 2. For the deluxe edition of *Ulysses* and its audience, see J. Howard Woolmer, "Ulysses at Auction, with a Preliminary Census," *James Joyce Quarterly* 17 (1980): 141–148. See also Chapter 2. On Eliot's plans for a deluxe edition of *The Waste Land*, see Chapter 3. On the deluxe editions of *The Cantos*, Lawrence S. Rainey, "A Poem Including History: The Cantos of Ezra Pound," *Paideuma* 21 (Spring/Fall 1992): n.p., but 199–220.

17. A telling symptom of the change is the poor sales and profits of *A Draft of XXX Cantos* issued by Nancy Cunard and her Hours Press in 1930; see Rainey, "A Poem Including History," 212–214.

18. The figure is from Boughn, "The Bibliographic Record of H.D.'s Contributions to Periodicals." In the category of nonfiction prose, Boughn adds seven items to the previous canon of thirty-seven items by H.D., as listed by Bryer; Boughn's additions, using his reference numbers, are C96, C128 (conjectural), C129 (conjectural), C157, C159, C162, and C174. Boughn also removes one item given by Bryer, "[Review of] On Being Creative, by Irving Babbitt," *Criterion* 12 (1933): 714; most likely he is correct in supposing it to be the work of another author with the same initials, because it shows a lexical range untypical of H.D. Also, it should be noted that the two bibliographies differ on which articles by H.D. are actually signed by her. Boughn reports that C102, H.D.'s "[Review of] *Little Novels of Sicily* by Giovanni Verga," is signed, but Bryer reports that it is "unsigned" (655). Boughn reports that C105, H.D's "[Review of] *The Polyglots*, by W. Gerhardi," is "unsigned," and Bryer states the opposite. I note these details to anticipate a subsequent discussion on H.D.'s critical prose.

19. Bryher to H.D., 23 December 1918, Yale University, Beinecke Library, Yale Collection of American Literature, Mss. 24, Box 3, Folder 80.

20. Perdita Schaffner, "Introduction" to H.D., *The Hedgehog*, viii.

21. Perdita Schaffner, "The Egyptian Cat," in H.D., *Hedylus* (Redding Ridge, Conn.: Black Swan, 1980), 143.

22. When Weaver closed her firm four years later in 1923, she had managed to sell 224 copies; see *DMW*, 464–465.

23. Recent literary studies have slighted the roman à clef because its referential character violates the presuppositions of academic criticism. The classic study on the formation of the genre in the wake of Honoré d'Urfé's *L'Astrée* (1607–1627) is still Fernand Drujon,

Les livres à clef (Paris: E. Rouveyre, 1888). For a more recent survey, see Georg Schneider, *Die Schlüsselliteratur* (Stuttgart: Hiersemann, 1951–1953), 3 vols.

24. Charles Molesworth, *Marianne Moore: A Literary Life* (New York: Atheneum, 1990), xiv, describing Enid Bagnold.

25. Friedman, "Hilda Doolittle," 131.

26. Friedman, "Modernism of the 'Scattered Remnant,'" 104.

27. "Expressed a progressive politics," ibid., 94; all other quotations, ibid., 114–116.

28. Friedman, "Hilda Doolittle," 130.

29. The *Norton Anthology* also informs readers that "the outbreak of World War II inspired three long related poems about the war . . . which appeared together as *Trilogy*." True, but the three poems did no such thing during the lifetime of H.D., for no volume bearing that title was issued until 1973, twelve years after her death. Even the claim that *Trilogy* was "inspired" by "the outbreak of World War II" conceals complications. One scholar has reported that H.D. wrote *The Walls Do Not Fall*, the first part of *Trilogy*, in 1942, three years after the war's outbreak (see Robinson, *H.D.,* 305). That claim, in turn, requires qualification. It was in April 1942 that H.D. published three sections (1, 21, and, 22) of what later became the third part of *Trilogy* (or *The Flowering of the Rod*) in *Life and Letters Today*. Six months later, in October 1942, she published another section (ultimately section 4 of *The Flowering of the Rod*), again in *Life and Letters Today*, and in November 1942 yet a fifth section (ultimately section 6 from *The Flowering of the Rod*), once more in *Life and Letters Today*. In other words, only five sections from all 129 sections of *Trilogy* were published by November 1942. And other data concerning the poem's composition and publication make the *Norton Anthology*'s claim that the poem was inspired by the war's outbreak still less tenable. What is now the first poem of *Trilogy* was not published until April or May 1944. What is now the second poem of *Trilogy* was composed in "the last two weeks of May" 1944, as H.D. explained to Norman Holmes Pearson (see Norman Holmes Pearson, "Foreword" to H.D., *Trilogy* [New York: New Directions, 1973], ix), and remained unpublished until 1945; what is now the third poem of *Trilogy* was composed, apart from the five sections published in 1942, largely between September and December 1944 and first published only in 1946. H.D. herself described the second part of *Trilogy*, *Tribute to the Angels*, as "a sort of premature peace poem," suggesting that it was inspired not by the outbreak of the war but by the opposite—the prospect of its end. (H.D.'s comment is quoted in Pearson, "Foreword," p. ix.) The same is true of the poem's last part, written when the conclusion of the war was but five months away. In short, the *Norton Anthology*'s misrepresentation of basic information about the poem's genesis directly bears on the field of interpretive possibilities that it also advances. As for the commentary for individual poems, it too is striking. What is one to make of an annotation that describes Helen as "the wife of Agamemnon" (poor deluded Menelaus!) and "the product" of Zeus's "union . . . with the moral [*sic*] woman Leda"?

30. Friedman, "Who Buried H.D.?" 803, 811. It may be a bit reductive to suggest that "the two world wars" were the outcome only of "the dominance of masculine values." Historians have advanced accounts of the two wars' origins that are slightly more complex.

31. Friedman, "Hilda Doolittle," 130.

32. Still the best close reading of the poem's syntax is given by Leo Spitzer, "On Yeats' Poem

'Leda and the Swan,'" *Modern Philology* 51 (1954): 271–276. For references to other studies, see note 36.

33. Friedman, "Hilda Doolittle," 130.

34. Ian Fletcher, "'Leda and the Swan' as Iconic Poem," *Yeats Annual* 1 (1982), 85; see also his references to earlier discussions of both the poem and the iconic background (110n.1 and 111n.13).

35. Keats, too, was fond of this rhyme when he was twenty-two, using it three times in *Endymion* (1:652–653; 2:807–808; and 4:663–664). But then, as he stated in his preface, he recognized that "the reader" would "soon perceive great inexperience, immaturity, and every error denoting a feverish attempt rather than a deed accomplished" in this work, and he especially censured the "mawkishness" of the adolescent imagination that such rhymes epitomized.

36. Robert von Hallberg, *American Poetry and Culture, 1945–1980* (Cambridge: Harvard University Press), 22.

37. Alicia Ostriker, "No Rule of Procedure: The Open Poetics of H.D.," *Agenda* 24, no. 3–4 (Autumn/Winter 1987/88), 151.

38. Ibid., 153.

39. Cyrena Pondrom, "Trilogy and Four Quartets: Contrapuntal Visions of Spiritual Quest," *Agenda* 24, no. 3–4 (Autumn/Winter 1987/88), 164.

40. Ibid., 162.

41. "Let no one argue," "my single, necessarily subjective perspective," and "prejudiced political and cultural categories," Friedman, "Who Buried H.D.?" 813; "a misogynist set of," ibid., 807; "distortions of a literary work," ibid., 813. It is not explained why "political and cultural subjectivity" will distort the reputations only of writers from "different races, nationalities, classes, and . . . sex." Surely similar distortions would also affect the reputations of writers from one's own race, nationality, et cetera.

42. Robinson, *H.D.,* 339.

43. Michael Davis, "Saving Walter Benjamin: Adrienne Monnier, Sylvia Beach, and Bryher," an unpublished paper that includes all the extant correspondence between Benjamin and these three. Benjamin and Bryher shared an interest in memories of childhood, and Benjamin was an appreciative reader of a childhood memoir that Bryher published only in a French translation by Beach and Monnier. I am grateful to Michael Davis for sharing his distinguished essay with me.

EPILOGUE

1. The fullest treatment of the aesthetic and its contradictoriness is Terry Eagleton, *The Ideology of the Aesthetic* (Oxford: Blackwell Publishers, 1990).

2. Anthony Giddens, *The Consequences of Modernity* (Stanford: Stanford University Press, 1990), 15–16; Ian Hacking, *Rewriting the Soul* (Princeton: Princeton University Press, 1995), 21, 61, 68, 239.

Index